"The result of Valle Junior's patient excavations is a Lacanian theoretical scaffold that, like a patient analyst, works through the libidinal consequences of capitalist, scientific modernity. It reframes and starts responding to Freud's famous question, 'what do queers want?', with a political economy of sexuality that is centred on desire and enjoyment rather than on identity and normativity."

Maria Aristodemou, *Professor Emerita; author, Law, Psychoanalysis, Society:*
Taking the Unconscious Seriously (Routledge)

"In his book, *Queer Theory, Lacanian Psychoanalysis, Sexual Politics: From Norm to Desire*, Luiz Valle Junior risks tackling questions both delicate and thorny – hallmarks of the desire that animates them – in language that is deliberately accessible. The effect is riveting... Thanks to Valle Junior's intervention, we can approach with renewed curiosity and concern what follows from asserting that Lacanian clinics have sexual politics, avowed or not."

Dr. Shanna Carlson de la Torre, *author, Sex for Structuralists:*
The Non-Oedipal Logics of Femininity and Psychosis (Palgrave Macmillan)

"Luiz Valle Junior's conceptual reorientation of queer theory and psychoanalysis resets the terms for the discussion of capitalism's libidinal reality that we need to be having today. With remarkably clear and compelling prose, he demonstrates how each field addresses an impasse in the other."

Professor Jodi Dean, *author, Democracy and Other Neoliberal Fantasies*
(Duke University Press)

Queer Theory, Lacanian Psychoanalysis, Sexual Politics

Queer Theory, Lacanian Psychoanalysis, Sexual Politics is a consideration of the relationship between LGBTQIA+ politics, Lacanian psychoanalytic theory, and queer theory.

The book argues, through readings of Judith Butler's *Gender Trouble* and Lee Edelman's *No Future*, that core queer categories – such as normativity and antinormativity – sidestep questions that are crucial not only to contemporary sexual politics but also to psychoanalytic thinking and clinical work. Luiz Valle Junior attends to the queer account of the political shortcomings of the contemporary LGBTQIA+ movement, as well as to the inadequacies of the queer reception of Lacanian psychoanalysis and makes a case for the ongoing relevance of Lacanian psychoanalysis to thinking through a renewed sexual politics. The book reflects on the potentiality of a Lacanian theory of sexual politics to challenge the dominance of identity in contemporary LGBTQIA+ activism and in the queer theoretical archive. Valle Junior shifts the discussion of sexual politics from the terrain of normativity and identity to the terrain of desire and enjoyment, and questions enduring heteronormative positions that contemporary Lacanians continue to espouse, against Lacan's own position.

Queer Theory, Lacanian Psychoanalysis, Sexual Politics will be of great interest to academics and scholars of queer studies, psychoanalysis, and in the LGBTQIA+ movement, and more broadly in the relation of identity analytics to contemporary psychoanalytic and political thought.

Luiz Valle Junior is Assistant Professor (Lecturer) in Law and Criminology at Northeastern University London, UK. He holds a PhD in Law from Birkbeck, University of London. He writes on queer and psychoanalytic theory and on the images of sexual normality promoted by LGBT+ activism and international human rights law.

The Lines of the Symbolic in Psychoanalysis Series

Series Editor: Ian Parker, Manchester Psychoanalytic Matrix

Psychoanalytic clinical and theoretical work is always embedded in specific linguistic and cultural contexts and carries their traces, traces which this series attends to in its focus on multiple contradictory and antagonistic 'lines of the Symbolic'. This series takes its cue from Lacan's psychoanalytic work on three registers of human experience, the Symbolic, the Imaginary and the Real, and employs this distinctive understanding of cultural, communication and embodiment to link with other traditions of cultural, clinical and theoretical practice beyond the Lacanian symbolic universe. The Lines of the Symbolic in Psychoanalysis Series provides a reflexive reworking of theoretical and practical issues, translating psychoanalytic writing from different contexts, grounding that work in the specific histories and politics that provide the conditions of possibility for its descriptions and interventions to function. The series makes connections between different cultural and disciplinary sites in which psychoanalysis operates, questioning the idea that there could be one single correct reading and application of Lacan. Its authors trace their own path, their own line through the Symbolic, situating psychoanalysis in relation to debates which intersect with Lacanian work, explicating it, extending it and challenging it.

Ornette Coleman, Psychoanalysis, Discourse
Movements in Harmolodic Space
A.L. James

The Origin of the Subject in Psychoanalysis
Rethinking the Foundations of Lacanian Theory and Clinic
Alfredo Eidelsztein

Decolonization and Psychoanalysis
The Underside of Signification
Ahmad Fuad Rahmat

Queer Theory, Lacanian Psychoanalysis, Sexual Politics
From Norm to Desire
Luiz Valle Junior

For more information about the series, please visit: https://www.routledge.com/The-Lines-of-the-Symbolic-in-Psychoanalysis-Series/book-series/KARNLOS

Queer Theory, Lacanian Psychoanalysis, Sexual Politics

From Norm to Desire

Luiz Valle Junior

Routledge
Taylor & Francis Group

LONDON AND NEW YORK

Designed cover image: © Freud Museum London

First published 2025
by Routledge
4 Park Square, Milton Park, Abingdon, Oxon OX14 4RN

and by Routledge
605 Third Avenue, New York, NY 10158

Routledge is an imprint of the Taylor & Francis Group, an informa business

British Library Cataloguing in Publication Data
A catalogue record for this book is available from the British Library

ISBN: 9781032543819 (hbk)
ISBN: 9781032543802 (pbk)
ISBN: 9781003424604 (ebk)

DOI: 10.4324/9781003424604

Typeset in Times New Roman
by Taylor & Francis Books

Contents

Acknowledgements

This book started out as a PhD thesis (though I hope it no longer reads like one) and has accordingly been several years in the making. Many more people than I can mention have contributed to its present form. Special thanks are owed to Prof. Emerita Maria Aristodemou for her insightful and useful comments on my sometimes hermetic PhD drafts; and to Dr Eddie Bruce-Jones for his support, kindness, and patience while I tried to clarify those same hermetic drafts. Prof. Emeritus Peter Frosh and Prof. Peter Goodrich's comments on and their criticism of the thesis were also extremely helpful. Thank you to Serene (and Sinan) Richards, Letícia Paes, Moniza Rizzini Ansari, Nathan Moore, Philipp Kender, Sara Paiola, and several other friends Birkbeck has given me who knowingly or unknowingly helped me to clarify aspects of the book's argument over too much wine. Georgia Golebiowski of 9 S.R. was patient enough to listen to outlines of at least three different versions of Chapter 3, for which I am grateful. Thanks to the IRI/PUC-Rio psychoanalysis reading group, and especially to Dr Paula Sandrin, for their thorough reading of Chapter 1 and for the stimulating discussion. And thanks to Rafael Moscardi Pedroso, 'vibe Marxism' consultant who will, I hope, approve of Chapter 4. I would also like to collectively mention the folks at the 2023–24 CFAR Psychoanalytic Studies programme and in-person reading group for their patient reading of *Seminar X*, the useful discussions, and for their grounding clinical experience. Thanks are also owed to my analyst, Astrid Zeceña, for reminding me a few times a week that there is indeed an unconscious. Thank you to all the friends who have, usually through collective, in-person or remote alcohol consumption, helped to see me through the process of settling in London, surviving a global pandemic and its ongoing effects, becoming a doctor, and acquiring and maintaining the privilege of selling my labour in a more or less tolerable way, of which this book is a kind of culmination: Thais Bakker, Luciana Martinez, Balgiisa Ahmed, Alice Helliwell, and several Toms, to name but a few. And thanks to my parents, who have believed in me despite not knowing how to explain what I do to everyone else in the family. In all honesty, I have a hard time of it, too.

Series Preface

You will not find in this book an attempt to 'normalise' queer theory, to render it in terms that will be understandable and acceptable to psychoanalysts who pretend to serve as the guardians of what a human subject should be when they are allowed to navigate the symbolic. Such normativity, which plagues much psychoanalysis, including Lacanian psychoanalysis, always carries with it a correlative pathologisation of the kinds of subject, those sometimes condemned as less than subject, who do not fit in. To 'normalise' queer theory, to find ways of turning it into the kind of 'norm' that could be welcomed into the symbolic universe that comprises contemporary psychoanalysis would also, while seemingly generous, institute exactly the kinds of conceptual boundaries that Freud, and then Lacan, questioned.

Psychoanalysts routinely do not only stipulate what the signifier 'queer' amounts to, with the most paranoic and reactionary traditions pinning it to their closed word-puzzle box of pretend analysis along with all the others they have decided are objectionable, those who are 'trans*', say, or those who are insufferably, unutterably 'woke'. There are those who claim the mantle of Lacan who do not actually return to Freud but to pre-Freudian psychiatric diagnostic categories, precisely those that chime with the neoliberal specification and securitisation of 'identity' they think they deconstruct, and they complement their understanding of what the symbolic 'really' is with a deliriously angry imaginary, something they evidently feel to be wrong.

This book is a timely intervention into a field that is riven with misreadings of Freud and of Lacan and, indeed of LGBTQIA+ politics, and it shows us not only that there are real stakes to these misreadings but that the way to go is to encourage these misreadings to proliferate, to 'queer' them. Instead of closing the lid on the box, shutting down the many ways in which we become human subjects, the way to go is to open it up, open up movement between the letters LGBTQIA+, and create space for desire.

Psychoanalytic clinical and theoretical work circulates through multiple intersecting antagonistic symbolic universes. The Lines of the Symbolic in Psychoanalysis series opens connections between different cultural sites in which Lacanian work has developed in distinctive ways, in forms of work that question the idea that there could be a single correct reading and application. This series provides a reflexive reworking of psychoanalysis that transmits Lacanian writing from around the world, steering a course between the temptations of a metalanguage and imaginary reduction, between the claim to provide a god's eye view of psychoanalysis and the idea that psychoanalysis must be the same everywhere. And the elaboration of psychoanalysis in the symbolic here grounds its theory and practice in the history and politics of the work in a variety of interventions that touch the real.

Ian Parker
Manchester Psychoanalytic Matrix

Introduction

Queer Theory, Lacanian Psychoanalysis, Sexual Politics

I Queer Theory and the Politics of Homosexuality

Queer theory is now over 30 years old. Many scholars of sexuality – myself included – have never known an academic world without the eclectic mix of French (post)structuralism, deconstructionism, literary criticism, media theory, psychoanalysis, and so on that has come to be identified with the 'queer' label. Many of us have been swayed by queer theory's unwavering political-normative commitment to the 'underdog' (Love 2021): its presumption to question, denature, deconstruct, and to oppose any and all regimes of the normal; its playful attitude towards the strictures of high theory; its minute attention to minor topics, such as bad emotions and the fine print of gendered self-presentation; and its exploration of sexuality's potential to unsettle certainties about oneself even as sexual identity is touted by the mainstream LGBT+ movement as the very anchor of one's personality.

Unfortunately, queer theory's age may have started to show. Some scholars and activists, as Heather Love (2021) has remarked, now even regard it as a bit passé. I want to linger briefly on why. On the one hand, queer perspectives have acquired a certain degree of academic currency, and not unusually feature in undergraduate syllabi in the humanities and social sciences, even as the field has certainly not become institutionalised to the same degree as, say, gender studies or African American studies in Anglophone academia. A discourse that defines itself as caring about the odd and the maladjusted – indeed as looking at the world from the perspective of those who have no place in it – can hardly keep its transgressive allure if every 'Introduction to x' course has a session dedicated to 'Queer approaches to x'. The increasing participation of queer approaches in notoriously conservative social scientific disciplines – such as, to stick to a couple of examples from my own academic and professional universe, criminology and international relations – would seem to compound that impression even further (for instance, Weber 2016; Buist and Lenning 2023).

On the other hand, and more problematically, the social and political respondents of queer theory – politicised gays and lesbians with university

DOI: 10.4324/9781003424604-1

degrees – are apparently not all that queer anymore, at least not in North American and Western European countries. As Love (2021) cogently asks, how queer can queers even be in a world of gay marriage? Can gays and lesbians continue to claim to fall outside majoritarian norms when enough of a viewership – presumably not all made up of homosexuals – can be mustered for a dozen seasons of RuPaul's *Drag Race*? In the contemporary West, in other words, there may be a real risk that queer has reached its 'sad finish', as Judith Butler (1994, 21) put it early on in the queer venture, in that those who might answer to that label are increasingly realising the impossibility of regarding themselves as anything but ordinary.

There is a complex history behind this latter claim, comprising legal, social, economic, epidemiological, and a great deal of other factors, which I can only partly gesture towards in this chapter. But the evidence that makes it at least feasible is not too difficult to find, nor is the claim itself, I think, particularly contentious (although it should be subject to some important qualifications). For example, in a recent international study of opinion surveys, Andrew Flores collates the results of various major surveys containing questions on the acceptance of LGBT+ people (primarily gay men and lesbians) around the world and arrives at the conclusion that, in Western Europe and North America at least, the trend towards more positive social attitudes in respect of LGBT+ people is clear and has also tended to be both sustained and significant over at least the past three decades (Flores 2021).

If such surveys are not sufficient evidence of a greater degree of societal acceptance, legally, the trend towards liberalisation is likewise clear. To stick to the British example, a brief list of landmark turning points might include the following: England and Wales decriminalised lawful sexual acts conducted in private between same-gender, consenting adults in 1967, in accordance with the 1957 Wolfenden Report's recommendations. In 1980, Scotland followed suit, and Northern Ireland in 1982. The age of consent was made equal (at 16 years) in England and Wales for homo- and heterosexual partners in 2000. Civil partnerships between same-gender partners across the United Kingdom were recognised in 2004, and finally marriage in 2013. Various other forms of discrimination on the grounds of sexual orientation, including in respect of employment, education, and others, are explicitly illegal (Stonewall 2016). Beyond the UK, according to the Human Rights Campaign (n.d.), 36 countries now recognise marriage between partners of the same gender, whether through judicial decisions or through explicit legislation.

This list is by no means exhaustive, but it is hopefully sufficient to say that there is a feasible case to the effect that Western LGBT+ people or, more realistically, more or less affluent, White, Western European and North American gays and lesbians, may well have accrued enough social and legal capital that they can now claim full, or almost full, sexual citizenship. I do not mean to discount the importance of ongoing homophobic abuse and violence, or the deplorably unequal access by more marginalised sexual minorities to whatever counts as full sexual citizenship, nor indeed do I mean to minimise the importance of the fact that the greater part of the world is far less (legally) welcoming to sexual minorities than the North Atlantic West. These are all very important qualifications to my entire argument in this chapter, as is the fact that, throughout this book, I devote little attention to other aspects of queer theory's development – for instance, its intersectional sensibilities (although I do take issue with its basic inability to take political economy into account in Chapter 4). I do mean to say, however, that much of queer theory's appeal as an 'underdog'-type discourse has started, retrospectively, to look like it was almost entirely a function of the explicit, systematic, and often murderous exclusion of gays and lesbians (the argument here applies to a much lesser extent, if at all, to trans and intersex people) from the basic entitlements of citizenship. This, in turn, means that all those queer theoretical propositions that either assume or propose that gays and lesbians are in some sense 'outside', or even 'against', heteronormative society, have lost much, if not all, of their intuitive appeal, now that gays and lesbians are patently no longer excluded from the entitlements one accrues when one belongs to that society – or, at least, not to the same degree, and not for the sole reason that they are gay men and lesbians.

These and other indexes of a greater acceptance of homosexuality in the West are partly a result of the tremendous success of the LGBT+ movement over the past few decades. They have, however, come at the cost of a whittling down or a de facto ban on associating certain issues with contemporary LGBT+ communities and identities. For example, the issue of intergenerational sex, once discussed (more, rather than less, ashamedly) in gay political circles, has been dropped by the movement and redefined entirely as a criminal justice issue. Similarly, the movement has largely disavowed the association between the LGBT+ communities and sexual practices centred around BDSM, leather, or kink, with each June bringing in a new flurry of online activity over whether kink belongs at Pride. Meanwhile, the broader left-wing sympathies of earlier gay liberation movements, for instance their association with the anti-war, anti-colonial, and anti-racist movements, have ceded ground to human rights-type claims couched in the language of the universal dignity of man.

It is a strong index of the historical change in the LGBT+ movement that some of its once-important discussions are no longer seen as being worthy of debate. Whatever one might think about these issues, their dropping out of the picture signals a relevant set of political choices made by the movement at large such as to assure its mainstream appeal, and in order that its claims could reasonably make it into serious policy discussions. Queer thinkers have tended to diagnose the accommodation of the LGBT+ movement to mainstream politics through various concepts derived from Lisa Duggan's notion of 'homonormativity'. Duggan defines this phenomenon as the pursuit of a sexual politics 'that does not contest dominant heteronormative assumptions and institutions, but upholds and sustains them, while promising the possibility of a demobilized gay constituency and a privatized, depoliticized gay culture anchored in domesticity and consumption' (Duggan 2003, 50). 'Homonormativity' and associated concepts have indeed proliferated to a remarkable extent: one can now speak, for example, of a Gay International (Massad 2006), of homonationalism (Puar 2017), queer liberalism (Eng 2010), global homocapitalism (Rao 2015), homotransnationalism (Klapeer 2017), and more generally of a 'homonormative turn' (Beam 2018, 20) in LGBT+ politics. Each of these concepts describes a regional instance of the more general process whereby LGBT+ politics has ceased referring to, and advocating on behalf of, a marginal, alternative gay lifeworld and has started working under the premise that gays and lesbians, if they are not yet fully perceived to be normal, are working towards, and perhaps are even close to reaching, that goal (which is, moreover, a desirable one).

That the concept of homonormativity and its offshoots are a general, and generally appropriate, description of the state of LGBT+ politics across the West today is, it seems, uncontentious among queer theorists, and I agree with many aspects of their diagnosis. However much success it may have achieved, it is difficult to contest that the contemporary LGBT+ movement is too professionalised, too middle-class, too single-minded in its pursuit of legal safeguards against employment discrimination, hate crimes, and of full relational recognition (marriage). I also agree that the movement's focus on these issues obscures many others: for example, it is all well and good that LGBT+ people be protected from discrimination in the workplace, but that does little to change the fact that labour is increasingly precarious for everyone, including for sexual minorities. More generally, the movement's choice to pursue an increasingly narrow political agenda fails to consider the fact that LGBT+ people are subject to the same social, political, and economic pressures as everyone else (in addition to the specific issues posed by variances in sexual orientation and gender identity). However, I also find it interesting, from a scholarly perspective, that queer theory, probably the most important contemporary intellectual project more or less explicitly arrogating itself of the perspective of LGBT+ people, is nevertheless against the larger part of the LGBT+ movement, despite credible evidence of its success. Surely this point requires explanation.

Much of the thrust of queer theory's distaste for LGBT+ politics is practical. The mainstream LGBT+ movement's demands for legal recognition obviously do not amount to a robust social critique, let alone to a particularly transformative political programme. Recognition, put simply, is always recognition by and within a pre-existing system, order, or hierarchy, and therefore does not necessarily entail a change of that order. Whether gay men and lesbians are legally protected from discrimination in employment, it should be repeated, does not change the fact that they have to work in increasingly precarious conditions, or that even people in full-time employment are finding it increasingly difficult to pay their rent. This is not to mention the issue that a change to legislation does not necessarily entail a change in people's material circumstances (there may be enhanced sentences for hate crimes but a reluctance to prosecute hate crimes, for example), nor does it follow that those changes that do transpire will be positive ones; for instance, if more hate crime legislation gives more leverage to punitivist, carceralist discourses (Thoreson 2022). So, speaking of the U.S. LGBT+ movement after the 1980s, Dean Spade argues that the movement's agenda has become so narrow that it can be pursued almost technocratically:

> The key agenda items became anti-discrimination laws focused on employment … military inclusion, decriminalization of sodomy, hate crime laws, and a range of reforms focused on relationship recognition that increasingly narrowed to focus on the legal recognition of same-sex marriages. Participatory forms of organizing, such as nonprofessional membership-based grassroots organizations, were replaced by hierarchical, staff-run organizations operated by people with graduate degrees.
>
> (Spade 2015, 30)

Spade is certainly right to critique the narrowing of the LGBT+ movement's agenda, even if it has won a large number of victories by so narrowing it, and he is also right to point out that the interests of people with graduate degrees are inevitably coloured by their class position, which makes them less likely to adopt the point of view of the most deprived of the LGBT+ population. Nevertheless, I think there is more to queer theory's unwavering critique of the LGBT+ movement than this. I think the queer distaste for the 'predominantly political' (Picq and Thiel 2015, 9) tactics of the LGBT+ movement is also partly due to a quirk of the field's normative position, namely its oppositional commitment, which means that queer theorists can only coherently countenance something one might call a politics of refusal. Queer theorists call this position 'antinormativity', or the presumption that queer politics is always a politics against a given regime of the normal, against a way of apportioning what counts as normal and what counts as pathological within a given field of human interest – medicine, for instance, or society. Indeed, queer theory is full of endorsements of people and groups who refuse to integrate, normalise, and ultimately settle for the heteronormative world as it is (most notably in the so-called antisocial tradition), usually without much regard to the question as to whether that refusal really is all that ethically or politically expedient.

In this respect, queer theory is an obviously, though not always self-consciously, moral discourse (see Chapter 2). One defining feature of all those perspectives that have arrogated themselves the label 'queer' is that all of them have worked under the presumption that queers ought to act in such a way that they subvert, refuse, implode, or whatever other term one might choose, (hetero)normativity. Antinormativity, in other words, is something of a queer categorical imperative, in the sense that it is the core, grounding, central rule disciplining the creation of all the other rules that allow one to pronounce on the queerness or otherwise of a perspective, group, or political programme. The problem with this perspective, to my mind, is not so much that it is more or less obviously a moral position (as Gilles Deleuze once said, a 'moral' perspective is always, in some sense, legislation from above, always theological in form; Deleuze and Eribon 1995, 100), but that it has not allowed queer theorists a full appreciation of some crucial questions for any political movement purporting to change the way people live. For example, queer theory has barely any reflection about the classical ethical question, 'what does it mean to live a good life?', just as it has generally failed to appreciate the ways in which any representation of sexual personhood and identity – including the ones that go by 'queer' – is, at least partly, attributable to strategic and contextual circumstances (Huffer 2013).

Queer theory, finally, has coalesced around a judgement of the LGBT+ movement based less on its contextual, strategic considerations and effects – the extent to which it has improved people's lives or changed societal attitudes, for instance, in a climate that has always been hostile to it – than on the intentions its core categories supposedly betray, that is, their always-already accomplished capitulation before heteronormativity. Queer thinkers are all closet deontologists, in this sense: the queer worth of an act is to be judged by its compliance with the antinormative rule. For example, representations of LGBT+ identity that rely on the proposition that being gay or a lesbian is a characteristic determined at birth, immutable throughout one's life, and essential to one's sense of personhood are consistently and mercilessly opposed by every queer theorist, yet they are unquestionably a central piece of the LGBT+ movement's contemporary strategy – and are certainly also part of the reason why it can claim such impressive successes among the new social movements. The queer critique is of course justified: the essentialism of sexual identity does very much flatten people's sexual experiences (many people have sex with their same-gender peers growing up, yet relatively few go on to self-proclaim, or indeed to live as, gays and lesbians, for instance), and it can shore up a veneer of respectability that makes LGBT+ rights conditional on a performance of LGBT+ normality that probably excludes many more LGBT+ people than it actually helps. However, these claims have become so routinised and commonsensical in queer theory that queer theorists can quite reasonably be faulted with exempting themselves from the normativity they purport to combat, as if they were content with knowing better and could not acknowledge the fact that queer (that is, non-straight) lifeworlds themselves, like any human lifeworld, could definitionally only be constituted around norms and normativity. The truly difficult queer question, in other words, and the question queer theory has little to nothing to say about, is not whether one can live with fewer norms, but rather which norms serve one better and why. As Robyn Wiegman and Elizabeth Wilson succinctly put it, in their much-needed reminder that, under a Foucauldian (queer) framework, there can be no such thing as a social position outside the norm: 'antinormative stances project stability and immobility onto normativity. In so doing, they generate much of the political tyranny they claim belongs (over there) to regimes of normativity' (Wiegman and Wilson 2015, 13).

There is, therefore, a need to rethink queer theory's core political commitments, as well as aspects of its conceptual arsenal. The conundrum signalled by the motif of homonormativity – how can queers be so relentlessly opposed to ordinary LGBT+ life and the LGBT+ movement? – is what led me to become interested in the subject of this book: where might a queer discourse, and a corresponding politics, premised on an apologia of transgression, subversion, etc., go when its referent is seemingly no longer that outrageous? Is there even a point to queer theory in an era of gay marriage, of RuPaul and Conchita Wurst, of 'gay rights are human rights'? Must a theory of sexual politics be so singularly invested in identity and its critique? Or is there another way? I wrote a PhD thesis on this topic, still under the assumption that what was needed was to rescue the queer apologia of transgression from the decline of its social, empirical, juridical, and political referent, and that a sufficiently articulate theory could at least get the ball rolling on that debate (and on what Lacanian psychoanalysis had to offer it). I no longer think that it is an interesting proposition, let alone a way forward, and at any rate there is already an entire queer theoretical, and gay political, scholarly and activist tradition that does what I had originally set out to do much better than I could (see, for instance, Hocquenghem 1993; Bersani 1995; Edelman 2004). Rather than propose a way forward to queer theory and politics, then, this book contents itself with presenting the result of some work that springs from a turn to psychoanalysis' understanding of what one might call, for the heuristic value of the concepts, sexual identity and sexual politics, although these terms are (not entirely, but mostly) foreign to the psychoanalytic tradition I am most interested in, namely Lacanian psychoanalysis. The book's ambition is merely to do some conceptual work towards a psychoanalytically informed discussion of sexual politics, including the sexual politics of the Lacanian clinic and movement (and both the Lacanian clinic and movement do have a sexual politics, regardless of their alleged political neutrality or their acknowledgement of their analysands' singularities), in a homonormative era in which queer arguments have lost much of their social and political appeal. In this sense, what will hopefully emerge by the end is a partial picture of the queer misreadings of Lacanian work, of the sexual politics implicit (or explicit, as the case may be) in that work, the shortcomings of that sexual politics from a queer vantage point; and, finally, a return to the question of what Lacan has to offer a theory of sexual politics centred on the concepts of desire and enjoyment (*jouissance*) rather than those of identity and normativity. Before I turn to these issues, a brief account of the feminist and queer engagements with Lacanian psychoanalysis is in order.

2 Lacan, Feminism, and Queer Theory

The publication of introductory essays by Jacqueline Rose and Juliet Mitchell to their selection of Lacanian texts on women's sexuality may be said to constitute something of a point of departure for the Anglo-American reception of a queer and feminist Lacan. As Rose argues in her essay, the difficulty feminists might have with Lacan is a difficulty inherent to the disjunction between language and the body, which is precisely the object of Lacan's discourse. For Rose, Lacan calls upon us to hold together three difficult propositions, namely that the sexual difference represented in the unconscious is not natural, since it is structured around the presence or absence of the penis (and not the presence of either a penis or a vagina, which would give each sex-gender its natural due); that the presence or absence of the penis is translated unconsciously as the possession or not of the phallus, which is first and foremost a symbol of desire, rather than of the actual penis; and that unconsciously recognising the difference in the social, political, and sexual roles of men and women does not solve the conundrum of human gender and sexuality, which remain, for all the cultural work that goes into domesticating them, without natural, preordained roles and objects (Rose 1982).

To enter the order of sexuality, which the discourse of analysands on the couch demonstrates is phallocentric, is to be caught between a rock and a hard place: man accepts his privileged 'having' only by knowing that what he does have to offer a woman is not really 'it', but only a penis; while woman accepts her role as phallic object only by knowing that she is not 'it', but a subject who disguises herself with 'its' allure. Both genders therefore consent to a theatrical display for the other's benefit, in at least partial cognizance that it is a display, but also knowing full well that there is no other option available to them. This generalised parading, it must be noted, plainly disadvantages women: their conundrum is not merely that they choose to parade as desirable, which would allow them some space for subjectivity, but that they are called upon to accept the role of an object (a status, of course, incompatible with full subjectivity).

One important implication of Rose's account is that there is no such thing as sexual normality: all sexuality is the effect of a parading that is furthermore often both experienced and consciously understood as a sham, a concerted pretending that nevertheless has the force of law. As Ellie Ragland-Sullivan has put it, '[e]ach analysis repeats endless variations on but one theme: Each subject feels in some way that he or she is a *failed* man or a *failed* woman' (Ragland-Sullivan 2004, 75, emphasis in the original). The core psychoanalytic intervention, in this sense, is not quite that Freud tells all other possible sexual variations that it is OK not to be normal, but rather that it problematises the very idea that normality is or can be an objectively satisfactory outcome to the conundrum that is sexuality. Rather, what psychoanalysis demonstrates, in this account, is that the experience of gender and sexuality is similar to the experience of participating in most other social and religious institutions – premised on the tacitly acknowledged, and forcibly maintained, necessity of a generalised make-believe for the benefit of others and, at the limit, for the maintenance of society as such.

It is clear how this insight might be particularly welcome to queer theory, given its investment in a theatrical and linguistic notion of performativity. If sexual identity is little but an I-pretend-I-have-the-phallus for the benefit of an I-pretend-I-am-the-phallus, maybe there is nothing behind the masks men and women put on for each other. Gender and sexual identity could then be understood as a ritualised make-believe given the force of law by the concerted action of those social institutions – family, school, university, the workplace, medicine, religion, advertising, etc. – that Louis Althusser called 'ideological state apparatuses' (Althusser 2001). This is precisely Judith Butler's intervention, whose work has been said to be marked by a disavowal of its Lacanian roots, which I scrutinise in Chapter 1 (Butler 1999; Kollias 2012). Gender and sexual identity, in this view, are not determined biologically; rather, they are the observable effects of an intricately coordinated, generalised compliance with the rules that must be followed so that one might participate in one or the other gender in the first place. The process whereby one is brought into this society-wide theatrical performance begins early on indeed: with a parent's desire to have a boy or a girl even before conception, with an ultrasound that allows for one's sex to be determined based on the presence or absence of a visible penis, or finally with the writing of a birth certificate that will mark one out juridically as male or female.

Many people have (wrongly) reproached Butler with advancing a 'voluntaristic' account of gender, as if people chose genders in the same way that they choose the day's outfit. This critique relies on the proposition that a linguistic and cultural account of gender is *ipso facto* more abstract, and therefore less real, than other possible accounts, such as those that rely on biological or economic categories (Morton 1996). These critiques are not particularly interesting or well informed. Lacanians, however, have had a different critique to advance against Butler's seemingly weak commitment to (whatever counts as) materiality. As Tim Dean has argued extensively, Butler's account of gender and sexuality is 'rhetoricalist', which might simply mean unaware of the limits of language (Dean 2000). For Lacanian psychoanalysis, even if gender and sexual identity are indeed cultural and linguistic constructs, there is something more fundamentally intractable about being human and taking up a sexual position than the idea that one only becomes a man or a woman, gay or straight, by learning the cultural codes and linguistic conventions societies ascribe to these identities and behaving accordingly. After all, in such 'hardcore' social constructionist approaches, the question can always be posed as to what is irreducible to language and culture: what 'real' do language and culture speak of? Which is a question to which they have no response.

Psychoanalytically inclined thinkers have provided a distinctive answer to that question, one that refuses to reduce 'sex' to either its biological substratum or culture. One thing that psychoanalysis takes to be axiomatic is that there is a sort of excess of sexuality over human (biological, cultural, social, political, etc.) environment and context. Contemporary Lacanians often address this excess in the context of discussions of sexual difference. As Patricia Gherovici explains, '[s]exual difference is neither just the body (as biological [substratum]) nor the psychic introjections of the social performance of gender (a socially constructed role)' (Gherovici 2010, 230), but a problem having to do with their point of contact. What is at issue for psychoanalytic accounts of sexuality is therefore not one's phenotypical traits, nor one's deeply felt sense of self, nor yet one's behaviour as constrained by social norms, although psychoanalysis can take all of these into account. Rather, the fundamental problem for psychoanalysis is that the process whereby one takes up a sexual position puts two mutually incompatible series – sex and gender, the body and language, nature and culture, etc. – in direct contact with one another. As Gherovici goes on to write, '[s]ince sexual difference is neither sex nor gender, sex needs to be symbolized, and gender needs to be embodied' (Gherovici 2010, 230).

The difficulty in putting together nature and culture in sexuality is not merely an epistemological problem for the psychoanalytic subject, but one in which everyone has skin in the game. This is because one's entrance into language and culture has to be paid for in a currency Lacan calls enjoyment or *jouissance* (I discuss this term in greater detail in Chapters 2 and 4). *Jouissance* is a difficult term to translate: *jouir* means 'to orgasm', and *jouissance* can refer to that height of pleasure, but the word also has a (somewhat neglected by Lacanians) juridical meaning of 'the legitimate enjoyment of something' – a title, property, etc. In the context of discussions of sexual difference, enjoyment can mean at least two things. On the one hand, it may refer to a body's singular way of enjoying itself, which calls up the question as to what the highest enjoyment possible to a natural body might be – a question for which the shape of one's reproductive apparatus might be relevant, but not determinant. On the other hand, it may refer to the legitimate or illegitimate use of the body of another, which engages the problematic of whether the one whose body I enjoy enjoys themselves in turn.

How one enjoys and how one's enjoyment relates to that of others are two of the major questions posed by sex and gender in the psychoanalytic clinic. They are also two core questions in respect of which culture is called upon to make sex and sexuality intelligible for us, to make them rule-bound and therefore less intractable. The paradigmatic example of the subjection of enjoyment to culture is the prohibition of incest, but this prohibition, in psychoanalytic thinking, is both a proxy and a metaphor for a much wider point. For example, masturbation is a taboo in many societies, sometimes even on par with incest; and marriage is almost universally the juridical precondition for the legitimate enjoyment of (typically a woman's) body (Godelier 2004). For a Lacanian, these are good examples of how the fact of belonging to a social group demands payment in enjoyment: the body's capacity to relate to itself and to other bodies 'immediately', as it were, must be filtered through a linguistic and cultural code and emerge fundamentally changed on the other side – at the cost of whatever enjoyment was, in fact or in fantasy, possible in the beginning. Accordingly, reconstructing the subject's payment history in respect of enjoyment will be part of any psychoanalysis, which most often attracts people who have, knowingly or otherwise, objected to the renunciations their society imposes on its newcomers.

However, there is one quirk to the Lacanian account of enjoyment that makes it different from a theory that might simply denounce society's excessive demands on the libido. Enjoyment, for Lacan and Lacanians, is presumed to be threatening. It must be warded off by the intervention of language as the precondition for any sort of predictable, orderly experience of pleasure (as opposed to enjoyment per se). In this sense, enjoyment is not necessarily positive. It consists in and through one's private fantasies of bliss, but one's path towards it, if one chooses to follow it too far, accompanies intolerable pain. There is a long theoretical justification for this argument that takes up a large part of Lacan's *Seminar VII* (Chapter 2) but, in brief, enjoyment can be threatening to the subject in part because of the prolonged helplessness of the human infant, which suspends much of their earliest experience of their bodies to the caretakers' caprice; and, in part, because the caretaker dominates not solely the satisfaction (or otherwise) of the infant's needs but also their acquisition of the linguistic means to designate those needs and to articulate demands of their own. Owing to this original dependency, as I demonstrate in Chapters 1 and 2, Lacan sees the situation established between caretaker and infant as determining an elementary logic through which the caretaker will become not only the fantasised seat of all possible satisfactions but also the holder of the means to designate the infant's very experience of themselves. They preside, in other words, over the infant's entire world, which invests them with a sort of omnipotence and accordingly also a threat of unrestrained power over, and enjoyment of, them.

The earliest caretaker, Freud had already intuited, is the prototype of God: loving and terrible at once. Faced with this terrifying entity on which one is nevertheless dependent for one's survival as well as for one's experience of the world, Lacan argues that the infant must find a way out, a semblance of autonomy, by developing their own desire. Desire drives a wedge between subjectivity and enjoyment (which is both their own and the caretaker's enjoyment of their body, since these are indistinguishable for the infant early on), in such a way that the experience of the body-subject-to-the-caretaker ceases being overwhelming by being refracted through a network of representations. In this sense, desire is called upon to mortify and to socialise enjoyment, for the very simple reason that desire can be spoken, communicated to, ratified by, and put to use on behalf of a community, whereas the live, so to speak, enjoyment presumed in the caretaker-infant situation cannot. To return to my earlier examples, masturbation is a problem to so many social groups, from this perspective, not because it is to debase oneself by treating one's own body as a sexual object, but because societies implicitly reason that masturbation stages an enjoyment akin to that threatened by the caretaker-infant situation, that cannot be put to socialised use. The same might be said of homosexuality: homophobic thinkers very often call up the fantasy of the end of mankind to justify their homophobia, and in doing so they are drawing precisely on the Western heteronormative tradition that unconsciously views in homosexuality a form of antisocial enjoyment (Edelman 2004).

In this sense, Lacan proposes an interesting reversal of the traditional assumption that desire is an orientation towards a desirable object: on the contrary, the entire point of desire is to keep the subject at an appropriate, respectful distance from an enjoyment they and their society are at pains to integrate. In light of this concept, it becomes clear why it is that Lacanians take issue with Butler's alleged rhetoricalism: for Butler, the body as such, as well as the rapport of a body to itself or to another – all of which falls under the ambiguous heading of enjoyment in contemporary Lacanian work – can only appear as a sort of inert prerequisite of desire. Enjoyment for a scholar following in Butler's footsteps is what is leftover when there is nothing else to say about what codes one is reciting in one's ongoing performance of one's gender identity, and it is therefore by and large uninteresting. This judgement is easily confirmed by the fact that none of Butler's major queer work discusses sexual enjoyment or indeed activity, presumably something that quite specifically sets queers apart from everyone else. If anything, Butler's work invites one to consider sex and pleasure merely as functions of the performances that constitute gender and sexual identity. For the psychoanalyst, of course, enjoyment is not and cannot simply be the inert material out of which desire is made. It is precisely the interactions between the loss of enjoyment, the representations that keep it at bay, and the hope of retrieving it that give the performance of gender roles its seemingly imperative character – investing it with the shame that accompanies our falling short of gendered ideals, for instance, or generating the terrible sense that the fulfilment conjugal love promises is, in fact, impossible. As Lacan put it, castration 'means that *jouissance* has to be refused in order to be attained on the inverse scale of the Law of desire' (Lacan 2006c, 700). This is precisely what the neurotic, who Lacan construes as someone who has refused to integrate part of their social reality psychically, cannot really do: the neurotic refuses to 'sacrifice [their] castration to the Other's *jouissance*, by allowing [their castration] to serve the Other' (Lacan 2006c, 700). In other words, the neurotic does not wish to renounce their enjoyment (their enjoyment and/or the mother's enjoyment of them), and in this sense they do not consent to it serving the social Other.

For many Lacanian scholars, then, the insight that sets Lacan apart from other structuralist and post-structuralist thinkers is that he allows one to think of that something in sexuality that resists every system in place to domesticate it, yet also something that is the precondition to any such system. In this sense, Lacan's theory provides a different way into this issue than the usual terms of the nature/nurture debate, which still suffuse so much thinking and debate on gender and sexuality. There is, for Lacanian thinkers, some enjoyment that stubbornly resists being reduced to an attribute of the body as a biological system, as well as to the cultural codes that determine how gender is embodied and what an acceptable sexuality looks like. This perspective is a challenge both to traditional, conformist discourses surrounding gender and sexuality, including but not limited to those that would reduce either term to biology, as well as to radical queer perspectives that would bracket the intractability of enjoyment in favour of an exploration of the cultural and political vicissitudes of gender and sexual identity as if they were endlessly malleable. However, the Lacanian account contains elements of both views, and the difficulty reconciling these two sides to it will become most obvious in a normative context, that is, whenever the question as to what psychoanalysis aims at is posed. I will consider this question as approached in some contemporary queer applications of Lacanian theory one might call theories of singularity, with which the remainder of this book is broadly in conversation.

3 A Theory of Singularity?

In respect of the conformist side to Lacan's work, it is important to be clear that the classical Lacanian theory of 1951–7 (Zafiropoulos 2010) treats virtually all kinds of subjective suffering as problems of conformity in relation to available social scripts disciplining gender, sexuality, and kinship.[1] Lacan's operative hypothesis throughout this period is that, if something fails in respect of the subject's assent to the symbolic fictions and structures regulating these domains, other aspects of the individual's experience might be called upon to compensate for that failure – so, for example, a symbolic problem in respect of the subject's placement in the web of kinship might call for a real or an imaginary compensation, such as the hearing of voices, in the case of the psychotic, or an identification to someone of the 'wrong' gender, in the case of the hysteric. Crucial to this contention is Lacan's version of the

Oedipal situation, to the extent that it must ensure that the subject locate themselves appropriately in relation to the father as the representative of social and symbolic authority. In brief, a normative end to the Oedipus complex would require that the phallus – signifier of desire (Chapter 1) – be the father's possession, such that the subject's access to it might become premised on their effort to become loveable to him, rather than to the mother's alleged caprice. This would, finally, entail submission to a minimal set of social dicta, chiefly expressed in the subject's acquiescence to the norms constituting what would now be called their gender, or their (gendered) ego-ideal.

Let us consider two classical examples where homosexuality is a central aspect of the clinical picture for Lacan, Dora and the young homosexual woman. Broadly speaking, Lacan's reading of Freud's Dora locates her symptoms as resulting from a breakdown of the circuit implicating her in her father's relationship to Frau K. and Herr K. Dora's father is having an affair with Frau K., Herr K.'s wife, and must, according to Lacan's adaptation of Lévi-Strauss's account of the exchange of women, give a woman in return. So, he gives Dora away to Herr K., making her into a desirable but exchangeable object, a status she does not understand and cannot accept. Failure to accept one's status as an object might, according to Lacan's operative 'compensation' hypothesis, result in some form of imaginary solution (in Dora's case, an identification with a man) that allows the subject to forge a social link by the wrong means. Dora therefore identifies with Herr K., so she may ask herself the question: 'what is it about Frau K. that makes her a desirable woman?' (Lacan 2006a), the answer to which would also be an answer as to 'what does it mean that I, Dora, am a woman, and therefore desirable to men?' This allows her to take her place in the circuit of exchange (she is given over to Herr K.) as well as to interrogate that place through her attachment to Frau K. (who her father loves and who, through her identification to Herr K., she also loves). Dora's solution breaks down once Herr K. tells her that he does not love his wife, at which point the interest of Dora's set-up – which is conceived in order to interrogate what it is that makes Frau K. desirable to her father, and so what makes Dora herself desirable to him and other men – dissolves (if she is not desirable then neither is Dora). At that point, her symptoms become a hindrance to her integration within the father/Frau K. = Herr K./Dora circuit, and she is taken to Freud for treatment.

Lacan's reading of the case of the young homosexual woman equally determines her (alleged) perversion to result from a sort of masculine identification. Her seemingly chaste lesbian affair with a woman of dubious reputation was itself motivated by the slight she had suffered, as a teen, at her father's hands: he gave her mother a child, thereby scorning her (Lacan 2014, 2020). The young homosexual woman's problem is different to that of Dora: she consents to being an object to a man but wants to receive from her father what she was promised from the outset of the Oedipal situation, namely a child that is equivalent to the phallus she has accepted she does not have, as a gift that would prove his love for her. It is because something in her family context gets in the way of her bringing the complex to its normative end, which would mean she must take up a symbolic position as recipient of the phallus from a man who is not the father, that her homosexuality assumes its later shape. For Lacan, it is the birth of a little sibling that makes the Oedipal set-up too real, and therefore not appropriate to symbolic resolution: once the young homosexual woman's father gives her mother a real child, what is at issue is no longer his symbolic role as bearer and giver of the phallus or the young homosexual's repressed wish for his child, but the real child the young homosexual was imaginarily denied by her father's preference for the mother. The young homosexual woman cannot countenance the father's preference except by incorrectly assuming that the mother has something – perhaps some sort of phallic attribute – she herself did not have. This means that she can no longer accomplish the Oedipal task, which would involve realising that the mother does not have the phallus, repressing the wish for the father's child and, later, displacing it onto another man. Instead, she sets up an elaborate *mise en scène* aimed at compensating her for what she believes was the father's incapacity of loving her as he should have, as if she were saying to him: 'I will show you what it means to love a woman, by giving myself over to her despite her not having the phallus. I will become for her the object you denied me when you preferred my mother over me. And, in my gift of myself, she will have it'. Once the father sees the couple on the street and makes his disapproval clear, the young homosexual woman's partner breaks things off with her, whereupon the interest of the *mise en scène* breaks down – no one actually wants the object she embodies and presumes is the only really desirable thing – and she, having lost her place in that *mise en scène*, throws herself onto a railway line in suicidal acting out.

On the one hand, then, the Lacanian account of Freud's case studies leads back to the question of subjects' integration into the social groups to which they belong. This integration, furthermore, is presumed to be accomplished via gendered and sexual normalisation, a process of which the family, and especially the father, will be the pivot. On the other hand, however, precisely in its theoretical and clinical concern with the infinitely creative ways in which people depart from the available gendered and sexual scripts, psychoanalysis demonstrates the importance of enjoyment – and of a subject's willingness or otherwise to part with it or to renounce it by subjecting it to some extrinsic, 'pro-social' ordering principle – to the maintenance or disruption of the very sexual and gendered scripts that define normality. Indeed, the Lacanian framework, in some senses despite itself, allows not only for a political theory of subversion and resignification of the Butlerian kind, but also for a theory of singularity, precisely because a subject's unwillingness to renounce enjoyment might lead to 'creative' (and not merely pathological) effects in respect of available gendered, sexual, and generational structures, identifications, and fantasies. These departures, furthermore, may be determined to be eminently liveable, or 'viable', in queer theory's parlance, as fully fledged modes of life (Ruti 2012, 2017). I would suggest that there are two versions to this theory of how people depart from gendered and sexual scripts, one of which tends to be espoused by Lacanian clinicians who are versed in the poststructuralist canon, while the other is espoused by cultural theorists of a Lacanian persuasion. Both perspectives might (more or less justifiably) be called theories of singularity.

The clinical version speaks of all those ways in which a subject might fashion some means of handling their enjoyment while departing, to a greater or lesser degree, from normatively prescribed solutions to the questions 'who am I, what do I want?' within a given familial, cultural, and social order. Such solutions allow for some accommodation with that order, or indeed against that order, but are, of course, never wholly unrelated to it. I associate this theory with thinkers who have a clinical practice because, in their case, professional rules constrain how much leeway they might really give to a subject's 'singularity' – which may very well be disturbing and harmful, even as Lacan was clear that there was no reason why analysts should act as 'guarantors of the bourgeois dream' (Lacan 1992, 303). Clinicians sometimes pursue the motif of singularity under the heading of the *sinthome*, a concept introduced in Lacan's work on Joyce in *Seminar XXIII*. I will not go into the intricacies of this concept here, partly because I do not think the concept is needed to say what contemporary analysts want to say with it[2] and partly because I think it takes Lacan's earlier theory – which is always at once a social theory – in a too individualistic direction. For the purposes of this book, let us simply define the *sinthome* as these scholars use it: the way a subject makes up for a problematic rapport with the Name-of-the-Father by means of a creative practice likened to a practice of self-nomination.

The paradigmatic example of the *sinthome* comes from Lacan's reading of James Joyce as having managed to avoid overt psychosis through his writing and his experimentation with the limits of language and, in this sense, having 'made his [own] name', rather than accepting the father's (an expression that gives Roberto Harari's book on the late Lacan its title, to which most scholars refer; see Harari 2002). Although it is based on Joyce, this is not necessarily a theory of the Great Man, nor is it exclusive to psychosis. For example, to simplify a vignette from Patricia Gherovici's work, Linda, a bulimic analysand who is not quite psychotic, but who has a 'looser' rapport with the Name, begins her analysis under the spell of the universal proposition that 'all food is my mother's attempt to silence my demands and make me into an object'. The bulimia and some psychosomatic issues are found to be so many protests against the mother's excessive proximity and her imperious enjoyment of Linda. The analysand finally finds some relief from her symptoms when she starts a chocolate-making business. This new career choice subjects the original universal proposition to the exception, 'some food is a commodity', which allows the analysand to articulate her own desire through a demand (for money and recognition) and to escape the threat of being a silent object of her mother's enjoyment (Gherovici 2010, 207–8). In the process of arriving at this sublimatory solution (the chocolate-making is a socially valued, creative practice), the subject also manages to draw on traditional techniques that locate her as part of her maternal and paternal lines, thus compensating for the weakly installed Name. In this sense, through her analysis, Linda gives consistency to her social being, and manages to make something of a name for herself, thus particularising her existence and desire (as Linda the chocolatier) and sacrificing something of her (mother's) enjoyment (of her) in the process. Linda, in other words, compensates for the relative weakness of the father function through a creative sublimation that is (supposedly) singularly hers.

The second account of singularity one finds in the literature is more closely associated with various poststructuralist perspectives in the humanities. It emphasises enjoyment (and other aspects of the Lacanian real, if there are any) and investigates it negatively. On this account, is 'singular' whatever is leftover or whatever escapes a subject's (or a society's) imaginary self-image or symbolic position. 'Singularity', in this sense, has a basic affinity with the notion of enjoyment. It 'relates to those pieces of being that stick out of, interfere with, undermine, or otherwise disturb the subject's pursuit of stable self-identity. It is the "inhuman" (or not fully human) excess ... [that] muti-lates the subject's "humanity"' (Ruti 2012, 4). The word also occurs in Lee Edelman's definition of the concept: '[t]he *sinthome* ... speaks to the singu-larity of the subject's existence ... [and] implies from the outset its relation to ... the constitutive fixation of the subject's access to *jouissance*' (Edelman 2004, 35). There are different degrees of commitment to this negative concept of enjoyment in the literature. Some scholars, such as Lee Edelman and other antisocial theorists, see enjoyment as a political weapon: it is precisely our political merit as queers to demonstrate that there is some enjoyment that is and will remain inaccessible to the circuits of exchange that constitute the social and to put it on display (Edelman 2004). Other thinkers understand this point differently and argue that enjoyment is interesting precisely because it can be leveraged towards creative effects in respect of gendered and sexual norms (Ruti 2017). It has even been suggested that, in light of the creative intractability of enjoyment, the very concept of sexual difference as entailing two and only two genders and their respective modes of enjoyment could be understood as a structuring fantasy that is ripe for traversal (Coff-man 2022). The gist of this perspective, then, is that whatever it is that resists symbolisation absolutely can be leveraged either towards social change, per-haps even revolutionary change (however one might like to define it), or towards resistance to processes of normalisation.

For the moment, I want merely to note a few deficiencies in the framework of these new queer Lacanian theories that I believe the remainder of this book will do some work to addressing. It should be noted from the outset that the scholarship centring some notion of singularity makes a valid and necessary point, if contextualised as a riposte to the kind of Lacanism that sees in the 'symbolic' or in the notion of 'sexual difference' some sort of God-given, transcendental standard according to which every sexual position must be judged (Chapter 3 and Conclusion). The enormous variety of ways in which people negotiate familial, gendered, and sexual norms, including if they are heterosexual, makes a mockery of any attempt to reduce gender and sexuality to the signifiers 'man' and 'woman' (which are, whatever else they might be, words invested with some seemingly divine power to polarise and to captivate). Yet these theories are not unproblematic. Indeed, they tend to gloss over what is undoubtedly one of the most important interventions psychoanalytic theory makes in respect of human life, summarised in Freud's argument that '[i]n the individual's mental life someone else is invariably involved, as a model, as an object, as a helper, as an opponent; and so from the very first individual psychology … is at the same time social psychology as well' (Freud 1955, 69). Theories of singularity, in other words, tend to downplay the fact that subjectivity as such is always already collective, and therefore the fact that it engages society (and our theories of society) necessarily rather than incidentally.

This downplaying of society has important consequences across all spheres of psychoanalytic and queer work. For example, it merely re-poses the timeless problem of the end of analysis: when can one tell if a given 'solution' to the problem of enjoyment is singular? What are the criteria whereby one might decide that an analysand or a political subject has arrived at something that is uniquely and inextricably *them* and *theirs*, and not merely a regular old symptom resulting from an interpretable conflict, for instance, between a repressed desire and some censoring instance modelled after a social authority? As of 2024, there does not seem to be any particularly defensible answer to this question, even as Lacanian work not only multiplies the instances of its use of enjoyment and the symptom/*sinthome* as an index for a subject's uniqueness, but also expands its catalogue of enjoyments (and it should be noted in passing that the fact that Lacan and Lacanians treat enjoyment as something that *can* be catalogued and differentiated is already an inconsistency in respect of the alleged 'ineffability' of enjoyment, as well as a sidestepping of the very real philosophical problems posed by the notion of singularity). As Darian Leader has quipped, the use of these concepts raises a certain suspicion:

> [W]e can't help noticing that if someone spends however many years in analysis with two-minute sessions, it isn't so surprising that they eventually buy into the idea that signifying elaboration is ineffective and that they just have to make do with their symptom!
>
> (Leader 2021, 129)

Theories of singularity also present problems for scholars concerned with politics. These perspectives make it difficult for us to ask some quite traditional, but necessary questions. To what extent, for example, should someone's singular enjoyment be encouraged if it leads to conduct that is plainly harmful to others? What is the relation to one's subjective singularity with shared ideals as to what counts as a life well lived? In what respects, in other words, is singularity an ethical ordeal not only for an individual, but also a political one for a society or culture? Should not a defensible ethics demand the renunciation of enjoyment and the adoption of run-of-the-mill social ideals, at least in some circumstances? Paradoxically enough, queer theories of singularity have largely disallowed this kind of question, which has traditionally animated ethical and political inquiry. Clinicians have an easier time with these issues, but only because they adopt professional norms that lead them to instinctively adopt certain ambient social ideals and dissuade their analysands from acting on what may well be considered the most singular aspects of their subjective constitution. To take a banal example from analytic work with gay men, virtually every Lacanian case study presumes that it is better to have penetrative sex with a stable partner than it is to derive sexual enjoyment from, for instance, mutual masturbation with a series of anonymous partners (Conclusion). Accordingly, analysts tend to rate an analysand's gravitation away from non-traditional enjoyment as a step forward in the treatment. Even as most of us would agree with that judgement, broad consensus does not suddenly make it any less of a judgement as to what counts as a better sexual life, and this judgement has strictly nothing to do with an analysand's purported singularity. Similarly, case studies work with an implicit judgement as to how dangerous an individual's sexual practice is – a thorny issue for many gay men and women, who sometimes have (relatively) unprotected or unconventional sex with multiple and sometimes anonymous partners – on the assumption that the safer the sex, the better the outcome. (This is, of course, a relative judgement: analysts might still be happy if a woman marries a man, even though it is a statistical fact that heterosexual marriage is an extremely dangerous situation for a woman). Again, whatever one might think about this issue, there is little room to argue that analysts make no *a priori* judgement as to what is better sex for an analysand and therefore what constitutes some sort of positive step in the treatment. More generally, what is singular and what is good are different things, which is part of the reason why being a good psychoanalyst and being a good clinician may not always be the same thing. Yet, again, theories of singularity do not even give us the vocabulary to pose these questions, since they start with a *parti pris* for singularity over the good. In respect of the current state of queer Lacanian literature, I will be satisfied if this book at least catalogues some of the reasons why there is considerable interest in recentring the 'classical' social Lacan (and what I will argue is a more Marxist version of him between 1968 and the mid-1970s), rather than the later 'singular' Lacan, for a queer perspective to contemporary sexual politics.

4 The Book

This book tries to hold together three threads: queer theory, Lacanian psychoanalysis, and a broad notion of sexual politics, defined vaguely as all those collective efforts that have some describable incidence – efforts and incidences that may be conscious or otherwise – upon human sexuality. Broadly speaking, in the chapters that follow, I present a critique of the queer understanding and application of (Lacanian) psychoanalysis, and then a critique of Lacanian psychoanalysis' inability to engage honestly with some core LGBT+ and queer theoretical problematics, out of which emerge, I think, some suggestions towards what Chapter 4 alternately calls a libidinal economy, or a political economy of enjoyment. On the queer side, I hope to suggest that the partiality of queer theorists' engagement with psychoanalytic thought may very well account for some of the field's more glaring blind spots and dubious political and theoretical commitments. So, for example, I purport to show in Chapter 1 that Judith Butler's reading of Lacan's 'The Signification of the Phallus' largely ignores one of the main problematics Lacan sought to address with the concept of the phallus, namely the intricacies of the disjunction between language and the body, which are emphatically not reducible to Butler's *Bodies That Matter* claim that the body's materiality is not independent of how it is spoken about. Chapter 2 critiques Lee Edelman's *No Future* as a summation of the antisocial thesis, ostensibly the most psychoanalytic of queer traditions, through a reading of Lacan's 1959–60 *Seminar* as presenting an ethics of desire appropriate to the psychoanalytic clinic. That Lacan's ethical thought is centred on desire, and that it is appropriate for the psychoanalytic clinic, means that it cannot provide a basis for the queer idea of an ethics of enjoyment (*jouissance*), self-shattering (*ébranlement*), and other queer antisocial favourites. However, an ethics of desire cannot lend credence to the pseudo-utopian moralism that much 'anti-antisocial' queer thought has sought to develop either. Rather, Lacan proposes a subversion of either perspective: the famous motto of not ceding ground on one's desire means at once acknowledging the dignity of one's particular fate – tied to family, culture, and the accidents of one's upbringing – its inescapability as well as its radical contingency, and acknowledging the internal limits to desire as such, inasmuch as desire is intrinsically bound up with death and its irrepresentability. As Lacan put it elsewhere, analysis, from an ethical point of view, is a long judgement that allows one to regard oneself as subject to the Other's desire and, on that basis, to decide whether one 'wants what [one] desires' (Lacan 2006b, 571).

On the psychoanalytic side, contemporary Lacanism has had a hard time confronting the challenges posed not only by queer critique but also by the changes that Western societies have undergone in the past century, including those societies (notably France, but arguably also the UK and parts of the United States) in which Lacanian approaches have some clinical and scholarly traction.[3] Changes to the legal and social status of women and homosexuality; the advent, popularisation, and/or greater acceptance of various means of technically manipulating sex, gender, sexuality, and procreation (for instance, contraception, abortion, etc.); new patterns of sexual activity and forms of sexual relationships; the evolving legal regulation of kinship and its dominant social forms; the metamorphoses of the capitalist mode of production, of the labour market, and of the (gendered) experience of labour; and many other social, scientific, and political phenomena are all relevant to psychoanalytic theory and practice, yet are usually quite superficially addressed in much Lacanian literature. Lacanian work that purports to make some sociologically or historically informed intervention tends to propose an incredibly simplistic bipartition of the history of the world between the 'good old days' when there was a consistent Other and everyone believed in the role and the power of the Father-who-art-in-Heaven; and a scientific-capitalist modernity in which the Other becomes inconsistent or inexistent. This depiction of history and society as a 'before and after science and/or capitalism', it goes without saying, is overly simplistic, even if it might illuminate aspects of the contemporary clinic. Particularly problematic is the impression one gets while perusing this literature that, even when the relevance of the major societal upheavals of the 20th century (let alone of the rest of human history!) is acknowledged, it is not understood as contradicting any Lacanian claims. If my impression is correct, this is an odd position to take, since Lacan himself was explicitly a historicist in respect of core psychoanalytic categories (which also makes Anglo-American work claiming otherwise suspect; see Copjec 1994), and indeed in respect of psychoanalysis itself. Early on in his career, he claimed, for instance, that the Oedipus complex was a product of the conjugal family form: which should, but mostly does not, lead Lacanians to ask what processes of normalisation (rather than their absence) look like today, in societies that are quite different from 1938 Paris (Lacan 2001; see also Tort 2007).

I discuss some of these issues, as they pertain to the Lacanian version of the Oedipus complex and its rapport with society, through an exploration of the various incarnations of the Lacanian concept of the father in Chapter 3. My main contention there is a painfully simple but, I think, a very important one, namely that Lacanians simply cannot do without an articulate theory of society, whether implicit or explicit. This is because, as I demonstrate through a reading of Lacan's early and classic teaching and of his sources, Lacan consistently defines the father functionally as, whatever else he might be, the pivot of the child's sexual normalisation – whence, Lacan presumes following Mauss and Lévi-Strauss, follows their inclusion into their society, language, and culture. Any theory of the father, therefore, must have an explicit account of what is needed for inclusion into society. If my argument is correct, and if Lacanians fail to provide an explicit theory of society, they *ipso facto* adopt Lacan's implicit one, which Lacan did have between 1938 and 1950, and then between the early 1950s until roughly 1968, and which was conservative as well as heteronormative.

Lacan's earlier theory was adapted first from the French sociological tradition, then, in the 1950s and 1960s, from Freud's *Totem and Taboo* and Claude Lévi-Strauss's *The Elementary Structures of Kinship*. In either case, it was not merely gendered but radically heteronormative: whenever Lacan discusses society or history from 1938 until the 1960s his assumption is that the basic unit of Western society and/or the normative standard for the regulation of sexuality is the conjugal family composed of the virile-male and virginal-female partners to a married, reproductive, cisheterosexual couple and their minor children (see Zafiropoulos 2001, 2010; Verhaeghe 2009; Robcis 2013). It follows that normality is not merely incidentally tied to one's capacity to form a heterosexual family, but essentially so tied, and that it is a substantive ideal to be strived towards. This diagnosis does not change by force of the (correct) argument that Lacan problematises and subverts the notion of normality, for instance by positing that there is no sexual rapport: everyone can agree that the perfect conjunction between man and woman is impossible while still holding that some failures are better than others, and Lacan very explicitly thought that conjugal heterosexuality was the 'most elegant and the easiest' such failure (Lacan 2023, 376, my translation). This is the version of the Lacanian Oedipus that queer theorists are most familiar with, and the one they have correctly argued to be unacceptably reductive and heteronormative. I take care to present my evidence for this argument in the form of long quotations, in anticipation that it will be controversial, but I hasten to note that I do not think this is Lacan's last word on this issue.

In fact, Chapter 4 charts Lacan's turn away from this rather crude and quiescent take on society and the Oedipus complex, as he starts to centre his theoretical reflection on the issue of *jouissance* or enjoyment and, importantly, its discursive capture. I argue that this is a pivotal moment in Lacan's work, because it entails Lacan's shift from a Lévi-Straussian, anthropological-structuralist theoretical axis towards a Marxian, political-economic one. This shift becomes all the more important when one notes that the notion of the father all but disappears in Lacan's post-1968 theory, to be explicitly collapsed under that of the phallus as a metaphor for renounced male enjoyment in *Seminar XIV* (see Chiesa 2007 and Chapters 1 and 3). Conceptually, this means that Lacan no longer considers the father to be a sort of extralinguistic power assuring that signifiers and signifieds correspond to one another (and, importantly for queer theorists, that the phallus corresponds with penis, woman, or child in Oedipalised subjects), but rather something immanent to, and circulated in, discourse. I argue, finally, that this move inaugurates the promise of a political economy of enjoyment in Lacan's theory, one that remains to be systematically developed (beyond the excellent philosophical statement made in Tomšič 2015, 2019), but has generated some definite insights about the way capitalism and science have libidinal consequences that queer theorists have all but ignored. Finally, I return to these problems in the Conclusion, where I situate and critique a few recent texts by Jacques-Alain Miller (Lacan's son-in-law and main intellectual legatee) and other French Lacanians that amount to a defence of a collective politics of Lacanism as conservative-liberal and hostile to the LGBT+ movement.

I hope that this book might serve as a sort of epistemological intervention in respect of some partialities of both queer theoretical literature and Anglophone Lacanian literature, especially within cultural studies and similar disciplines. On the queer side, the exploration that follows purports to step away from the queer theoretical commitment to an antinormative ego-ideal that all too often bears little resemblance or reference to how people negotiate sexual rules, ideals, and activities in the personal, social, and political planes. I concur with scholars who argue that queer work has relied far too much on its credentials as a sort of academic-activist radical chic and that, over time, this has translated into a disciplinary *a priori* – rather than a research programme or a set of observations – stating that 'queer' is, by virtue of being 'queer', subversive, revolutionary, the locus of resistance to heteronormativity, or whatever other formulation one might prefer. This has led commentators to argue – correctly and, to my mind, damningly – that queer theory all too often bears little reference to empirical reality, where non-straight people are often concerned with surviving and having fun (and what's wrong with that?) rather than with the radical subversion of gendered norms (see, for instance, Morton 1996; Browne and Nash 2010).

Conversely, on the Anglophone Lacanian side, I want this book to participate in a movement away from an overwhelmingly 'philosophical' contextualisation of Lacan (and indeed queer theory) towards a more 'social scientific' contextualisation of Lacan (see Zafiropoulos 2001, 2010; de la Torre 2018). As recent queer Lacanian work makes clear, the Anglo-American reception of Lacan remains rooted in the poststructuralist tradition and has, for over 30 years now, been hopelessly stuck in a philosophical debate between particularism (pro-identity analytics) and universalism (anti-identity analytics). It seems to me that this debate has become routinised and that it has, like queer theory more broadly, lost any systematic reference to social reality, sexual politics, and indeed to the practices, desires, taboos, and fantasies that constitute sexuality proper (see, especially, Penney 2014; Ruti 2017; Coffman 2022). While I have much respect and admiration for this literature and understand the enormous stakes of this debate, it is perhaps time that queer scholars interested in Lacanian theory start asking themselves whether what Slavoj Žižek and Alain Badiou think about women and sexual minorities is so urgently important that it deserves such impassioned commentary.

Since I am intervening into two scholarly fields with their own distinctive and often conflicting conceptual constellations, interpretive techniques, historical problematics, and fields of application, not to mention the strictures implied in the fact that Lacanian psychoanalysis is not merely a theory but also a clinic and social movement, I have made the decision to not assume that the jargon of either field is intelligible to the other. This has had a few consequences for the book, some of which are merely formal, and some substantive. I hope, on the formal front, that the book is, if not accessible *tout court*, at least more accessible than much extant Lacanian and queer work. Much of the literature in this area is notoriously opaque – Lévi-Strauss once remarked that 'understanding' to the Lacanian acolyte seemed to mean something very different than what it meant for him (Eribon and Lévi-Strauss 1991) – and, to my knowledge, little English-language work has sought to make the queer problematic intelligible to a Lacanian audience, and vice versa, at a basic conceptual level (although see Gherovici 2010; and the essays collected in Giffney and Watson 2017; and in Gherovici and Steinkoler 2023). On a more substantive note, I acknowledge that my scholarly apparatus could have been more robust, precisely because I have opted for more intelligibility rather than more comprehensiveness. Specifically, I have decided to discuss certain ideas and concepts at length, including their context and often also their sources, and sometimes accompanied by long quotations, rather than assume a reader with too much specialised knowledge. The result has been that some literature that could have received greater elaboration was either left out, or only briefly touched on, but also hopefully given a sufficiently clear exposition.

I would like to make some remarks about my own reading practices, since the following chapters give Lacan extensive exegetical treatment and since I do not touch on this topic in the chapters themselves (although I do give reasons for my choices in respect of the queer theoretical archive there, and so will not discuss them here). There are plenty of ways to categorise the 'moments' of Lacan's work, including, but certainly not limited to, the 'standard' early/imaginary, mid/symbolic, and late/real Lacanian schema that has been largely canonised by now. Personally, I find this schema less useful than most commentators in tracking the momentous changes, not merely in emphasis but in substance and theoretical axis, that Lacan's work undergoes throughout his life and teaching. Specifically, this tripartition seems to presume that these concepts provide some sort of stability to Lacan's work, which would require them to mean more or less the same thing as Lacan's teaching goes on. This is patently untrue: for example, the notion of the real until the mid-1950s is just a common-sense notion of 'reality' and will be given a technical meaning no earlier than in the 1959–60 *Seminar VII*. What I have sought to do in the readings that follow is to isolate sections of Lacan's work in which I take his formulations about the topics I am most interested in to be more or less stable, or moments in which they undergo significant and more or less isolatable changes.

These sections are of quite variable length. Chapter 1 pays close attention to what Lacan has to say about the father, the phallus, and sexual normalisation in the 'classical' period between *Seminars III* and *V*, held between 1955–8, whereas Chapter 2 looks almost exclusively at the 1959–60 *Seminar VII*. Chapter 3 follows Zafiropoulos (2001, 2010) and Chiesa (2007) in isolating three broader and fuzzier 'moments' of Lacan's theory of the father, one running from 1938–50, another important one throughout the 1950s, and yet another 'undercurrent' beginning in 1958–9 and reaching its highest point in 1966–7. Chapter 4 includes Lacan's scattered pronouncements about capitalism made from 1968 to Lacan's death in 1981, while the Conclusion considers aspects of the post-Lacanian doxa between the 1990s and today. Even if they might vary wildly in length, it is my contention that, in respect of the issues that concern each of the chapters, my preferred sections correspond to moments when Lacan is following a set of definite threads that can be isolated and the progression of which can be tracked through the characteristic discontinuities of the *Seminar*, which often drops topics from one session to the next, and picks them up at sometimes much later dates, and throughout which Lacan's opinion on various issues changes, sometimes abruptly. My choices are guided by the topics I am interested in, and accordingly the sections I isolate make no further claim in respect of the continuity of Lacan's problematics in other respects. Thus, other ways of partitioning Lacan's work are possible in respect of different problematics to the ones I pursue here in ways consistent with my method.

Finally, I refer to the *Seminar* and to the written works with no presumption that the one is more important than the others. In retrospect, however, it would be dishonest not to recognise that my interpretation probably relies more on the *Seminar* than on the written work. I can only really give personal reasons for this. Personally, I find the *Seminar* much more interesting, precisely for the qualities that make it arguably less rigorous: the reader of the seminar gets a better feel for how Lacan's public engagement is a sort of live experimentation with ideas and knowledge, which makes it not entirely unlike the analytic itinerary itself. Additionally, the very open-ended form of the *Seminar*, as well as Lacan's reiterated (and most often unheeded) requests for the cooperation of his audience, serve as a reminder that Lacan left most of the work of developing the implications of his various theoretical systems (which are systems, and which are many) to his auditors and readers – a task, it seems to me, that has been only very timidly taken up since his death over 40 years ago. Finally, the *Seminar* includes a great deal of digressions and commentary on current events, which provide sometimes useful indications of the concrete issues from the standpoint of which Lacan is considering his rather abstract systems.

Finally, insofar as this book makes an intervention in respect of which parts of Lacan's work are more representative of his 'doctrine' – and I am not entirely sure that it does – it is the following: it would perhaps be more in keeping with the spirit of the *Seminar* that scholars start to think of Lacanism as a method of reading for the desire encoded in a text or practice (such as Freud's, or the analytic itinerary), rather than as a fixed set of concrete propositions constituting a knowledge.[4] However, this is not to reject the point that privileging the written work might yield the opposite contention, of course, and that doing so might be methodologically valuable (as in Jean-Claude Milner's brilliant *L'Oeuvre claire* 1995).

Notes

1 Some Lacanians might object to this formulation and reframe this problem as one having to do with language acquisition and the imposition of linguistic schemata on pre-existing drive excitations. In this view, the problem is not the child's sexual normalisation, presumed to prepare them for social life, but rather their ability to tame the excessive organic and inborn excitation they experience through a sort of shield made up of a set of (linguistic) representations (see Verhaeghe 2009). This objection is, of course, valid, but it smuggles in a negative biological argument (specifically that biology, here represented in 'the drive', is the limit of psychoanalysis) that Lacan found suspicious, and it fails to take seriously the question as to where the protective representations the infant is meant to acquire come from. For Lacan, and this throughout his work, these come from society via the family, and so every Lacanian claim about subjectivity is also and simultaneously a social claim.

2 Any symptom in Lacan, including during his classical Lévi-Straussian phase, can be defined as a more or less successful compensation (*suppléance*) for a deficient Name-of-the-Father (see Zafiropoulos 2010). The new writing for the *sinthome* adds little but a topographical dimension to this Lacanian concept (i.e. the *sinthome* is not the expression of an unconscious conflict) and, to my mind, does not do much to help us to think about the rapport between subjectivity and society.

3 I exclude other major centres of Lacanian thought and practice – notably Brazil and Argentina – from this list partly because I am publishing this book in English, but also because the psychoanalytic literature issuing from these countries strikes me as more politically aware than that issuing from Western Europe and the United States. I would suggest that this greater awareness of social and political concerns is possibly due to these countries' postcolonial nature and to the recent authoritarian history of Latin America (for an exploration of the Brazilian case, see Alves Lima 2021).

4 I owe this suggestion to Prof. Emerita Maria Aristodemou.

References

Althusser, Louis. 2001. 'Ideology and Ideological State Apparatuses'. In *Lenin and Philosophy and Other Essays*, translated by Ben Brewster, 1st ed., 85–126. New York: Monthly Review Press.

Alves Lima, Rafael. 2021. *A Psicanálise Na Ditadura Civil-Militar Brasileira*. Doctoral Thesis, São Paulo: University of São Paulo. https://www.teses.usp.br/teses/disponiveis/47/47133/tde-12082021-220350/publico/lima_do.pdf.

Beam, Myrl. 2018. *Gay, Inc: The Nonprofitization of Queer Politics*. Minneapolis, MN: University of Minnesota Press.

Bersani, Leo. 1995. *Homos*. 1st ed. Cambridge, MA: Harvard University Press.

Browne, Kath, and Catherine Nash. 2010. 'Queer Methods and Methodologies: An Introduction'. In *Queer Methods and Methodologies*, edited by Kath Browne and Catherine Nash, 1st ed. London: Routledge.

Buist, Carrie, and Emily Lenning. 2023. *Queer Criminology*. 2nd ed. London: Routledge.

Butler, Judith. 1994. 'Introduction: Against Proper Objects'. *Differences* 6 (2/3): 1–26.

Butler, Judith. 1999. *Gender Trouble: Feminism and the Subversion of Identity*. 2nd ed. New York: Routledge.

Chiesa, Lorenzo. 2007. *Subjectivity and Otherness: A Philosophical Reading of Lacan*. 1st ed. Cambridge, MA: MIT Press.

Coffman, Chris. 2022. *Queer Traversals: Psychoanalytic Queer and Trans Theories*. 1st ed. London: Bloomsbury.

Copjec, Joan. 1994. *Read My Desire: Lacan Against the Historicists*. 1st ed. Cambridge, MA: MIT Press.

De la Torre, Shanna. 2018. *Sex for Structuralists: The Non-Oedipal Logics of Femininity and Psychosis*. 1st ed. London: Palgrave Macmillan.

Dean, Tim. 2000. *Beyond Sexuality*. 1st ed. Chicago, IL: University of Chicago Press.

Deleuze, Gilles, and Didier Eribon. 1995. 'Life as a Work of Art'. In *Negotiations*, translated by Martin Joughin, 94–102. New York: Columbia University Press.

Duggan, Lisa. 2003. *The Twilight of Equality? Neoliberalism and the Attack on Democracy*. Boston, MA: Beacon Press.

Edelman, Lee. 2004. *No Future: Queer Theory and the Death Drive*. 1st ed. Durham, NC and London: Duke University Press.

Eng, David. 2010. *The Feeling of Kinship*. 1st ed. Durham, NC: Duke University Press.

Eribon, Didier, and Claude Lévi-Strauss. 1991. *Conversations with Claude Lévi-Strauss*. Chicago: University of Chicago Press.

Flores, Andrew. 2021. *Social Acceptance of LGBTI People in 175 Countries and Locations, 1981 to 2020*. Los Angeles, CA: The Williams Institute.

Freud, Sigmund. 1955. 'Group Psychology and Analysis of the Ego'. In *The Standard Edition of the Complete Psychological Works of Sigmund Freud*, vol. XVIII, translated by James Strachey, 65–133. London: The Hogarth Press.

Gherovici, Patricia. 2010. *Please Select Your Gender*. 1st ed. New York: Routledge.

Gherovici, Patricia, and Manya Steinkoler, eds. 2023. *Psychoanalysis, Gender, and Sexualities: From Feminism to Trans**. 1st ed. London: Routledge.

Giffney, Noreen, and Eve Watson, eds. 2017. *Clinical Encounters in Sexuality: Psychoanalytic Practice and Queer Theory*. 1st ed. Santa Barbara, CA: punctum books.

Godelier, Maurice. 2004. *The Metamorphoses of Kinship*. Translated by Nora Scott. 1st ed. London: Verso.

Harari, Roberto. 2002. *How James Joyce Made His Name: A Reading of the Final Lacan*. Translated by Thurston Luke. 1st ed. New York: Other Press.

Hocquenghem, Guy. 1993. *Homosexual Desire*. Translated by Daniella Dangoor. 1st ed. Durham, NC and London: Duke University Press.

Huffer, Lynne. 2013. *Are the Lips a Grave? A Queer Feminist on the Ethics of Sex*. 1st ed. New York: Columbia University Press.

Human Rights Campaign. n.d. 'Marriage Equality Around the World'. https://www.hrc.org/resources/marriage-equality-around-the-world.

Klapeer, Christine. 2017. 'Queering Development in Homotransnationalist Times'. *Lambda Nordica* 2–3: 41–67.

Kollias, Hector. 2012. 'Queering It Right, Getting It Wrong'. *Paragraph* 35 (3): 141–163.

Lacan, Jacques. 1992. *The Seminar of Jacques Lacan, Book VII: The Ethics of Psychoanalysis*. Translated by Dennis Porter. 1st ed. London: W. W. Norton.

Lacan, Jacques. 2001. 'Les complexes familiaux dans la formation de l'individu'. In *Autres écrits*, 1st ed., 23–84. Paris: Seuil.

Lacan, Jacques. 2006a. 'Presentation on Transference'. In *Écrits*, translated by Bruce Fink, 1st ed., 176–187. New York: W.W. Norton.

Lacan, Jacques. 2006b. 'Remarks on Daniel Lagache's Presentation: "Psychoanalysis and Personality Structure"'. In *Écrits*, translated by Bruce Fink, 543–574. New York: W.W. Norton.

Lacan, Jacques. 2006c. 'The Subversion of the Subject and the Dialectic of Desire in the Freudian Unconscious'. In *Écrits*, translated by Bruce Fink, 1st ed., 671–702. New York: W.W. Norton.

Lacan, Jacques. 2014. *The Seminar of Jacques Lacan, Book X: Anxiety.* Translated by A.R. Price. Cambridge: Polity.

Lacan, Jacques. 2020. *The Seminar of Jacques Lacan, Book IV: The Object Relation.* Translated by A.R. Price. 1st ed. Cambridge: Polity.

Lacan, Jacques. 2023. *Le Séminaire, Livre XIV: La logique du fantasme.* 1st ed. Paris: Seuil.

Leader, Darian. 2021. *Jouissance: Sexuality, Suffering, and Satisfaction.* 1st ed. Cambridge: Polity.

Love, Heather. 2020. 'Interview with Heather Love'. *Interalia* 15. https://interalia.queerstudies.pl/wp-content/uploads/InterAlia_5-2000_Heather-Love.pdf.

Love, Heather. 2021. *Underdogs: Social Deviance and Queer Theory.* 1st ed. Chicago, IL: University of Chicago Press.

Massad, Joseph. 2006. *Desiring Arabs.* 1st ed. Chicago, IL: University of Chicago Press.

Milner, Jean-Claude. 1995. *L'Oeuvre claire.* 1st ed. Paris: Seuil.

Morton, David. 1996. 'Changing the Terms: (Virtual) Desire and (Actual) Reality'. In *The Material Queer: A LesBiGay Cultural Studies Reader*, edited by David Morton, 1st ed., 1–34. Boulder, CO: Westview Press.

Penney, James. 2014. *After Queer Theory: The Limits of Sexual Politics.* London: Pluto Press.

Picq, Manuela Lavinas, and Marcus Thiel. 2015. 'Introduction: Sexualities in World Politics'. In *Sexual Politics and International Relations: How LGBTQ Claims Shape International Relations*, edited by Manuela Lavinas Picq and Marcus Thiel, 1st ed., 1–22. New York: Routledge.

Puar, Jasbir. 2017. *Terrorist Assemblages: Homonationalism in Queer Times.* 2nd ed. Durham, NC and London: Duke University Press.

Ragland-Sullivan, Ellie. 2004. *The Logic of Sexuation.* 1st ed. New York: SUNY Press.

Rao, Rahul. 2015. 'Global Homocapitalism'. *Radical Philosophy* 194: 38–49.

Robcis, Camille. 2013. *The Law of Kinship: Anthropology, Psychoanalysis, and the Family in France.* 1st ed. Ithaca, NY: Cornell University Press.

Rose, Jacqueline. 1982. 'Introduction – II'. In *Feminine Sexuality*, edited by Juliet Mitchell and Jacqueline Rose, 1st ed., 27–56. London: Macmillan.

Ruti, Mari. 2012. *The Singularity of Being.* 1st ed. New York: Fordham University Press.

Ruti, Mari. 2017. *The Ethics of Opting Out: Queer Theory's Defiant Subjects.* 1st ed. New York: Columbia University Press.

Spade, Dean. 2015. *Normal Life: Administrative Violence, Critical Trans Politics, and the Limits of Law.* 1st ed. Durham, NC: Duke University Press.

Stonewall. 2016. 'Key Dates for Lesbian, Gay, Bi, and Trans Equality', 26 July. https://www.stonewall.org.uk/key-dates-lesbian-gay-bi-and-trans-equality?gad_source=1.

Thoreson, Ryan. 2022. '"Discriminalization": Sexuality, Human Rights, and the Carceral Turn in Antidiscrimination Law.' *California Law Review* 110: 431–488.

Tomšič, Samo. 2015. *The Capitalist Unconscious.* 1st ed. London: Verso.

Tomšič, Samo. 2019. *The Labour of Enjoyment.* 1st ed. Berlin: August Verlag.

Tort, Michel. 2007. *La fin du dogme paternel.* 1st ed. Paris: Flammarion.

Verhaeghe, Paul. 2009. *A Radical Reconsideration of the Oedipus Complex.* 1st ed. New York: Other Press.

Weber, Cynthia. 2016. *Queer International Relations.* 1st ed. Oxford: Oxford University Press.

Wiegman, Robyn, and Elizabeth A. Wilson. 2015. 'Introduction: Antinormativity's Queer Conventions'. *Differences* 26 (1): 1–25.

Zafiropoulos, Markos. 2001. *Lacan et les sciences sociales: Le déclin du père.* 1st ed. Paris: Presses Universitaires de France.

Zafiropoulos, Markos. 2010. *Lacan and Lévi-Strauss or the Return to Freud (1951–1957).* Translated by John Holland. 1st ed. London: Karnac.

Chapter 1

To Φ or Not

Gender Trouble and the Phallus (1955–9)

1 Engendering Desire

It is impossible to say anything queer in a theoretically sound fashion without bringing up Judith Butler's work. Indeed, *Gender Trouble* and its follow-up, *Bodies That Matter*, have generated such an immense amount of enthusiasm that Butler's thinking on normativity and identity has undoubtedly become something like a cultural, in addition to an academic, staple. In the same way that one cannot seem to stop using Freudian categories such as identification, repression, castration, and other tools of the Freudian arsenal, when one speaks of psychology each day, it appears that one cannot stop using Butlerian categories to speak about modes of sexual and gendered expression either. Everyone acknowledges that gender and sexuality are performative, or at the very least that they are socially constructed and, often enough, that even sex (usually understood as biological) will not escape the tyranny of the norm. In queer circles, Butler's deconstruction of the gender binary and of the sex-gender distinction has indeed become canonical to the point where to question it is to run the risk of being seen as an artifact from another era.

For an inquiry into the issue of Lacan's reception in queer theory, however, Butler's work does not represent an easy or convenient way in. Lacan's name was first approached in queer theory through Butler's powerful critique of the alleged heteronormativity of his account of desire. Butler's well-known argument is twofold. While Butler recognises that Lacan is right in approaching gender and sexuality from the vantage of symbolic positionings, first, Butler claims that he continues to uphold a form of essentialism in that there are only two (male and female) positions to be taken before the signifier denoting all possible meaning-effects in respect of desire (the phallus – more on this definition later); and, second, Lacan's position on the purportedly insurmountable character of symbolic determination amounts to political quietism insofar as it does not allow any room for the proliferation of desires that are not ultimately reducible to a heterosexualised gender binary. Put simply, Butler argues that Lacan remains too faithful to Freud's belief

DOI: 10.4324/9781003424604-2

that analysis can only aspire to bring its analysands to the bedrock of castration – that is, to acknowledge one's penis envy, if one is a woman, or one's castration anxiety, if one is a man (Freud 1964). Lacan may indeed radicalise this argument, Butler suggests, by positing that the phallus one will always and necessarily either demand to plug up one's lack-of-penis (or fear that it may be chopped off) as the central building block of culture in its entirety.

In light of Butler's crucial queer challenge to Lacanian thinking, this chapter advances three interrelated arguments. My first argument is that *Gender Trouble* – and this changes very little with Butler's subsequent work – is theoretically inadequate if measured by its reading and critique of Lacan. The poverty of *Gender Trouble*'s engagement with Lacanian psychoanalysis has been pointed out more than once since the book's publication (Copjec 1994; Dean 2000; Penney 2014; Rae 2020). *Gender Trouble* directly quotes only a single text from Lacan's *Écrits*, namely 'The Signification of the Phallus', composed around the time of *Seminar V* and dealing with themes from *Seminars III, IV,* and *V*. My second argument is that there are grounds to suspect that even Butler's reading of 'The Signification of the Phallus' is, if not wrong, at least damagingly partial or misguided. My third argument is that Butler's reading in *Gender Trouble* would remain theoretically inadequate even had Butler considered more of Lacan's own work of this same period in his *Seminar*, for the reason that Lacan's thinking undergoes an important shift in *Seminar VI*. This final suggestion introduces the problematic with which the next chapter is concerned.

This sustained reconsideration of the Butlerian critique of Lacan is important for my overarching point in this book. Specifically, I intend to suggest that Lacanian theory offers a more interesting basis for thinking about sexual politics than LGBT+ and queer theorists have so far recognised. Part of this itinerary involves the suggestion that it is at least arguable that Lacan's theory is not necessarily sexist, patriarchal, and heteronormative, although there is ample scope to interpret it as such (Chapter 3). In what follows, I argue that Lacan's accounts of the phallus and of the Oedipus complex allow for readings that do not reduce psychoanalysis to the *epos* of the father. In other words, there is a case to be made that, for Lacan, 'psychoanalysis is not the Oedipal rite' (Lacan 2006e, 693). Before elaborating upon these arguments, the question must be asked as to what motivates me to revisit this apparently well-trodden ground. A core consideration in this regard is that most well-known attempts to provide a more nuanced picture of Lacan's thinking on sexual difference have focused on his later theory of sexuation, which relates it to the concept of enjoyment and to his reworking of contemporary and Aristotelian logical categories (Zupančič 2018; Copjec 1994), and have left his considerations on the Oedipus complex from the 1950s relatively untouched. Similarly, few attempts to take Lacan's thinking on sexual identity seriously within queer theory seem to have grappled with Butler's reading of Lacan on its own terms. Finally, thinking through Butler's early[1] engagement with Lacan, and especially if one takes into account the progression of Lacan's thinking across the 1950s, is particularly important since it appears that Butler's argument has lent credence to something of a dismissal of Lacan in queer and LGBT+ circles (an argument that extends to Butler themselves, whose theoretical development, for one, has been said to be marked by a disavowal of its debt to Lacan; see Kollias 2012).

A non-heteronormative reading of Lacan's take on these issues requires a lengthy excursus into Lacan's dialectical and developmental explanation of the Oedipus complex. In hyper-condensed form, the gist of the argument is that, for Lacan, an infant does not have the linguistic resources to designate what they want, such that their demands will all be translated back to them by the caretaker, who is moreover responsible for the satisfaction or otherwise of the infant's needs and demands. Since, from the perspective of the infant, all satisfaction comes from the caretaker, the satisfaction of all needs and demands becomes coterminous with the caretaker's presence. It follows that, later, if the child can become what the caretaker lacks, the caretaker's presence is assured, and uninterrupted satisfaction with it. Therefore, because of the conditions of their early infancy, the child will try to identify with whatever they think the caretaker lacks – the sum of which Lacanians call the phallus, and which represents, at this stage, the object of the caretaker's desire.

At this early stage, then, there is a confusion between successfully being the phallus for the caretaker and the fantasy of an impossible assurance of satisfaction. 'If I am the phallus, which is what the caretaker wants, the caretaker does not leave me, and I am satisfied'. The problem with this satisfaction is that it is paradoxically dissatisfying: because the caretaker originally cannot be sure that the objects provided to the child are really what they want, and because the caretaker must nevertheless 'contain' every satisfaction for the child, the child gives up the specificity of all objects granted them by the caretaker and transmutes those objects into proofs of love. There accordingly comes about, at this stage, a sort of mismatch between the specific object of need and the unspecifiable object of demand: the object of need must come from a limited repertoire (water, food), whereas the object of demand can be anything at all, inasmuch as it is always *a priori* proof of the caretaker's love. One result of this mismatch is precisely desire, to the extent that it persists only insofar as the object demanded is not what is capable of satisfying, since it (the object) is merely a proof of love. Another such result is the repurposing, so to speak, of the phallus as a signifier to a hypothetical object that would overcome that mismatch. Henceforth, it may be said that the phallus becomes the signifier to the object of desire, but only insofar as it is recognised that it refers to an absence or impossibility, specifically the impossibility of particularising the object that might satisfy a demand for the caretaker's love as if it were an object of need (indeed, the object of all needs).

In this sense, I argue that the role of the phallus in one's earliest upbring-ing has nothing *a priori* to do with gender and sexual identity. What will forcibly place the phallus in these contexts is the father, the Lacanian account of which, I argue, must be characterised as a particular (rather than a universal) subjective solution as well as a sociopolitical technology. For the Oedipus complex to decline normatively, the father must give proof that what the mother (who must, at this point, be a mother, and not just any caretaker) lacks, and what the child strives to be for her, lies securely in his possession. The father breaks apart the game of identifications and counter-identifications the child had been engaged in in their rapport with the mother by stating: 'your mother lacks a penis, which I have, and which she wants; you, the child, have or do not have one, depending on whether you are a boy or a girl, but at any rate it is nothing compared to mine – you will be able to use yours when you are a man like me, or you will get a child as a substitute for your lack of one when you are a woman, so long as you respect the rules of the game by acting like a grown man or woman'. The father, in this sense, transmits the prerogatives and norms of one's gender and sex by enforcing the basic categories and taboos accruing to kinship, and it is only in this transmission that the phallus takes on the heteronormative clothing it has been given by Butler and other queer thinkers. Finally, then, Lacan's account of the Oedipus complex is not necessarily heteronormative, although, in fact, his elaboration of it in *Seminars IV* and *V* is, making it all the more impor-tant that Lacan shifts gears as early as *Seminar VI*, with the proclamation that there is no Other of the Other.

2 Judith Butler: The Heterosexual Matrix

Judith Butler's momentous intervention in *Gender Trouble* (1999) laid the theoretical and conceptual groundwork for queer theory. It first established a kind of axiomatic that is still followed, almost verbatim, by many queer and queer-adjacent thinkers. I believe it is useful to offer a condensed statement of that book's argument, as follows:

1   Gender, sex, and desire are socially constructed.

    a   Gender, then, is not to culture as sex is to biology – rather, (biological) sex was (cultural) gender all along.

2   Gender, sex, and desire, all of which are cultural, entertain complex relations to one another, and these relations can be uncovered discursively.

    a   There is a norm of alignment joining together gender, sex, and desire.

    b   This norm of alignment is presumptively heterosexual, which is to say that it privileges an alignment of gender, sex, and desire amounting to a certain idealised image of the two parties to the heterosexual couple.

3   Gender is not merely socially constructed, but performative – strictly speaking, there is no set of attributes with which one may describe (any given) gender in a way that holds across times and places.

   a   'Performative' is to be understood both in its theatrical sense – of performing a role – and in its philosophical sense – as a speech act that does something by virtue of nothing but its utterance.

   b   The ritualised repetition of norm-governed behaviour (e.g. the performance of a role) called 'gender' retrospectively conjures up – performatively – the illusion of a gendered agent standing prior to the ritualised repetition itself.

   c   This retrospectively conjured up agent of a norm-governed behaviour is gender identity, or more aptly 'a man' or 'a woman'.

4   The norms which determine the ritualised repetition of behaviour (which in turn conjure up the illusion of a gendered agent behind it) are themselves a function of power.

   a   Power has both a repressive and a creative function, which is to say that it 'engenders' the subjects it 'genders'.

   b   Power, however, cannot be ascribed a subjective intention; it is no more than 'a reiterated acting' (Butler 2011, xviii) out of which norms emerge and become entrenched in time.

Gender Trouble opens to a critique of the various understandings of gender that were available to feminists working in the late 1980s. Broadly speaking, Butler finds the dominant representation of gender as a set of cultural meanings superimposed upon an objectively existing biological substratum (called 'sex') inadequate for the purposes of a transformative sexual politics. Feminists tended to articulate their project of equality or emancipation as acting upon gender, rather than sex. So, as the feminists Butler disagrees with tended to see it, women objectively existed as a sex – they were human individuals with breasts, vaginas, XX chromosomes, uteruses, etc., and could be systematically differentiated from men on this basis – but from these characteristics alone it was impossible to account for women's political and economic subordination. Rather, feminists tended to agree that to account for women's oppression was only possible via the concept of gender, which was accordingly understood as a set of cultural, political, or ideological meanings attached to the pre-existing material of sex which objectively predated gendered meaning.

Understanding gender in these terms accomplished at least two important goals: first, it showed that women were not naturally subordinated to men, since it was cultural gender, not biological sex, that accounted for women's subordination. So, feminists could claim that gender was actually a function of women's oppression, rather than the converse – that is, rather than the claim that it was due to women's biological femaleness that they were oppressed. Accordingly, change in the relations between the genders was not only possible – because these relations were not rooted in women's biology and accordingly not subject to the whims of the *longue durée* of evolution, which would put them outside of our political reach – but imperative. Second, to understand gender and sex as distinct from one another guaranteed that women who were discriminated against on the basis of gender were still a unitary group-subject, inasmuch as they shared a sex defined as biological. It was not the case, then, that the sexed nature of women dictated that they would be dominated by men; rather, it was men's domination that designated 'feminine' characteristics as *a posteriori* justifications for the domination of those who displayed them; yet women were still unproblematically a distinctive social group by virtue of the sex they shared.

One issue with this representation of the sex-gender distinction is that it tended to overlook the great diversity of possible social positions occupied by women. So, for instance, to speak of a womanhood that was universally shared – that is, to suggest that people who had breasts, vaginas, and other such phenotypical traits, were all on average bearers of certain gendered characteristics inculcated into them, and to which they were subjected by virtue of their sexed characteristics – was at once to obscure the fact that the issues that mattered to, say, a white, upper-middle class feminist in London were certainly very different from those facing a seamstress from the Global South. If women were oppressed on the basis of gender yet were still recognisably women by virtue of their sex, there was no need to acknowledge the differences among various modes of being a woman. While feminists had undoubtedly recognised the silences a presumptively white-first-world-middle-class, etc., feminist theory and politics tended to perpetrate, there seemed to be no theory of gender capable of accommodating the increasingly precarious status of the 'woman' subject without making reference to some essential womanhood, whether cultural or biological, that would subtend that concept (at the cost of minimising the importance of the differences among women).

This, then, is the terrain Butler purported to intervene upon with *Gender Trouble*: feminism needed a subject, yet the subject of feminism was under siege from all sides, and all attempted solutions had until then been defeated by their own universalising pretentions. Butler's solution to this conundrum, in a nutshell, is to 'empty' the central category of feminism, that of 'woman', of any content. For Butler, gender is a highly regulated, ritualised repetition of behavioural and aesthetic norms, and not some substantive identity rooted in some culture or other, nor indeed in any set of biological or anatomical characteristics. It is only in complying with the behavioural and aesthetic norms of gender that an individual might, in becoming a subject, accede to social recognition, which is to say to become intelligible from the standpoint of a given social formation, and accordingly to be deemed to live a worthy or liveable life. Predictably, these norms are biased towards a quite specific iteration of gendered and sexual identity, namely heterosexual masculine-presenting men and feminine-presenting women who were so designated at birth (and not subjected to any surgical 'correction') and who never much questioned that designation.

This ambitious contention is substantiated in *Gender Trouble* by a compelling reconstruction of the hegemonic schema of the gendered and sexualised criteria through which intelligible subjects were, Butler claims, constituted throughout the history of Western philosophy. In one of *Gender Trouble*'s most enduring legacies, Butler approaches the constitution of the 'intelligible' – that is, capable of social recognition – subject as a result of compliance with the heterosexual matrix. The heterosexual matrix is, at minimum, a relation of entailment among the three (socially constructed) categories of sex, gender, and desire. To count as an intelligible subject under the heterosexual matrix, a given subject would have:

1   A sexed body that presents itself unambiguously as having either a penis or a vagina (or a determinate set of XX or XY chromosomes, or a particular reproductive apparatus, or whichever criteria are preferred for determining sex at a given historical juncture; see, on this point, Fausto-Sterling 2000).
2   A gendered self-presentation corresponding to the meanings attributed to their morphology (that is, one must be a masculine man with a penis or a feminine woman with a vagina).
3   A desire for the opposite sex-gender (a man desires a woman who desires a man).

In the matrix's completed form, then, a masculine man with a penis desires feminine women with vaginas, while a feminine woman with a vagina desires masculine men with penises, and these two oppositional but complementary positions pose as an exhaustive description of what it means to be a person. Axiomatically, everyone has a sex, a gender, and a desire that align in this neat fashion (Butler 1999). Conversely, anything that eschews that direct relation of entailment – say, a (gay) man with a penis who desires other men with penises, a (lesbian) woman with a vagina who desires other women with vaginas, or any other such permutation – is coded as unintelligible, that is, said to exist only as a pathology within the terms of the heterosexual matrix.

Concretely, the effect of this manner of regulation of gender and sexual identity is that certain lives will be deemed worth living and fostering, whereas others – those that fail to comply with the alignment demanded by the heterosexual matrix – will not. The immediate implication is that the social regulation of gender and sexual expression has historically tended to produce heterosexual and cisgendered men and women who acted manly or femininely and were capable and desirous of reproduction, and to admit of no variation to this motif. *Gender Trouble* goes on to trace the influence of the heterosexual matrix in some of the most refined theories that attempted to account for gender and sexuality over the course of the 20th century, particularly those associated with structuralism and poststructuralism. One of Butler's targets is Lacan.

3 Judith Butler: The Phallus, the Symbolic

To reconstruct Butler's reading of Lacan, one must first turn to Lévi-Strauss's *The Elementary Structures of Kinship*, an ambitious endeavour to systematise the logics subtending the varied kinship systems prevalent in non-modern societies. It is also simultaneously a general hypothesis about the origin of human society and its coincidence with the origin of symbolic thought. For Lévi-Strauss, what founds kinship relations, supposedly the most basic bond that humans establish with one another in that it subjects sexuality (a human need requiring the participation of another) to a norm of functioning, is the prohibition of incest. This prohibition, Lévi-Strauss surmises, founds culture, as it were, out of nature:

> [T]he prohibition of incest is in origin neither purely cultural, nor purely natural, nor is it a composite mixture of elements from both nature and culture, it is the fundamental step because of which, by which, but above all in which, the transition from nature to culture is accomplished.
>
> (Lévi-Strauss 1969, 25–6)

As Gayle Rubin argues in her 'The Traffic in Women', Lévi-Strauss had built on Marcel Mauss's previous work on the gift as the basis of social reciprocity by putting forward the notion 'that marriages are a most basic form of gift exchange, in which it is women who are the most precious of gifts' (Rubin 1975, 173). For Lévi-Strauss, the prohibition of incest is so important precisely because it ensures this exchange. It is only because one cannot marry a mother or a sister (with occasional exceptions; see Godelier 2004) that one is compelled to engage in exchange with another social group, which will similarly have women available yet forbidden on grounds of incestuality. Had that prohibition not existed, no intercourse between these two hypothetical groups would take place, since, at least from the point of view of sexual relations, neither group lacked something (a woman) which might force them to solicit the other. As Lévi-Strauss puts it,

> the prohibition on the sexual use of a daughter or a sister compels them to be given in marriage to another man, and at the same time it establishes a right to the daughter or sister of this other man ... Like

exogamy, which is its widened social application, the prohibition of incest is a rule of reciprocity.

(Lévi-Strauss 1969, 51)

The end result is nothing short of the basic institutions of kinship, to the extent that what emerges from the transaction of a woman 'is more profound than the result of other gift transactions, because the relationship thus established is not just one of reciprocity, but one of kinship. The exchange partners have become affines, and their descendents will be related by blood' (Rubin 1975, 173).

The fact that it is women who are exchanged in this account should naturally raise suspicion. The schema of exogamy could conceivably work just as well under a female-dominated society in which men are exchanged, a topic Lacan claims to have broached with Lévi-Strauss, to which the latter responded that this might indeed be the case, but that empirically men still hold political power everywhere (Lacan 2020, 183). Read in conjunction with the claim that incest is the transcendence of nature into culture, it becomes clear that Lévi-Strauss thus leaps from the empirical observation that men in most known societies hold political power and have property-like claims over women to the rather metaphysical statement that the exchange of women, which presupposes the incest taboo, is the very basis of society. In this sense, Rubin argues facetiously that, from Lévi-Strauss's exposition,

it can be deduced that the world historical defeat of women occurred with the origin of culture, and is a prerequisite of culture. If his analysis is adopted in its pure form, the feminist program must include a task even more onerous than the extermination of men; it must attempt to get rid of culture.

(Rubin 1975, 176)

Since it is likely that the destruction of culture would also entail the destruction of humanity, Lévi-Strauss's claims have to be relativised, if not abandoned outright. Rubin's response, insofar as *The Elementary Structures of Kinship* is concerned, is to claim that 'the exchange of women is a profound perception of a system in which women do not have full rights to themselves' (Rubin 1975, 177) and, accordingly, that it can be mobilised as a critique of any such system.

Rubin's suggestion that accepting Lévi-Straussian anthropology is at once to accept the proposition that culture and the subordination of women are born simultaneously is mirrored in Butler's reading of Lacan's 'The Signification of the Phallus'. For Butler, Lacan's account of the Oedipus complex relies on a primary prohibition through which, by the intervention of the father, the child will be separated from the mother's nourishing body and come into the social world as a man (who will, in time, be handed a claim to a woman) or as a woman (who will be offered to a man in response to a prior claim). Lacan, unlike Lévi-Strauss, is interested primarily in the subjective basis and effects of kinship structures, and he will intervene upon Lévi-Strauss's scheme for his own purposes already at the level of terminology. Specifically, for Lacan (as Butler interprets him), the structure of kinship relations determines that a man only becomes a man once he has a claim to what Lacan calls the phallus – which, in this context, may be broadly understood as the designation of the object called 'that which a man is owed for having renounced the use of his mother (or sister)', and which he desires. In turn, a woman will become a woman only in attempting to symbolise the phallus for a man (and Lacan is explicit that her 'femininity', which in this context means something closer to 'her personality', has to be renounced in order for her to symbolise it; see Lacan 2006d, 583).

Prima facie, this would seem to be a perfectly sustainable situation. A man is owed a woman, who only became a woman by being owed to a man in the first place, such that the social order can move along perfectly on the basis of an endless series of mutual obligations (a man receives a woman who was promised to a man; their union generates more women who will be exchanged on that same basis or more men who will be owed women, and so on). The order arising from this endless series – that is, the whole web of kinship obligations subtending human togetherness as such – is what Butler (1999) calls the capital-S Symbolic. If the symbolic requires that women be exchanged as property, it is misogynistic at a basic conceptual level, which makes tenable the claim that Lacan and Lévi-Strauss consider society as such to exist only inasmuch as misogyny exists. Butler's point would be fully made out if one stopped short of interrogating how Lacan reads Lévi-Strauss. However, Lacan is a psychoanalyst, not an anthropologist. For Lacan, what is of interest is the subjective dimension of this process through which culture (and, with it, gender) emerges not solely at the level of the human species, but also at the level of the individual. For Lacan, the relationship arising from these apparently complementary positions is thoroughly unsatisfying at the subjective level, since no woman can become equivalent to 'that which a man is owed' (if for no other reason than that no woman is an object), and since the shadow of what man has renounced in the figure of the mother, daughter, and sister will always loom large in his dealings with his partner.

While Lacan thus recognises that, in this sense, everyone is dissatisfied with the core institutions of kinship, Butler claims that he still recognises these institutions as necessary. Recall Freud's ambivalent relation to culture, his stance towards it in 'Civilisation and its Discontents' being something like 'can't live with it, can't live without it' (Freud 1961). In the same vein, Butler sees Lacan as extending Lévi-Strauss's insight to men and women's sexual lives, in addition to their formal and legal family dealings, ultimately to no one's benefit. Everyone has to enter the order of kinship, but women are doubly debased in doing so – not only will they, like their brothers, fathers, and husbands, have renounced their own incestual maternal and fraternal objects, they will also have been called upon to become nothing but their objecthood (a task they will inevitably fail, since, of course, they remain people). As Butler puts it:

> 'Being' the Phallus and 'having' the Phallus [respectively, the feminine and the masculine positions for Lacan] denote divergent sexual positions, or nonpositions (impossible positions, really), within language. To 'be' the Phallus is to be the 'signifier' of the desire of the Other and to appear as this signifier. In other words, it is to be the object, the Other of a (heterosexualized) masculine desire, but also to represent or reflect that desire. This is an Other that constitutes, not the limit of masculinity in a feminine alterity, but the site of a masculine self-elaboration.
>
> (Butler 1999, 56)

Evidently, this is an unsatisfactory position to arrive at if one is looking for an adequate representation of the feminist subject. Women, in Butler's reading of Lacan, are nothing but the symbolisation of an ageless promise allowing men to assert their own bond of 'manliness' through it – providing an easy explanation, for instance, for various forms of male parading, such as bragging about how many sexual partners one has had, or indeed for stereotypical male infidelity. (It should also be noted that Lacan constantly mocks men – his attribution of the 'having' to them is certainly not evidence of his sympathy.) In short, for Butler, while Lacan's reading has the merit of at least never being reducible to biology or to what Butler calls the 'metaphysics of presence' (the presumption that some feminine or masculine 'substance' stands behind the acts one sees as gendered), and while Lacan is himself critical of the purported complementarity between men and women, he still ascribes a subordinate position to women. Lacan may even go further: according to Butler, he claims that this subordination is a structural feature of language, to the extent that language, as far as gender is concerned, is coextensive with the Symbolic, which, in turn, is coextensive with kinship relations. If this is the case – and, accordingly, if any individual who speaks is always already trapped in the fake reciprocity of the 'to be or to have (the phallus)' for another – then any feminist presumption must be abandoned from the outset. Language itself is heteronormative, and the gender binary is akin to the rules of grammar (in that it may change from language to language, but any language has it).

Butler supports this position with two arguments: on the one hand, surely it cannot be accidental that this purportedly structural relationship, that commands that one must 'have' or 'be' this symbol conveniently called the 'phallus', privileges men.[2] There is a strong prima facie case, then, that Lacan arrives at this position through the same procedures as Lévi-Strauss: that is, by jumping from an empirical observation (issuing in this instance from the psychoanalytic clinic rather than ethnographic work) to an undue ontological statement. On the other hand, and relatedly, Lacan ultimately exposes a certain irony in heteronormativity, in that a woman can never truly be the phallus for a man, nor can a man ever truly have the phallus in a woman, such that the pseudo-relationship between these two positions does not admit of any resolution or higher dialectical synthesis. For Lacan, there is no happy ending, and the fate of all sexual relationships is foretold in advance – failure. As Butler puts it, in this context,

> this structure of religious tragedy in Lacanian theory effectively under-mines any strategy of cultural politics to configure an alternative ima-ginary for the play of desires. If the Symbolic guarantees the failure of the tasks it commands, perhaps its purposes, like those of the Old Tes-tament God, are altogether unteleological – not the accomplishment of some goal, but obedience and suffering to enforce the 'subject's' sense of limitation 'before the law'.
>
> (Butler 1999, 72)

Put simply, then, Butler charges Lacan with two classical heterosexist operations: first, the assumption that sexual dimorphism is ontological (that is, that there are two and only two sexes that are divinely ordained to seek out one another); and, second, that men are always and necessarily structu-rally superior to women, if for no other reason than that this has over-whelmingly been the case in existing societies. From these two operations, in turn, follows the likewise classical presumption that any desire that cannot immediately be understood to be heterosexual is defined as a pathology, a developmental accident on the way to the *telos* of an (admittedly rather disappointing) 'ideal' heterosexuality.

4 Lacan: 'The Signification of the Phallus'

Butler's direct source into Lacanian theory in *Gender Trouble* is Lacan's 'The Signification of the Phallus', a piece that somewhat ironically appears to anticipate Butler's critique:

> Let me make it clear that my emphasis on man's relation to the signifier as such has nothing to do with a 'culturalist' position ... It is not man's relationship to language as a social phenomenon that is at issue ...
>
> What is at issue is to refind – in the laws that govern this other scene (*ein anderer Schauplatz*), which Freud, on the subject of dreams, desig-nates as the scene of the unconscious – the effects that are discovered at the level of the chain of materially unstable elements that constitutes language.
>
> (Lacan 2006d, 578)

So, Lacan, in a piece that explicitly deals with the concept of the phallus, refuses it the status of a cultural artifact – even if one may be ready to grant this artifact a foundational status in regard to culture. The phallus is not, then, simply and straightforwardly the (cultural) designation of a woman inasmuch as a woman is promised to a man as compensation for his having given up enjoyment of his mother and sister. Lacan is even more explicit in one of the most often quoted fragments of this piece:

> In Freudian doctrine, the phallus is not a fantasy, if we are to view fantasy as an imaginary effect. Nor is it as such an object (part-, internal, good, bad, etc.) inasmuch as 'object' tends to gauge the reality involved in a relationship. Still less is it the organ – penis or clitoris – that it symbolizes ... it is the signifier that is destined to designate meaning effects as a whole, insofar as the signifier conditions them by its presence as signifier.
>
> (Lacan 2006d, 579)

The phallus is neither social nor cultural, neither a fantasy nor an object, and not even whatever organ it purports to symbolise. What does it mean to argue that the phallus is a signifier – and an exceptional one at that, a signifier that designates nothing short of the entire set of meaning effects, inasmuch as they are conditioned by the signifier? Answering this question demands a brief detour through the work of the father of structural linguistics, Ferdinand de Saussure. Saussure was commonly regarded in Lacan's time to have provided a secure foundation for the human sciences. There is no need to go into the long, complicated, and contested history of the structuralist movement here (see, for a summary, Milner 2002). What matters is one of the core distinctions Saussure elaborates upon, that between the signifier and the signified, inasmuch as their interconnection becomes a sign. Saussure's work provides an interesting decoupling between language and representation. For Saussure, 'a linguistic sign is not a link between a thing and a name, but between a concept and a sound pattern' (Saussure 2011, 76). Language, in other words, does not per se refer to the real world outside of it, nor is it immediately reducible to a set of representations of that world; rather, sound patterns relate to concepts the referential function of which need not be assumed at all, such that there will always be words and concepts that do not refer to things that are 'out there' in the world. Furthermore, the link between a concept and a sound pattern is arbitrary. There is no necessary relationship, as Saussure points out, between the concept 'sister' and the sound sequence that purports to designate it – the French *soeur* denotes 'sister' just as well as the English 'sister' does, such that nothing makes the sound sequence 'sister' more appropriate to the concept 'sister' than any other sound sequence. As such, 'the initial assignment of names to things, establishing a contract between concepts and sound patterns, is an act we can conceive in the imagination, but no one has ever observed it taking place' (Saussure 2011, 83).

However, Saussure goes even further: he claims that linguistic signs are not fixed, individual entities existing independently of one another. Rather, for Saussure, a sign is only truly distinguishable from other signs to the extent that it is different to all the others. For instance, English speakers do not eat sheep, but mutton, whereas the French both eat and rear *mouton*. Accordingly, in order to understand what the signified called upon by the signifier 'sheep' comprises for an English speaker, it is not enough to note that it is the same mental image called upon by a French person on hearing the French *mouton*. Rather, it is necessary to interrogate the relationship of that particular sign to all other adjacent signs; otherwise, one may begin to eat sheep rather than mutton, or cow rather than beef, or flesh rather than meat. Yet, if the scope of this inquiry is expanded further and one starts asking, for instance, about the difference between sheep and other farm animals, one quickly notices the need to take into account a great many signs in a given language to give any given concept a sufficiently precise meaning. Sheep are sheep, in other words, not solely through their identity to sheepness, but also through their non-cowness, for instance, and they are different from mutton in their (exclusive) aliveness or their non-edible character, and so on. The same can be said about each 'level' of the sign: the sound patterns (signifiers) that copulate with their respective signifieds in order to form the sign are only themselves in their difference to others, as are the concepts with which they copulate, etc.

To return to our original topic: the phallus, then, is a signifier, which means that it is a constituent part of language, notionally reducible to a given sound pattern which is itself reducible to nothing but its difference from all the others. Lacan introduces a crucial difference to Saussure's schema when he claims that the signifier 'conditions' the signified 'by its presence as signifier' (Lacan 2006d, 579). For Saussure, the signifier and the signified were like two flows, constantly moving past one another, and only joining together in a hypothetical contract through which a set of signifiers once came to correspond to a set of signifieds (a contract Saussure designates as 'tradition'). Implied in this image is a kind of 'ontological' independence of one order to the other; signifiers and signifieds exist separately from one another, although they only ever appear in any empirical language already joined together in the sign. For Lacan, the flow of the signifier takes logical precedence – it decides, conditions, and ultimately creates the signified as a representation more or less appropriate to it. In this, Lacan follows Lévi-Strauss, who proposes that the structuralist method

> is not a matter of translating an extrinsic given into symbols, but of reducing to their nature as a symbolic system things which never fall outside that system except to fall straight into incommunicability ...

symbols are more real than what they symbolise, the signifier precedes
and determines the signified.

(Lévi-Strauss 1987, 37)

In other words, the signifier and the signified do not copulate to yield the
sign as the final unit and unity of meaning (a word designating a concept
designating a thing). Rather, a series of signifiers refers to other signifiers
according to some discoverable logic (a grammar, for example), and the
impression one might get of having understood something someone else said
is nothing but an effect of this rule-bound referral of one signifier to the next
which, finally, can only be arrested by reference to the totality of the system
of signifiers and its constituent rules. The best intuitive approximation of this
referral and deferral is probably that of looking up the meaning of a word in
the dictionary:[3] each word there will be described by other words, which will
themselves be contained in the dictionary and described by and as other
words, etc. A dictionary never delivers a signified directly, much less an
unmediated and exterior reality, but only more signifiers that relate to each
other according to a grammar. The point that Lacan and Lévi-Strauss are
making is that it is, in principle, possible to discover the grammar just by
reading the dictionary – there is no need to ask a native speaker, as one
would be forced to do if one wanted to start out from the signified. Moreover, it is in response to the pre-existing grammar that various mental concepts (signifieds) are created and give it some consistency in ordinary
experience. Finally, language as a structure, and indeed anything else that
might be modelled as a structure, for instance kinship systems or other such
social systems, exists independently of any individual's representation of the
meanings of words. The fact that 'mother' means 'mean old hag' to someone
is a signified that fills up that pre-existing relationship in someone's kinship
structure, making it meaningful. However, the equation 'mother = mean old
hag' means nothing to the society's kinship structure, which exists independently of any actor's representation of it, and indeed forces them to try to
represent it by imaginary means.

The phallus, then, designates the sum of these signified effects, the promise
of a conceptual content adequate to one's symbolic environment. However,
the phallus is not an intervention into the field of linguistics. Lacan is a
psychoanalyst, and this must be taken into account. The phallus finds its
place in a conceptual edifice designed to give desire its proper place in psychoanalytic thinking. For Butler, the phallus is always and necessarily gendered, to the extent that it is a promise a woman must come to embody – it is
the proposition 'I am owed to a man', if one is a woman, and 'I am owed a
woman', if one is a man. Accordingly, desire for Butler's Lacan is reducible
to the signifier to a masculinist cultural norm, since it is the means by which
and the reason why women have to be circulated as objects capable of satisfying male desire. Lacan's actual theory incidentally includes that contention,

but also more than it: for Lacan, the phallus is only conceptually justified if one attends to how desire differs from both biological need and from every possible demand for an object. Lacan's itinerary ultimately suggests that the phallus, at least insofar as it is a properly psychoanalytic concept and not a strictly anthropological one, is not *a priori* gendered.

Consider the following simple, mundane scenario: a human baby is born into the world and thereupon emits a series of cries, whether for food, warmth, or for the ceasing of the terrible pain of filling their lungs with air for the first time. In comparison with other mammals, humans spend an inordinately large part of extra-uterine life entirely dependent on caretakers. A baby cries to alert their caretakers that they require something – food, cleaning, warmth, an end to some vague discomfort, or whatever other internal or external stimuli one might imagine them wishing to escape. The baby's world is, furthermore, permeated by language from the start; care-takers speak to one another in some language, and they also address the baby directly. Yet the baby is incapable of language in any strict sense; their cry signifies nothing in particular, as evidenced by the great disarray of caretakers who, often enough, are clueless as to what input (food? warmth?) will yield the desired output (a quiet baby). Parents will most often have a set of things they might believe the child to want – milk, water, etc. – but they can never be sure, even after they have provided everything they can think of, whether the baby craves something else entirely. Maybe the baby wishes to hear a specific sound they had previously enjoyed, for instance, or some other thing no one would reasonably assume a baby wants. What matters, then, is that the baby is thrown into a world of language without the capacity for meaning, yet they must communicate their needs and wants. It might be said that the baby has some access to the order of the signifier – the sheer materiality of language, phonemes, rhythms, tones, etc. – but not to the sig-nified (it is implicitly axiomatic for Lacanian psychoanalysts that humans have no ingrained reservoir of pre-made meanings, however much infants do have a behavioural repertoire that can only be described as instinctual). The baby, in other words, is like a translator chancing upon an unheard-of dead language, yet they will be immersed in that language from the start.

So, the baby's first cry, the earliest demand for a satisfaction, is ultimately a gamble: the cry does not mean anything, since the baby cannot translate their need into the appropriate sign in the same way that an adult might ask another to fetch them some water. The baby's inability to request the appro-priate object might then lead, for instance, to a demand for warmth being interpreted as a demand for food. An anxious caretaker might even treat the breast or the bottle as a universal solution to all of the baby's cries, which might then lead the baby to employ 'his refusal as if it were a desire' (Lacan 2006b, 524), for instance, by refusing to eat. At the origin of the baby's cry thus lies an untranslatable need, a pure opacity counterposed to the cry itself, which is only a pure demand for whatever is capable of sating an unspecified need's opaque 'pressure' (for instance, what one recognises, after having acceded to language, as hunger).

The first step in this exploration, then, leaves us with, on the one hand, an untranslatable need; on the other, an unspecified demand. However, the baby's demand will only ever be satisfied by another person, such that satisfaction of any need is at this stage coterminous with the presence of the caretaker. It is not necessary to ask, then, about the specifics of the need that motivates the cry, since the caretaker must, from the perspective of the baby as a term in the baby-caretaker system, be presumed capable of satisfying any need whatsoever. Demand is thus identical, at least at this early stage, with a demand for the presence of the caretaker, who 'contains' (as provider and interpreter) every satisfaction. (Note that this hypothetical caretaker is genderless; they are the earliest incarnation of the Other[4] and not strictly, as Anglophone Lacanians sometimes like to say, the mOther). For Lacan, this itinerary means that the progression of need to demand necessarily fails, first, because need as such is untranslatable (it comes from a hypothetical outside-language which can only be understood by the grown-ups if it is turned into a signifier the infant does not have, or if it is 'murdered' into language, as Lacan memorably puts it; see Lacan 2006a, 262). Second, that progression fails because demand cannot, in this context, be particularised: one cannot directly demand the object of the opaque need, since one's demand must be translated back to oneself. The baby's problem (I cannot speak but I must speak) must then be resolved logically. This, then, is the solution: since satisfaction, from the baby's perspective, always comes from the caretaker in response to a signifying act (for instance, the cry), the caretaker must be posited as containing everything that might lead to satisfaction – a positing that transforms every object given into both something that possibly sates a need and is proof of the caretaker's ongoing favour or, as is Lacan's preference, their love.

The earliest back-and-forth between need and demand leads into the coincidence of two lacks:[5] first, the need arising prior to language hopelessly wants for a sound pattern, for a way into the order of the signifier, so that need might be delimited and met, in its specificity. Second, the instance that 'metabolises' need into demand so it can be satisfied is missing the right sound pattern to designate that untranslatable something needed – since the child producing the cry does so from outside language and nothing assures the caretaker that they are giving the child the correct object apart from the child's silence, which may in fact signal nothing but a 'smothering' of the original need by the closeness and availability of the caretaker's body (by their love). It is from this earliest mismatch, Lacan claims in 'Signification', that desire will be born, even if it will only assume a more or less 'mature' form much later:

> [D]emand annuls (*aufhebt*) the particularity of everything that can be granted, by transmuting it into a proof of love, and the very satisfactions

demand obtains for need are debased (*sich erniedrigt*) to the point of being no more than the crushing brought on by the demand for love ...

It is necessary, then, that the particularity thus abolished reappear beyond demand. And in fact it does reappear there, but it preserves the structure concealed in the unconditionality of the demand for love. By a reversal that is not simply a negation of the negation, the power of pure loss emerges from the residue of an obliteration ... desire is neither the appetite for satisfaction nor the demand for love, but the difference that results from the subtraction of the first from the second, the very phenomenon of their splitting (*Spaltung*).

(Lacan 2006d, 580)

Desire, in other words, is the unconditional demand for love minus the appetite for the satisfaction of a need. What, then, is the object of this 'free-floating' demand, untethered, by the action of language, to the biological shackles that subtend need, and as insatiable as the lover's demand? Evidently, it is not something that well and truly exists in the world – one need only pose the question of what it is that might satisfy a demand for love to realise such an object would lead one into rather complicated terrain. Lacan's answer to the question of what this object might be is: nothing but a signifier, and specifically the signifier called the phallus, 'the signifier of this very *Aufhebung*, which it inaugurates (initiates) by its disappearance' (Lacan 2006d, 581). The *Aufhebung* (sublation or overcoming) that Lacan is referring to is the abolition of 'the particularity of everything that can be granted', 'the latency with which any signifiable is struck, once it is raised (*aufgehoben*) to the function of signifier' (Lacan 2006d, 581). The phallus, otherwise stated, is the designation of the mismatch between need and demand, the name of the meeting place between need's untranslatable object and the Other's lack of the signifier that might translate it. The object of the earliest need as a pure signifiable is overcome in demand as pure signification, and desire arises as the residuum of this overcoming, inasmuch as demand is 'infinitised' or made absolute through the very 'latency' striking the object of need, its becoming-signifier. The phallus is thus what the internal necessity of the progression of need, to demand, to desire comes to posit as desire's referent, the reason desire can claim it is not without object, even if nothing truly existing in the world or in language – no object that can be demanded outright – can satisfy it: a hypothetical object that, one must concede, would probably be much more (or indeed much less) than a penis or a baby, if it were possible. But, since it is not possible, it is nothing but that: a marker for what is not there, an acknowledgement that desire refers always and necessarily to the pure loss humans incur when they speak. This is precisely why psychoanalysts can see phalluses everywhere except in the penis: anything can be the phallus, because the phallus is not anything.

5 Gender and the Father

What emerges from this exploration is that the phallus need not *a priori* be understood as gendered, cisheterosexual, and patriarchal. It is, or can be interpreted as, prior to the existence of any gendered object, inasmuch as it is logically prior to the internalisation of the cultural repertoire which fills up the symbolic fact of gender roles, performatively transmuted into gender identities, as Butler convincingly analyses them. The phallus, and certainly that to which the phallus will come to provide a solution, is accordingly prior to gender, if one understands gender as a cultural artifact, as Butler does. None of this, however, is to say that Lacan himself refuses to place the phallus in the context of the gender binary and its attendant ideal of mono-gamous reproductive cisheterosexuality. For example, Lacan treats gender identity as a sort of response to the fact that neither man nor woman 'has' or 'is' the phallus. The attributes of masculinity and femininity are nothing but a seeming (*paraître*), a parade conducted by a subject by means of 'insignias' through which they can see themselves as loveable manly men or womanly women: each gender being, in this sense, a heraldry composed of the ideals a subject will have disengaged from parents' speech and desire (see Lacan 2017, 277, 2006d, 582–3). He also goes on to argue in 'The Signification of the Phallus' that the phallus is closely related to the image of the erect penis – because the penis's erectile capabilities are presumably the most 'salient' part of what can be 'grasped in sexual intercourse', and because it can serve as an 'image of the vital flows [that are] transmitted in generation', even if it can 'play its role only when veiled' (Lacan 2006d, 581). More simply, the phal-lus's elective affinity with the erect penis is due to the penis's heuristic char-acter: most of the time, one can reasonably say that there where there is an erection, there is desire, which presumably contrasts with the feminine body, which does not have as obvious or culturally significant a way of representing desire. As such, for the child, the mother's desire for the father and the father's continued performance are strong indications that the desire of the mother is symbolised in what the father has, and she does not. Lacan also considers the objection that this need not be the case (that the phallus need not be the penis, therefore possessed by men, therefore absent in women) in *Seminar IV*:

> Let's leave for a moment the terrain of analysis to take up a question I put to Monsieur Lévi-Strauss … So, I asked Lévi-Strauss, what if you were to describe this circle of exchange by turning it around, to say that the female lineages produce men and exchange them between one another? For, in the end, we are already aware that the lack that we have been speaking about in women is not a real lack. Everyone knows that they can have phalli, and what is more they produce them. They beget boys, phallophores. As a consequence, one may describe the exchange

down through the generations in a more straightforward way, in the opposite order. One can imagine a matriarchy whose law would be – I've given a son, I shall now receive a man?

Lévi-Strauss's reply is the following. From the standpoint of formalisation one could doubtless describe things in exactly the same way, symmetrically, by taking a reference axis, a system of coordinates founded on women or founded on men, but then a heap of items would remain inexplicable and in particular the following. In every case, even in matriarchal societies, political power is androcentric. It is represented by men and by male lineages. Very peculiar anomalies in these exchanges – a modification, an exception, or a paradox that might appear in the laws of exchange at the level of the elementary structures of kinship – can be explained only in relation and by reference to something that lies outside the interplay of kinship, and which has to do with the political context, that is to say, the order of power, and very precisely the order of the signifier, in which sceptre and phallus merge into one

(Lacan 2020, 183–4, translation modified)

This is a momentous acknowledgement. Empirically, it may be overwhelmingly the case that men exchange women – although there are arguable counterexamples, including societies that seem to lack marriage-like institutions (see Godelier 2004). Even so, as feminist scholars have long pointed out, this empirical fact does not in itself justify the generalisation that things are the way they are for a deeper, necessary, and structural reason. Rather, and Lacan's recounting of Lévi-Strauss's answer to his question suggests that Lévi-Strauss was willing to entertain this, the answer to the obvious 'why must women be the objects?' question is to be sought elsewhere: in the order of politics, for Lacan as for feminist theory, but also in different strata or levels, so to speak, of what Lacan calls the order of the signifier (the symbolic), which therefore includes much more than kinship. Lacan very much recognises this, claiming that the 'future' of the phallus in tying together normative desire and castration 'depends on the law introduced by the father in this sequence', which makes it a matter of the political efficiency, as it were, of the function of the father, and not merely of some intrinsic property of the penis or the phallic signifier (Lacan 2006d, 582).

Lacan's interrogation of the phallus therefore leads into the concept of the father, which for a time in Lacan's work was distinguished from that of the phallus. It is not often remarked upon that Lacan had a culturalist view of the Oedipus complex. In his early encyclopaedia article 'The Family Complexes' he had argued along the lines of a prominent conservative thesis that the function of the father – his authority enshrined in law, custom, and in the family form – had been on the wane in the West, and he had even suggested that this phenomenon would lead to something of a civilisational-moral weakening (Lacan 2001, 60–1; Zafiropoulous 2001, 2010; Chapter 3 in this volume). A casualty of this process, of course, would be the classical Oedipus complex in Western societies. No longer, in other words, would boys struggle with and ultimately yield to the power of their fathers over the mother's body, prompting them to enact the all-powerful father as an ego-ideal and thereafter become manly men capable of heightened culturally valued sublimations. The disappearance of this character-building rivalry would even, Lacan hypothesised, lead to men weak in moral fibre and to women unwedded to the virginal ideal – an apocalyptic scenario even for contemporary conservatives.

Lacan would forego parts of this rather unpalatable perspective soon afterwards – and there are about 20 years between 'The Family Complexes' and 'The Signification of the Phallus' – but his suspicion of the role Freud had ascribed the castrating yet endlessly loving father in the Oedipus complex was to remain. In *Seminar III*, Lacan suggested that the function of the father was not to be found in his purported threats to the effect that, if the boy kept touching 'it', he (the father) would chop it off. For Lacan, what came to matter over the father's empirical person was the paternal function's intimate relation to the origin of kinship as a signifying system dictating the outer bounds of what might be legitimately lived as sexuality. The function of the father, put simply, would provide Lacan with a link between the creation of the signifier – that of paternity, 'being a father', and, with it, the phallus as it presented itself as a virtuality in analysands' recounting of their sexual lives – and the sociocultural regulation of heterosexual coupling.

At the close of *Seminar III*, Lacan surmises that paternity is a more abstract entity than maternity. Fathers do not birth or carry children, and various societies seem to do just fine with no clear knowledge of the link between heterosexual coitus and pregnancy (the *locus classicus* of this thesis is Malinowski's *The Family among the Australian Aborigines* (1913), who Lacan cites in 'The Family Complexes'). For Lacan, then, paternity as it appeared to psychoanalysts was a purely signifying function:

> [T]he elaboration of the notion of *being a father* must have been raised by work that has taken place through an entire cluster of cultural exchanges to the state of major signifier, and this signifier must have its own consistency and status.
>
> (Lacan 1993, 293, emphasis in the original)

Lacan explicitly relates this novel signifier (paternity) to the phallus and to kinship. Still in *Seminar III*, Lacan argues that the phallus could be compared to a meteor. Lacan uses the word in an unusual, older sense, meaning any atmospheric phenomenon, any 'appearance' in the sky, for example, a rainbow. Lacan argues that what distinguishes meteors like the rainbow is that they exist solely in their appearance. There is no substance 'behind' rainbows; they subsist as rainbows only as artifacts of (the refraction of light as filtered through) our perception and, importantly, of the fact humans have named them. For Lacan, the phallus as discussed in the 'Signification' essay is exactly the same – a pure, insubstantial, and fleeting appearance, but one that must be granted substance and subsistence through the agency of the father. The father, Lacan claims, 'is that which … must exist in order for the phallus to be something other than a meteor' (Lacan 1993, 319): for instance, a penis, a baby, or (the claim to) a woman. Put simply, it is the father who assures the referentiality of the phallus as what signifies the (im)possible satisfaction of desire; the father gives the phallus a definite signified, he serves the same function as 'tradition' in Saussure, but in respect of the sexual order (or the Lévi-Straussian 'zero-value institution' in respect of sex; see Zafiropoulos 2010). In a more psychoanalytic register, the father allows the phallus to become the object of a demand, and to be integrated into a fantasy: it is the father who in some sense commands that woman and phallus coincide for the boy, just as he assures that penis, baby, and phallus coincide for the girl.

The father is therefore the reason why the endless cycle of kinship – give a woman, take a woman – keeps on going, and he ensures that it does so precisely by vouching for the consistency of the objects making binary cisheterosexuality possible, by allowing for the definition of kinship as the origin of sociability through a set of fundamental statements (for instance, phallus = penis = woman = baby). Father and phallus should thus be understood as tools to make sexuality – the laws regulating it as well as its proper and improper objects – intelligible at the individual level, and to allow the child-subject to come into their own as a more or less autonomous being within the field of sexuality. Lacan is reasonably clear on the point that the father is what lends strength to a given signifying structure in *Seminar V*, and relates father and phallus as signifier-to-the-system-of-signifiers and signifier-to-the-signified:

> Just as I have told you that within the signifying system the Name-of-the-Father has the function of signifying the entire system of signifiers, authorizing its existence, making it law, I will tell you that we frequently have to consider that the phallus enters into play in the signifying system when the subject has to symbolize, in contrast with the signifier, the signified as such – I mean signification.
>
> (Lacan 2017, 223)

The phallus, then, starts its journey as a variable x placed within an equation the child comes up with when they ask themselves the rather hopeless question: 'what does the caretaker want?', a question the child must answer if they are successfully to assure themselves that the caretaker has no reason to deny them their presence and therefore the satisfaction they provide. Should the standard Oedipal narrative hold good, the caretaker will have been the mother, and the child's longing for her presence will be transmuted by the father's intervention to the effect that daddy has a penis and likes women, mummy is a woman who does not have a penis but likes them, and mummy is only daddy's – the child can only get a replacement later, whether by becoming like daddy or by becoming an object likeable to daddy. The child then realises: 'I have it, I do not have it, but in either case I cannot be it for mummy'.

In this sense, the phallus participates in the order of kinship – the object, when all is said and done, of Butler's early work – only through the agency of the signifier 'father', of his Name, that is, through the creation of a wholly artificial signifier designating a strictly conventional family relationship along which certain prerogatives may be passed from the men of one generation to those of the next (specifically, the claim to a woman-who-is-not-mother). Lacan's reflection at the close of *Seminar III* suggests that he saw in this signifier no less than the triumph of culture over nature at the level of the human species, which demonstrates how the primarily symbolic bond of paternity comes to take precedence over the more natural, or at any rate certainly easier to establish, link of maternity (although this is obviously also a problematic claim, since 'maternity' is also a cultural artifact and subject to cultural variation (on the links between this claim, French family law, and conservative political thought, see Robcis 2013)). This claim, however, entails also that it is not the phallus per se that mandates the existence of men, women-for-men, phallus-penises, phallus-babies, and the entire paraphernalia of conjugal heterosexuality. Rather, the phallus-penis-woman-baby chain is preceded and determined by the invention, in some endlessly far-removed historical moment, of paternity as that which invests heteronormative kinship with the nature of a compulsion basic to human sociality – and it is paternity that ultimately commands and regulates the ongoing generational cycles in which each subjects has to insert themselves through the Oedipal crisis and its more or less successful resolution.

Finally, the heterosexual compulsion that language seems to inaugurate in the majority of human beings is not (conceptually) due to the phallus but to the concept of paternity which, in stringing together father, phallus, woman, penis, child, keeps the gears of the kinship-machine running. Lacan reconstructs the link joining paternity to the gender binary and to heterosexuality through Freud's (pseudo)scientific myth in *Totem and Taboo*:

> [T]he necessity of [Freud's] reflection led him to tie the appearance of the signifier of the Father, as author of the Law, to death – indeed, to the killing of the Father – thus showing that, if this murder is the fertile moment of the debt by which the subject binds himself for life to the Law, the symbolic Father, insofar as he signifies this Law, is truly the dead Father.

(Lacan 2006d, 464)

The motif of 'murder' and 'killing' in Lacan's work typically refers to the elevation of something to the status of signifier ('the symbol first manifests itself as the killing of the thing'; see Lacan 2006a, 262). One might then translate and complement this quotation thus: the Freudian myth in *Totem and Taboo* is about the creation of the signifier of paternity. This signifier appears in analysands' speech as the symbol of a debt to kinship, which humanises sexuality. This is the law such as psychoanalysis discovers it: you were born and given language by the agency of kinship, and you must pay for it by accepting to play its game – the only two moves are to have the phallus or to be it. The child's acceptance of the father-function as the pivot of their entrance into the kinship system, and of the phallus as the 'material' circulated in that system, would therefore at once be the metaphorical overcoming of the child's bondage to nature and the acceptance that the only two players in the game are men with penises and women without them.

6 There Is No Other of the Other

What I mean to suggest with this latter discussion is quite simple. Classical Lacanian sexual anthropology is premised on the notion that the penis (or the woman, or the baby) comes to be represented in the phallus only through the (very much accidental, contingent, happenstance) invention of paternity. In Lacan's account, heterosexuality, the gender binary, and their respective conceptual and social paraphernalia are a function of a specific iteration of paternity, of one specific form given to the conventional regulation of kinship, and not of the presence or otherwise of penises and vaginas in some people's bodies rather than in others'. This, as Michel Tort (2007) has argued, gives scope to interpret the father as a sociopolitical technology – albeit a subjectively useful one, since knowing who one is in a gendered and generational order allows for ready answers to the questions 'who am I?' and 'what do I want?', with which everyone is concerned. I elaborate upon this suggestion in Chapter 3. For now, I will take the definition of the father as a sociopolitical technology as axiomatic, and suggest that the traditional patrophallocentric-heteronormative version of Lacan's sexual anthropology is neither central to his theory of desire nor necessary to it.

Lacan's trajectory across *Seminars III, IV,* and *V* will work through his account of kinship in its relationship to the Freudian Oedipus and eventually arrive at a rather radical questioning of some core tenets of psychoanalysis. One basic question that I would advance that Lacan is working upon in these seminars is simply whether to uphold the idea that some ideal developmental model buttressed by the 'orthodox' Freudian Oedipus should serve as the substantive goal of an analytic itinerary, or indeed as the basis for a diagnosis of the social. Does an analyst, in other words, hope that an analysand will learn to desire as a 'normal' heterosexual should? Does an analytic itinerary demonstrate that to desire is always to desire Oedipally and according to the

pre-given, presumptively heterosexual mould of kinship norms such as supposedly dominate our societies? Should analysis do no more than help a patient
to arrive at a normal resignation before their childish Oedipal dramas, rather
than impotently struggle against them in neurotic fashion? To my mind, Lacan
will answer these questions in the negative, though not without some ambi-
guity. To accept that desire is always subject to the norms that constitute kinship is to subject desire to culture, and Lacan is adamant that doing so would
be to diminish the force of the desire psychoanalysis has consistently shown to
determine the speaking being down to the most seemingly insignificant minutiae
of their existence. As Lacan puts it in *Seminar VI*,

> psychoanalysis is not a simple reconstruction of the past, nor is it a
> reduction to pre-established norms; analysis is neither an epos [an epic, a
> story in narrative form] nor an ethos ... we [analysts] find ourselves in
> the paradoxical position of ... those who preside over [desire's] advent.
>
> (Lacan 2019, 485)

To allow a subject to encounter their desire in the absence of any normative,
'ideal' way to desire – in which theoretical consistency demands that one include
heterosexuality – is thus (part of) psychoanalysis's wager. The history of this
development can be concisely summarised in two contradictory formulations
Lacan presents between his fifth and sixth seminars (see Chiesa 2007). In
Seminar V, Lacan summarises his reinterpretation of the Oedipus complex:

> At the first moment and first stage, it is, then, a matter of the following –
> the child identifies in the mirror with the object of the mother's desire ...
>
> Second moment. I told you that on the imaginary plane the father
> definitely intervenes as the depriver of the mother, which means that the
> demand addressed to the Other, provided it's relayed as it should be, is
> referred to a higher court ... *What the subject effectively questions the*
> *Other about, provided he traverses it completely, will always encounter in*
> *the Other, in some ways, the Other of the Other, that is, its own law* ...
>
> The third stage is as important as the second, for the outcome of the
> Oedipus complex depends on it. The father testified that he was giving
> the phallus insofar as, and only insofar as, he is the bearer, or the sup-
> porter, if I may put it like that, of the law. Whether the maternal subject
> possesses this phallus or not depends on him.
>
> (Lacan 2017, 176–7, emphasis added)

One year later, the following appeared in *Seminar VI*:

> At **A** [Lacanian algebra for the Other, *Autre*] – which is not a being,
> but rather the locus of speech, the locus where the whole system of sig-
> nifiers, that is, a whole language, resides in a developed or envelope

form – something is missing. What is missing can only be a signifier …
The formulation that gives S(Å) [or, the signifier S of the barred Other
Å] its most radical value is as follows: the signifier that is missing at the
level of the Other.

This is the big secret of psychoanalysis, if I may say so myself. The big
secret is that *there is no Other of the Other*.

(Lacan 2019, 298, emphasis added)

These two fragments, roughly one year apart, index the significant shift
taking place in Lacan's thought at this time – a shift that would become
clearest in Lacan's *Seminar VII*, which Lorenzo Chiesa has called an 'in-
between two Lacans' (Chiesa 2007, 9). At the level of *Seminar V*, Lacan
expounds his theory of the Oedipus complex as it has traditionally been
understood. The child, always at risk of falling under the spell of their identification to the object of the mother's desire (identified in the earliest need-
demand dialectic as the phallus) must be forced into shared, social reality by
the father's 'no' and in his 'name' (the two words, *non and nom*, being
homophonous in French), the prohibition he will be deemed to have cast
over the gratification of the mother's desire. This process requires that the
father furnish proof that he holds the phallus, the (signifier to the) object the
mother desires, and that he is the one who can give it or take it away, such
that the child cannot become what the mother lacks without the father's say-
so, which entails that the child will submit to his law. The father, in this
schema, is the operator of the child's encounter with what Lacan calls the
Other of the Other, which is more or less implicitly equated with the order of
kinship. Finally, this impersonal order commands the ongoing cycle of
reproduction and kinship by designating women-other-than-the-mother (for
men), penises-other-than-the-father's, and babies-other-than-the-father's (for
women) as possible embodiments of the phallus. All that is left for the child
to do is to integrate themselves into this order so they may fulfil their role as
bearer or imitation of the phallus so the cycle can begin anew.

The *Seminar VI* fragment, on the other hand, is clear to the effect that this
Other of the Other – the father as guarantor, as support of kinship systems
that are supposedly the fundamental basis of society – does not exist. The
child's interrogation of the mother's desire no longer finds beyond her and
beyond the empirical father a timeless mandate that they become a man for a
woman or a woman for a man, but merely a provisional, artificial signifier
covering over the fact that there is no such mandate. Recourse to biology is
of no use here: the bewildering variety of sexual preferences in humans militates against any presumption that people are hard-wired to be turned on
only by potentially reproductive partners. Even further, technological mastery of nature already makes reproduction possible without heterosexual
coitus, let alone the juridical paraphernalia of conjugal heterosexuality,
which even heterosexual couples increasingly regard as unnecessary. Finally,

if the father is a (increasingly anachronistic) sociopolitical technology, it follows that his commands are not transcendental givens of social life, but that he fulfils a function many other things can fulfil. In 'Subversion of the Subject', Lacan writes:

> No authoritative statement has any other guarantee here than its very enunciation, since it would be pointless for the statement to seek it in another signifier, which could in no way appear outside that locus. I formulate this by saying that there is no metalanguage that can be spoken, or, more aphoristically, that there is no Other of the Other. And when the Legislator (he who claims to lay down the Law) comes forward to make up for this, he does so as an impostor.
>
> (Lacan 2006e, 688)

Therefore, the reason why the father's heteronormative command strikes so many as persuasive has to be looked for elsewhere than in the father's alleged exceptionality as a signifier. This 'persuasiveness' will soon be understood to come from enjoyment, or *jouissance* – a topic I discuss in Chapters 2, 3, and 4. For now, let us simply note that, if the father is no longer the guarantor of the order of kinship, if he is in no position to command that the child accustom themselves to occupying their place in the timeless generational cycle as a man- or a woman-to-be, then the classical Oedipus complex can no longer be accepted as the most basic truth of psychoanalytic discourse. No longer can psychoanalysts work under the assumption, for instance, that the ideal outcome of an upbringing (or indeed of an analysis) is that one end up a married, cisgendered heterosexual wallowing in one's common unhappiness, nor certainly can something like this heteronormative anti-ideal pose as the aim of the psychoanalytic cure (I hasten to note here that, while many Lacanians today will condescendingly disavow the history of their own discipline and claim that psychoanalysts never sought to change their analysands' sexual orientation, many of Lacan's contemporaries did think in these terms, and many contemporary Lacanians may credibly be presumed to do so too, from their public pronouncements about sexual diversity; see Lewes 1995, and Chapter 3 and Conclusion). In conclusion, as Lacan would later put it:

> The lack at stake [in the signifying chain] is one I have already formulated: that there is no Other of the Other. But is this characteristic of truth's Faithlessness really the last word worth giving in answer to the question, 'What does the Other want from me?' when we analysts are its mouthpiece? Surely not, and precisely because there is nothing doctrinal about our role. We need not answer for any ultimate truth, and certainly not for or against any particular religion.

It is already significant that I had to situate here [in S($\cancel{A}$)] the dead Father in the Freudian myth. But a myth is nothing if it props up no rites, and psychoanalysis is not the Oedipal rite.

(Lacan 2006e, 693)

The analyst, then, need not provide the analysand with an answer as to what the Other demands of them, whether a religious answer, or a nihilistic one, or a heteronormative one. This development is undoubtedly salutary, but it poses more questions than it answers. If not to lead a suffering subject into a common unhappiness that always more or less coincides with heterosexuality, what does psychoanalysis aim to do? If not to be brought to the bedrock of castration, whether to castration anxiety or to penis envy, why is it that analysands spend years and years on the couch? What, finally, does an analytic itinerary do, and what are its ethical stakes for the analyst and for the analysand? Lacan interrogated some of these questions in *Seminar VII*, which forms the axis of Chapter 2.

Notes

1 I focus on Butler's work until roughly 2004, the point at which Sam Bourcier argues that Butler's work becomes more conservative from the standpoint of the subversion of gender and sexual identity (Bourcier 2012).
2 Butler's terminological objection is not without merit. There are, however, compelling enough reasons to keep the Lacanian terms. On the one hand, the majority of analysands an analyst might expect to see are and are likely to remain homosexuals or heterosexuals raised by heterosexuals, often in quite traditional marriages. In this sense, their sexual positions and fantasies are likely to be described well enough by the gendered language Lacan was employing in the 1950s, regardless of how much the sexual-gendered-relational landscape may have changed since (see Chapter 3). Additionally, as queer theorists are abundantly aware, gay male as well as lesbian communities and couples liberally draw on traditional heterosexual categories for their cultural and sexual repertoire – tops and bottoms, butches and femmes, and many other concepts crucial to gay and lesbian self-understanding are all transpositions of such categories to a queer context. In this sense, these communities' innovations in respect of patro-phallocentrism are by no means absolute, such that there is little reason to assume that signifiers such as the phallus do not matter, or matter all that differently, to them. On the other hand, terms such as 'phallus', 'mother', or 'father' index the centrality ascribed by psychoanalytic theory to sexuality and the body as sources of metaphoricity. In this sense, several theoretically relevant aspects of the phallus do coincide with the usage of the penis. For example, the phallus is the signifier of desire partly because of the presumption that there where there is an erection, there is desire. The Lacanian clinic constantly highlights the importance of the father's potency – his erection being a way to demonstrate possession of the phallus the mother lacks. Similarly, Lacan will speak of castration as closely related to the fact that the penis tends to return to its flaccid state after ejaculation, signalling a sort of natural limit to pleasure and a metaphorical limit to enjoyment. In this sense, using more inclusive, non-gendered language might have the counterproductive effect of desexualising psychoanalytic reasoning, which would, in turn, diminish its queer interest.

3 There is also an interesting and largely neglected engagement here with information theory and the cybernetic field. There are good indications that Lacan's model for his notion of 'language' was not natural language as we speak it each day, but a notion closer to that of language as a sum of regularities implied in Claude Shannon's work on the statistical distribution of letters in the English language. A not dissimilar principle also informs artificial intelligence tools capable of composing text: such tools work only at the level of the signifier, of pure statistical regularities stripped of any reference to their meaning. See Lydia Liu's very interesting *The Freudian Robot* (Liu 2011).

4 The notion of the Other in Lacan designates the 'place of speech', or the place of what Lacan sometimes calls the 'treasure' of the signifier. It is a designation for the hypothetical space in which speech is 'processed', so to speak – in which the act of speaking determines itself as speech or gibberish, true or false, etc. This rather abstract notion is justifiable in at least two respects: one, each of us has been an infant, and thus our 'speech' (say, a cry) was elaborated back to us by someone else, who was therefore near-factually the Other; and, two, no one invents the language that they speak (including, of course, the mOther), such that whether what one has to say even counts as an utterance must be admitted into a logical space that is not coterminous with the simple relation between speaker and spoken-to, but includes the abstract place in which everything that makes language language is contained and 'enforced'.

5 It is more accurate to say that there are three lacks at stake. As early as *Seminar IV* Lacan's developmental account distinguished between privation, frustration, and castration, as real, imaginary, and symbolic forms of the lack of object, respectively. See the *Seminar IV* lesson on 'The Dialectic of Frustration' (Lacan 2020).

References

Bourcier, Marie-Hélène. 2012. 'Fuck the Politics of Disempowerment in the Second Butler'. *Paragraph* 35 (2): 233–253.

Butler, Judith. 1999. *Gender Trouble: Feminism and the Subversion of Identity.* 2nd ed. New York: Routledge.

Butler, Judith. 2011. *Bodies That Matter: On the Discursive Limits of 'Sex'.* 2nd ed. Routledge Classics. New York: Routledge.

Chiesa, Lorenzo. 2007. *Subjectivity and Otherness: A Philosophical Reading of Lacan.* 1st ed. Cambridge, MA: MIT Press.

Copjec, Joan. 1994. *Read My Desire: Lacan Against the Historicists.* 1st ed. Cambridge, MA: MIT Press.

Dean, Tim. 2000. *Beyond Sexuality.* 1st ed. Chicago, IL: University of Chicago Press.

Fausto-Sterling, Anne. 2000. *Sexing the Body: Gender Politics and the Construction of Sexuality.* 1st ed. New York: Basic Books.

Freud, Sigmund. 1961. 'Civilization and Its Discontents'. In *The Standard Edition of the Complete Psychological Works of Sigmund Freud*, vol. XXI, translated by James Strachey, 57–146. London: The Hogarth Press.

Freud, Sigmund. 1964. 'Analysis Terminable and Interminable'. In *The Standard Edition of the Complete Psychological Works of Sigmund Freud*, vol. XXIII, translated by James Strachey, 1st ed., 209–235. London: The Hogarth Press.

Godelier, Maurice. 2004. *The Metamorphoses of Kinship.* Translated by Nora Scott. 1st ed. London: Verso.

Kollias, Hector. 2012. 'Queering It Right, Getting It Wrong'. *Paragraph* 35 (3): 141–163.

Lacan, Jacques. 1993. *The Seminar of Jacques Lacan, Book III: The Psychoses.* Translated by Russell Grigg. 1st ed. New York: W.W. Norton.

Lacan, Jacques. 2001. 'Les complexes familiaux dans la formation de l'individu'. In *Autres écrits*, 1st ed., 23–84. Paris: Seuil.

Lacan, Jacques. 2006a. 'On a Question Prior to Any Treatment of Psychosis'. In *Écrits*, translated by Bruce Fink, 1st ed., 445–488. New York: W.W. Norton.

Lacan, Jacques. 2006b. 'The Direction of the Treatment and the Principles of Its Power'. In *Écrits*, translated by Bruce Fink, 1st ed., 489–542. New York: W.W. Norton.

Lacan, Jacques. 2006c. 'The Function and Field of Speech and Language in Psychoanalysis'. In *Écrits*, translated by Bruce Fink, 1st ed., 197–268. New York: W.W. Norton.

Lacan, Jacques. 2006d. 'The Signification of the Phallus'. In *Écrits*, translated by Bruce Fink, 1st ed., 575–584. New York and London: W.W. Norton.

Lacan, Jacques. 2006e. 'The Subversion of the Subject and the Dialectic of Desire in the Freudian Unconscious'. In *Écrits*, translated by Bruce Fink, 1st ed., 671–702. New York: W.W. Norton.

Lacan, Jacques. 2017. *The Seminar of Jacques Lacan, Book V: Formations of the Unconscious.* Translated by Russell Grigg. 1st ed. Cambridge: Polity.

Lacan, Jacques. 2019. *The Seminar of Jacques Lacan, Book VI: Desire and Its Interpretation.* Translated by Bruce Fink. 1st ed. Cambridge: Polity.

Lacan, Jacques. 2020. *The Seminar of Jacques Lacan, Book IV: The Object Relation.* Translated by A.R. Price. 1st ed. Cambridge: Polity.

Lévi-Strauss, Claude. 1969. *The Elementary Structures of Kinship.* Translated by James Harle Bell, John von Sturmer, and Rodney Needham. 1st ed. Boston, MA: Beacon Press.

Lévi-Strauss, Claude. 1987. *Introduction to the Work of Marcel Mauss.* Translated by Felicity Baker. 1st ed. London: Routledge.

Lewes, Kenneth. 1995. *Psychoanalysis and Male Homosexuality.* 1st ed. London: Jason Aronson.

Liu, Lydia. 2011. *The Freudian Robot: Digital Media and the Future of the Unconscious.* 1st ed. Chicago, IL: University of Chicago Press.

Malinowski, Bronislaw. 1913. *The Family among the Australian Aborigines: A Sociological Study.* London: University of London Press.

Milner, Jean-Claude. 2002. *Le périple structural: Figures et paradigme.* Paris: Seuil.

Penney, James. 2014. *After Queer Theory: The Limits of Sexual Politics.* London: Pluto Press.

Rae, Gavin. 2020. 'Questioning the Phallus: Jacques Lacan and Judith Butler'. *Studies in Gender and Sexuality* 21 (1): 12–26.

Robcis, Camille. 2013. *The Law of Kinship: Anthropology, Psychoanalysis, and the Family in France.* 1st ed. Ithaca, NY: Cornell University Press.

Rubin, Gayle. 1975. 'The Traffic in Women: Notes on the Political Economy of Sex'. In *Toward an Anthropology of Women*, edited by Rayna Reiter, 1st ed., 157–210. New York: Monthly Review Press.

Saussure, Ferdinandde. 2011. *Course in General Linguistics.* Translated by Wade Baskin. 1st ed. New York: Columbia University Press.

Tort, Michel. 2007. *La fin du dogme paternel.* 1st ed. Paris: Flammarion.

Zafiropoulos, Markos. 2001. *Lacan et les sciences sociales: Le déclin du père.* 1st ed. Paris: Presses Universitaires de France.

Zafiropoulos, Markos. 2010. *Lacan and Lévi-Strauss or the Return to Freud (1951–1957).* Translated by John Holland. 1st ed. London: Karnac.

Zupančič, Alenka. 2018. *What IS Sex?* 1st ed. Cambridge, MA: MIT Press.

Chapter 2

Queer (Im)Moralism and the Ethics of Psychoanalysis (1959–60)

1 Is There a Queer Ethics?

Chapter 1 revisited a foundational moment in the queer engagement with Lacanian psychoanalysis – Judith Butler's performative theory of gender and Butler's accusation that Lacan remained within Freud's patriarchal and heteronormative orbit. I argued that Butler's reading misses the mark, because Butler extracts from (aspects of) 'The Signification of the Phallus' a position that Lacan would soon nuance and presents it as all Lacan had to say about gender and sexual difference. In contrast, I have attempted to demonstrate that the concept of the phallus bears no necessary relation to any prescriptive object of desire (for instance, the penis or the baby, from women's perspective; women, from men's). Rather, the phallus is a signifier fashioned out of a mismatch between need and demand as it delineates itself in the early life of every speaking being to be. It is accordingly prior to the constitution of an object that may be described as gendered. That the phallus comes to coincide with a woman, for a man, or with a penis or a baby, for a woman, is a function of the father – which the classical Lacan endowed with an anthropological basis and a heteronormative role – and not a result of the phallus per se. This reflection, I suggested at the close of Chapter 1, would lead Lacan to interrogate the ethics of psychoanalysis anew.

Before turning to Lacan's ethical thought, one might note that queer theory, too, has a moral or ethical reflection. In her study of queer ethical thinking, *Are the Lips a Grave?*, Lynne Huffer wonders about 'the relative thinness of ethical thinking in queer theory' – directly traceable, Huffer claims, to sexual minorities' distaste for the kind of moral system subtending 'everyday thinking, professional ethics, and many traditional moral philosophies' (Huffer 2013, 29). As Huffer summarises her point, given 'the history of ethical systems that have condemned even the most benign forms of sexual deviation from the norm, the pervasive queer disengagement from ethics is not surprising' (Huffer 2013, 29). While Huffer is right to note that a distaste for traditional morality is queer theory's bread and butter, it is clear that Huffer overstates her case. Queer theory and LGBT+ politics, for one, have always had to deal with questions

DOI: 10.4324/9781003424604-3

everyone would readily recognise as moral and ethical. Birth control, abortion, the moral status of non-reproductive sexual activity, and the exact contours of marriage as a social institution are just a few prominent examples, and this list could be extended *ad nauseam*. Furthermore, it is difficult, if not impossible, to critique a moral standard without at least implicitly offering some other moral tenet in its stead. Queer theory has always, in this sense, at least arguably been a moral discourse, even if much of its theoretical thrust goes in the direction of a kind of endorsement of immorality.

Quite to the contrary of Huffer's suggestion, then, queer theory is at least arguably saturated by ethical thinking. Huffer's argument can be considered in another light, however, depending on how one goes about defining 'ethics'. In this new light, the problem with queer ethical thinking is not that it is simply not there, but that it is, even in its most radical moments, concerned with morality rather than with ethics. In an interview with Didier Eribon, Gilles Deleuze defines 'morality' as 'a set of constraining rules of a special sort, ones that judge actions and intentions by considering them in relation to transcendent values (this is good, that's bad)' (Deleuze and Eribon 1995, 100). Deleuze goes on to distinguish morality from ethics, which he treats as a set of optional rules that may be employed to gauge the appropriateness or not of our behaviour in relation to the 'ways of being' involved in a given situation. Moral rules are, then, perceived to come from above, from a legislator not subject to the restrictions of our earthly condition.

Based on Deleuze's definition, I would suggest that queer thought on the question of morality and/or ethics has tended towards the first term. Queer theory, in other words, is a moral, rather than an ethical, discourse – a discourse purporting to discover transcendental rules pitched from above, from a hypothesised higher legislator. This point is easily illustrated through one of the field's most contentious moments. In a 2005 Modern Languages Association roundtable dedicated to the so-called antisocial thesis in queer theory, two broad orientations coalesced around the question of whether queers were in some sense opposed to forming the same kinds of social bonds (familial, monogamous, reproductive, genital-centric, etc.) that heterosexuals form (Caserio et al. 2006). While the theme of the discussion was a reference to Leo Bersani's suggestion that 'inherent in gay desire is a revolutionary inaptitude for heteroized sociality' (Bersani 1995, 6), participants were chiefly concerned with Lee Edelman's just-published polemic *No Future*, which had argued against the notion of 'the future' as the ultimate normative *telos* of politics (Edelman 2004).

For Edelman, the easy appeal to 'the future' was always saturated in a distinctively anti-queer morality, an ideology of radical renunciation that was always presumptively heterosexual. Everyone fails to live now, *No Future* claims, because they are always living for the future children will inherit – and most children, of course, are born to straights. 'Queer', in this view, is what turns traditional morality, or widely held ideas of the good and the proper, on its head. If, in other words, one's default presumption is that it is good to build community, raise a family, have a happy marriage, etc., Edelman suggests that what is properly queer is to refuse any such presumption. Predictably, the examples of queers that *No Future* presents us with are not the kinds of characters one might sympathise with, ranging from anti-Christmas maverick Ebenezer Scrooge to Hitchcock's murderous birds. The unpalatability of this argument on queerness is by design (some have seen in it a queer manifesto; see Schotten 2018), and Edelman is clear to the effect that queerness's burden, as he paraphrases Guy Hocquenghem, is 'to figure an unregenerate, and unregenerating, sexuality … rejecting every constraint imposed by sentimental futurism' (Edelman 2004, 47). If there is a queer duty, then, it is to resolutely and publicly oppose traditional morality, to 'figure' (which is to say, to make visible, to embody) the downfall of those values that constitute 'proper' society.

While Edelman's views have generated much opprobrium in queer circles (see, for a sample of critiques, Dean 2008; Halberstam 2011, 149; Ruti 2012, 5–6; for analysis, Freccero 2006; Bernini 2017; Ashtor 2021), it is probably fair to say that the most important argument levelled against *No Future* is that of José Esteban Muñoz. Muñoz argues quite simply that Edelman's take on queerness, premised on themes of refusal, death, unproductiveness, and other forms of negativity, were all tired stylistic borrowings from a white, European, and gay male archive. This meant not only that Edelman's ideas were by and large unoriginal, but also that they contributed nothing to thinking about those who lived without a future *in* the here-and-now (by which Muñoz chiefly means non-white, U.S.-based LGBT+ people). In Muñoz's memorable quip, it had been clear to many that the antisocial thesis 'was the gay white man's last stand' (Caserio et al. 2006, 825; see also Muñoz 2009).

What I find interesting about Muñoz's suggestion, which undoubtedly won out in a discipline of queer studies that has increasingly defined itself as an outgrowth of intersectionality and other identity knowledges (Wiegman 2012; see also Nash 2019), is that it has a powerful moral and moralistic charge. Muñoz mobilises a by now canonical, and often only half-heartedly critiqued, move in identity knowledges – the appeal to the 'most oppressed' or some figure thereof as the worthiest of attention and, by that token, as the inevitable ushers of some utopian future fully inclusive of all minorities (a 'quasi-proletariat', in Rahul Rao's words, to which might be added: for the era of identity politics; see Rao 2020). Against Edelman's polemical immor-alism enjoining us to reject the presumption that the future is worth fighting for, in other words, Muñoz offers the upright-positioned moralism that, for some, nothing but the future is worth fighting for. The rather Christian tenor of the two positions (the remarkably explicit Manicheism, the covert citation of the maxim 'the meek shall inherit the earth') is, I think, an appropriate summation of the two extremes of queer (im)moralism: on the one hand, queer theorists following Muñoz's suggestion put forward a salvational and utopian discourse exalting the plight of those excluded from heteronormativity, whiteness, cisness, etc.; on the other hand, the antisocial thesis boils down to the advocacy of ever more revolting, and ever more politically sterile, forms of opposition to the values ascribed to 'The Straights' (for a discussion and critique of 'antinormativity', see Wiegman and Wilson 2015; for a fuller explanation see Edelman 2022).

The positions exemplified by Muñoz and Edelman dramatise an intractable disciplinary and political divide in LGBT+ politics and thought. Do queers want, with Muñoz, inclusion into the domain of legitimate lives with futures attached, and thus integration into what is likely to remain an only ever slightly enlarged heteronormativity? Or do they, with Edelman, revel in their marginality, deriving enjoyment not only from the increasingly debauched sex they allegedly have but also from flaunting their illicit pleasures before straight, respectable society? Are queers working to reform society in such a way that it becomes more welcoming not only of LGBT+ people but also of other minorities (non-white people and peoples, women, socioeconomically deprived people, etc.)? Or are they looking to drive home the point that a truly queer life refuses to produce and reproduce those social relations (work, marriage, reproductive sex, childrearing, etc.) presumed to assure the continuity of society, which, finally, is presumed to be of necessity heteronormative?

Such big, existential questions for LGBT+ movements probably do not admit of any one answer. Thankfully, what is at issue in this chapter is something else. Surprisingly, Edelman's *No Future* is often understood as a representative of 'Lacanian orthodoxy' (Caserio et al. 2006, 826), as Tim Dean has put it, within queer theory. Besides the inherent difficulty in claiming that there is such a thing as a Lacanian orthodoxy in light of the pulverisation of the Lacanian movement (Roudinesco 1997) and of the plain fact that no two Lacanians share the same Lacan, the suggestion that Edelman's thesis is orthodox in any sense (other than as a queer, antinormative orthodoxy) is rather puzzling, and especially so coming from one of the few queer theorists who have read Lacan with any care. In what follows, I argue that Lacan's ethics simply do not allow for a reading consistent with the antisocial thesis in queer theory. Indeed, the ethics of psychoanalysis is very much directly concerned with the need to move past any kind of (im)moralistic posturing if one is to have any hope of understanding the ethical stakes of desire as psychoanalysis understands it. In this chapter, I elaborate upon the claim that the ethics of psychoanalysis is an ethics of desire, such that the Lacanian position is irreducible to Edelman's antinormative immoralism as well as to Muñoz's utopian moralism.

2 Desire and Duty

Lacan's *Seminar VII* is an interrogation of the ethical implications of the psychoanalytic experience, especially in respect of its concept of desire. Yet the meaning of desire in psychoanalysis is far from intuitive; if my trajectory in the previous chapter suggests anything, it is that desire is thoroughly irreducible to a simple 'I want (or need) this or that'. Desire surfaces in the beyond of anything that might be demanded, a domain that is itself beyond what might be needed by a biological system. Desire is something else; it is made visible more often in phenomena that disturb an individual's self-image rather than in all those thoughts and impulses that appear to confirm it. This, indeed, is often what brings an analysand to the couch. In the first session of *Seminar VII*, Lacan wonders about this issue. An analysand would have no reason to subject themselves to the painful, tiresome, and costly analytic itinerary if something were not going awry in their lives. The initial demand addressed to an analyst – something like 'can you make my symptoms stop? Can you make me better?' – speaks of the difficulty the subject has, and structurally so, of spelling out the desire which, often repressed and unconscious, resurfaces symptomatically in ciphered form.

Lacan complicates this point further when he bluntly suggests that, for the subject who suffers, desire may appear only in symptomatic form – for instance, through the oppressive duties an obsessional subject might experience: intrusive thoughts, for instance, or senseless rituals such as the washing of hands of the double-checking of locks. Lacan wonders:

> Should [the 'I', the ego] or should it not submit itself to the half-unconscious, paradoxical, and morbid command of the superego, whose jurisdiction is moreover revealed increasingly as the analytical exploration goes forward and the patient sees that he is committed to its path?
>
> (Lacan 1992, 7)

This example, particularly apt in light of the experience of the obsessional, nevertheless retains some universal validity. As Lacan spells it out, '[t]he justification of that which presents itself with an immediate feeling of obligation, the justification of duty as such ... is at the heart of an inquiry that is universal' (Lacan 1992, 8). The questions delineating themselves at this early juncture of the seminar are crucial: what is this morbid command that may present itself alternately as duty or as desire, as an 'immediate feeling of obligation' within which a desire may be lodged, or through which it may be betrayed? How does one distinguish an 'autonomous' desire from acquiescence to the often arbitrary norms (and the impulse to violate them) everyone will have internalised from our parents and peers – that is, from what Freud called the superego? How, finally, are these questions related to what psychoanalysis discovered in the unconscious, and to what an analytic itinerary does?

It is debatable whether Lacan answers these questions satisfactorily, but they do provide a convenient entry point to the ethical problematic that psychoanalysis inaugurates with its concept of desire. One should, first, highlight how this notion of desire implies a different perspective to that of traditional ethical systems. Western ethical reflection is usually pitched against the kinds of things psychoanalysis recognises under the heading of desire – and, of course, typically also against the kinds of desire that queer theorists would find most interesting. Since at least Aristotle's *Nicomachean Ethics*, philosophers have been arguing that desire, the passions, and ultimately the set of those unruly impulses everyone (sometimes painfully) experiences ought to be disciplined, resisted, or even excluded entirely from the game, if one is to live a life worth living. For instance, happiness, the highest ethical goal in Aristotle, is precisely not the state of those who see their desire fulfilled at every turn; it is the activity of those who are virtuous and who are endowed with the means – wealth, slaves, friends, wives, boy lovers, children – to cultivate that virtue (Aristotle 2000, 20). Aristotle summarily excludes from the ethical domain a number of actions and affections that are central to psychoanalytic and queer thinking. Affections such as 'spite, shamelessness, envy, and, among actions, adultery, theft, homicide' do not even make the cut, as it were, of ethical inquiry, since they are always of necessity bad (Aristotle 2000, 31).

Aristotle need not concern himself with such debasements, since his objective is to assure his reader that there is a pleasure that comes with being virtuous, an experience in which pleasure and the Highest Good – the Good that is only ever aspired to for itself, and never in view of anything else – coincide. Lacan is clear to the effect that the true import of Aristotelian ethics is unintelligible to moderns, just as the ancient Greek ideal of the master – a philosophically inclined nobility, absorbed in leisurely contemplation and looking down on its labouring entourage – ceased to be possible at the dawn of modernity. Ethics for us moderns is no longer a science of character, no longer a function of virtue as Aristotle conceived it, no longer the means through which pleasure and the Highest Good meet through the intermediary of the master's happiness and the repression of all his unpalatable impulses. It is just as well, since Aristotle's inquiry ultimately relies on the hefty propositions that there is such thing as the Highest Good, that it is the object of ethics, and that its exercise procures a pleasure distinctive to it. A position reliant on this set of propositions always of necessity arrives at the notion that some objects are closer to the Good, and thereby are worthier of being desired than others – in the same way, for instance, that the heteronormativity queer theorists criticise would convince one that desiring someone of the opposite gender to one's own is better than to desire someone of the same.

Psychoanalysis refuses the assumption that there are objects that are (in themselves) more desirable than others and, accordingly, it refuses a core axiom of Aristotelian ethics. Lacan repeatedly and consistently went against any attempt on the part of those who carried forward the Freudian legacy to normalise their analysands, or to adapt them to reality, and ultimately to impose on them a Good that looks a lot like the analyst's own concept of the good. It is no accident, then, that Lacan locates the birth of modern ethical thought in Kant's *Critique of Practical Reason*. For Kant, it is well known that the criterion that must be employed to assess whether an act satisfies the dicta of morality is not that of utility, such that one ought to maximise, for example, earthly happiness to the greatest number; nor is it the conformity of one's action to one's place in the *polis*, such that there would be a virtue appropriate to a nobleman and another one entirely to his wife and slaves; instead, it is that of strictly rational universality. Moral action, in other words, is motivated by nothing but its capacity to satisfy the command 'so act that the maxim of your will could always hold at the same time as a principle of a universal legislation' (Kant 2002, 30).

For Kant, if the will is determined by anything other than this criterion of universality – for instance if one expects one's moral act to procure one some pleasure, or to realise some good, or to make oneself or someone else happy, etc. – whatever act follows it is already not moral. Kantian morality is thus premised on a rather curious notion of freedom as the autonomous acquiescence to rationally ascertained duty, one in which to be free is at once to accept the shackles of universal reason. Practical reason is autonomous only insofar as it alone determines one's actions, meaning that moral action requires that one act for no reason except to fulfil the duty one has recognised through the free use of one's reason – not for any interest exterior to it (or 'pathological', in Kant's terms; see de Kesel 2009, 111). Two of Kant's examples allow Lacan to think through the implications of his view. In a famous passage in the *Critique of Practical Reason*, Kant invites his reader to consider two scenarios:

[Scenario 1]
Suppose someone alleges that his lustful inclination is quite irresistible to him when he encounters the favored object and the opportunity. [Ask him] whether, if in front of the house where he finds this opportunity a gallows were erected on which he would be strung up immediately after gratifying his lust, he would not then conquer his inclination. One does not have to guess long what he would reply.

[Scenario 2]
But ask him whether, if his prince demanded, on the threat of the same prompt penalty of death, that he give false testimony against an honest man whom the prince would like to ruin under specious pretenses, he might consider it possible to overcome his love of life, however great it may be. He will perhaps not venture to assure us whether or not he would overcome that love, but he must concede without hesitation that doing so would be possible for him

(Kant 2002, 44)

Let us follow Alenka Zupančič (2003) and start with Kant's second example, in which a man is asked by his king to falsely testify against a peer who he knows has done nothing wrong on pain of death. This example is meant to prove the existence of the moral law, as well as its independence from and superiority over what is supposedly humanity's most basic and universal pathological motive – the attachment to one's own life. Kant surmises that everyone will at least stop to consider whether they should tell the truth and accept death, even if most people may still choose to lie and save their own skin. If this is the case, then everyone concurs that the voice of the moral law inhabits them, even if they might choose to disobey it. Lacan claims, however, that Kant's example is designed to mislead. Kant does not prove that the voice of conscience, the moral law, imposes itself inexorably, because the man's acknowledgement that he may answer truthfully and thereby give up his life may be explained not by his deeply felt sense of the moral law, but by a pathological interest in preserving the honest man that his false testimony would ruin. As Zupančič explains, Kant's example

> puts the categorical imperative (our duty) on the same side as the good (the well-being) of our fellow-man … the reader follows Kant here not because she is convinced of the inexorability of duty as such, but because the image of the pain inflicted on the other serves as a counterpoint.
>
> (Zupančič 2003, 54)

In other words, if I tell the truth and die in order to spare my fellowman, I may still be acting pathologically: it is not that I am fulfilling my duty to tell the truth for its own sake, but rather that the pain he will be unjustly caused is simply worse to me than my own death (or, alternatively, I might be acting for the narcissistic satisfaction I will procure through others' witnessing of my own altruistic death, or I may identify with my fellow-man such that a blow to him would at once be a blow to me, etc.).

Lacan offers a more appropriate example to Kant's ends, in which his hypothetical man would be prompted to denounce his own neighbour for subversive activities against the state – activities he is indeed engaged in, and which threaten the community. The question here is no longer 'should I tell the truth and preserve my innocent neighbour, even if it means giving up my own life?' – which places the good of the other on the same side as duty – but rather 'am I telling the truth out of duty, or am I balancing my neighbour's good against that of the community?' It is no longer a matter of discharging my duty because it coincides immediately with the good of the other; rather it is a matter of whether I am acting on the basis of my duty or on the basis of some consideration of the good. In this case the subject is presented with two choices:

Must I go toward my duty of truth insofar as it preserves the authentic place of my *jouissance*, even if it is empty? Or must I resign myself to this lie, which, by making me substitute forcefully the good for the principle of my *jouissance*, commands me to blow alternatively hot and cold? ...

Either I refrain from betraying my neighbor so as to spare my fellow man [that is, I choose my neighbour's good and lie, thereby going against my duty] or I shelter behind my fellow man so as to give up my *jouissance* [that is, I choose the community's good and tell the truth, but not because of duty].

(Lacan 1992, 190)

What is at issue, then, is whether I choose to base my decision on the moral law, or on some calculus of the good. Do I tell the truth and kill my neighbour by force of the duty of telling the truth – that is, without any consideration as to whether doing so would be a violation of my fellow man's rights, but in compliance with the moral law, which Kant claims tends towards the Highest Good or, for Lacan, enjoyment or *jouissance* [1] (better translated in this instance as the conjoining of happiness and virtue one might call 'bliss')? Or do I use my neighbour's or the community's good as the compass for my actions, in which case I am not reasoning morally in the Kantian sense? If I choose to betray my neighbour, how can I tell whether I am acting out of duty or because I prefer the good of the community over the good of my neighbour? The independent role of the moral law in the decision comes to the fore much more forcefully in Lacan's scenario. As Lacan puts it, and this is the first point he makes in respect of Kant's scenarios, 'there is no law of the good except in evil and through evil' (Lacan 1992, 190). In other words, since every moral choice can be formulated as a choice between one good and another, one can never truly know whether one is acting morally, because one can never truly know whether one acted out of compliance with the moral law or with some image of the good. Every moral choice, in other words, can be presumed to be pathological; that is, motivated by a consideration of the good, unless there is some other way to prove that one's will is determined by duty and duty alone.

Kant admits of just one exception to this problem, which has to do with those situations in which complying with the moral law will infringe every natural inclination and instinct, and will therefore cause pain:

What is essential in all determination of the will by the moral law is that, as a free will, and hence not merely without the cooperation of sensible impulses but even with rejection of all of them and with impairment of all inclinations insofar as they could be contrary to that law, it be determined merely by the law. Thus to this extent the effect of the moral law as an incentive is only negative, and as such this incentive can be cognized a priori. For all inclination and every sensible impulse is based on feeling, and the negative effect on feeling (by the impairment done to the inclinations) is itself a feeling. Consequently we can see a priori that the moral law as determining basis of the will, by infringing all our inclinations, must bring about a feeling that can be called pain; and here we have, then, the first and perhaps also the only case where we have been able to determine a priori from concepts the relation of a cognition (here a cognition of a pure practical reason) to the feeling of pleasure or displeasure.

(Kant 2002, 95–6)

What Kant suggests here is that there is an affective counterpart to the moral law, which is the displeasure felt when one does something one knows must be done out of duty, despite one's every other inclination. However, psychoanalysis demonstrates that there are cases in which the feeling of obligation or duty presents itself morbidly – for instance, the case of the obsessional, who experiences his rituals as unpleasurable, arbitrary obligations against which, try as he might, he is powerless to resist. What, then, does psychoanalysis make of these moments in which the sole affective sign of the moral law, namely the pain felt when one complies with it despite one's every pathological inclination, is actually a sign of something else, for instance, in the obsessional's case, of a repressed desire? What Lacan proposes next is to consider the consequences of this proposition – that duty can present itself morbidly, and that it is ultimately impossible to distinguish between a morbid presentation of duty and the normative presentation of duty – psychoanalytically.

3 On Evil

Turning to Kant's example of the lustful man, who is presented with his desired woman and the gallows waiting for him after he has satisfied himself, Lacan argues that its

> striking significance ... resides in the fact that the night spent with the lady is paradoxically presented to us as a pleasure that is weighed against a punishment to be undergone; it is an opposition which homogenizes them. There is in terms of pleasure a plus and a minus.

(Lacan 1992, 189)

For Kant, the choice of the lustful man is obvious, since it is obviously better to renounce the fleeting pleasure of sex now to avoid certain death. For Lacan, Kant fails even to introduce the problematic of duty in this example, since Kant only admits of the choice of postponing one's escapade, and since he makes either choice necessarily pathological, having to do with pleasure or displeasure. Lacan allows us to see, however, that there is a way to introduce the problematic of duty even in this example – Kant simply cannot entertain it, because he forces himself to ignore the question of evil.

All it takes, Lacan suggests, is to change the terms of the question: to frame it not as a matter of weighing up the expected pleasure from the sex against the displeasure of an early death, but as a matter of a decision between pleasure and enjoyment (*jouissance*) – let us define this term provisionally as the affect presumed to accompany the satisfaction of the psycho-analytic concept of desire (Chapter 1). This is the point at which Lacan joins up with the queer problematic once more in the question: why does enjoyment, the satisfaction of desire as such, as distinct from need and demand, engage the problematic of evil? The first thing to note here is that Lacan models his interrogation of enjoyment after the Kantian notion of the Highest Good. The Highest Good is the object of the moral law, a state that would become reality if and only if everyone always and everywhere obeyed the moral law to a perfect standard. If everyone were so virtuous that they could not fail to comply with the moral law, the Highest Good would materialise, and humanity's virtuosity would translate immediately into our happiness. The ethical subject needs to assume that this Highest Good exists, Kant claims, otherwise they would have no incentive to act morally. However, if the Kantian argument is read in light of what Lacan had to say about Kant's examples, the problem as to 'how does one know whether one is complying with the moral law?', to which Kant answers 'when it hurts to do so', becomes rather more difficult.

Reconsidering Kant's example of the lustful man in light of his theory of desire, then, Lacan suggests that 'anyone can see that if the moral law is, in effect, capable of playing some role here, it is precisely as a support for the *jouissance* involved' (Lacan 1992, 189). How does the moral law serve to support enjoyment? In this case, the moral law, because it ratifies the lustful man's assessment that the only real choice is for him to postpone his sexual encounter, serves precisely not to deter the encounter, but rather to elevate it into something more than merely pleasurable, but transgressively enjoyable ('utterly sinful', as Lacan quotes Saint Paul in reference to the relationship between the law and sin; Lacan 1992, 189, translation modified). The fact of contravening the subject's deeply held sense of the moral law might, in other words, itself become an incentive for the subject to choose the gallows, a way for the subject to raise the expected pleasure of the encounter to the rank of an enjoyment that is not merely pleasurable, but also suggestive of a higher satisfaction beyond pleasure. If the moral law can be thus 'libidinised', so to speak, it can become a sort of tool for the subject to support the fantasy of desire's ultimate satisfaction, enjoyment or *jouissance*, rather than something that directly determines the subject's will: the moral law might thereby become a means to further the subject's transgressive desire.

Indeed, despite Kant's view on this issue, Lacan successfully points out that it is not so difficult to imagine situations in which the lustful man might consent to dying. Literature, for instance, is littered with instances of people dying for the sake of love, and often for the sake of wholly hopeless love. Lacan reads these literary fantasies as sublimations of 'the feminine object', resulting from 'the exaltation we call love' (Lacan 1992, 109), and argues that they are one historical solution to the problem of desire and its impossible satisfaction. One makes enjoyment of the Lady (to reference Lacan's discussion of courtly love in this seminar) unattainable, at the limit by fantasising about dying for a single night with her, in order to safeguard the fantasy that possessing her would spell out the ultimate satisfaction. In this sense, the subject's consent to die would represent a contravention of the moral law, and this contravention would paradoxically be motivated by the moral law itself: it is because the moral law demands that the lethal night with the lady be renounced that the subject comes to desire it in the first place, since the contravention of the law would then become proof of the subject's infinite love for the Lady.

On the other end of the spectrum, there is the non-sublimatory solution of perversion: one might similarly imagine Kant's lustful man agreeing to the gallows if, for instance, he perversely craved 'the pleasure of cutting up the lady concerned in small pieces' (Lacan 1992, 109). In such instances, the perverse subject gets not merely the pleasure of the sex, but also a semblance of enjoyment supported by the contravention of the moral law that would have him act in self-preservation. In either case, sublimation and perversion, the moral law is employed as a means to safeguard the place of enjoyment, to preserve the fantasy that final satisfaction is attainable. Or, as Slavoj Žižek has put it, both cases accomplish a 'paradoxical reversal by means of which desire itself ... can no longer be grounded in any "pathological" interests or motivations ... so that "following one's desire" overlaps with "doing one's duty"' (Žižek 1998).

What Lacan is aiming at with his idiosyncratic reading of Kant, then, is that there is an ethical stratum deeper than the one Kant masterfully analyses, a stratum that might be described as the field of desire. If desire can indeed employ the moral law and its dicta as part and parcel of its own articulation, as Lacan suggests is possible through his examples of excessively sublimated love and murderous perversion, then desire cannot be done away with as a determining ground of the will, nor can it be simply and directly identified to the pathological. In fact, Lacan demonstrates, in his discussion of the Marquis de Sade, that Kant's own system can be rigorously followed in ways that would produce what Kant would have called diabolical evil. In Kant's *Religion within the Bounds of Bare Reason*, Kant argues that humans are incapable of adopting the reverse formula to the categorical imperative as a maxim guiding our actions. In other words, one cannot decide, at every turn, to determine what the moral law demands and then do the exact opposite, 'because the opposition to the [moral] law would thereby itself be elevated to an incentive (for without any incentive the power of choice cannot be determined), and thus the subject would be turned into a diabolical being' (Kant 2009, 39). Kant does not offer much by way of justification for this claim, which seems quite unusual considering his thorough argumentative style – surely there are plenty of reasons to imagine the world is full of diabolical beings. Why does Kant feel the need to dismiss this possibility so strongly, one might even say arbitrarily?

For Zupančič, Kant's rejection of this 'diabolical' kind of evil can be accounted for by the fact that Kant had sensed the uncanny proximity between his description of the worst kind of evil and his description of the moral law. This contention is relatively straightforward to support, to the extent that Kant's ethics can be interpreted (and I have more or less been following Zupančič's take in doing so) in purely formal terms; the requirements of the ethical act are simply that it should comply with the injunction to universality (i.e. that one wills it to be as necessary as a law of nature) and that an ethical act should be undertaken under no incentive but respect for the moral law. Since the question as to whether the effects of one's actions are recognisable by a finite agent as good or evil is a moot question for Kant, then this formalism may perfectly well be satisfied in the diabolical purity of evil if, unlike Kant himself, one dares to entertain its possibility. In an amusing flourish, Zupančič even rewrites Kant's description of the postulate of the immortal soul so as to apply it to diabolical evil:

> The achievement of the highest evil in the world is the necessary object of a will determinable by (im)moral law. In such will, however, the complete fitness of disposition to the (im)moral law is the supreme condition of the highest evil. However, the perfect fit of the will to the (im)moral law is the diabolical, which is a perfection of which no rational being of this world of sense is at any time capable.
>
> (Zupančič 2003, 91)

Zupančič concludes, then, that 'diabolical evil, the highest evil, is indistinguishable from the highest good … they are nothing other than the definitions of an accomplished (ethical) act' (Zupančič 2003, 92). Zupančič argues that not only must diabolical evil be taken into account as a possibility, its formal structure may even be identical to that of any truly ethical act. Lacan will not directly argue Zupančič's more radical point, namely that the Highest Good and Evil are the prototype of the ethical act (the *act* being a concept that Lacan introduces much later). Rather, Lacan will turn to Kant's contemporary, famous libertine thinker and inmate of the Bastille, the Marquis de Sade, and argue that beneath its veneer of debauchery Sade's violent licentiousness is a kind of staging of Kant's ethical system.

For Lacan, the Sadean categorical imperative is a parody of Kant's principle of humanity, that one ought to 'use humanity … always at the same time as an end, never merely as a means' (Kant 1996, 38), and can be called a right to *jouissance.* Maurice Blanchot expresses the Sadean imperative concisely as 'give yourself to whomsoever desires you, take from whomever you please' (Blanchot 1965, 37). In 'Kant *avec* Sade', Lacan goes on to argue that Sade's maxim (*pace* Blanchot) satisfies the core criteria of Kantian morality, namely through (1) its purging of any pathological interests that might determine one's act; and (2) the possibility that it could serve as a universally compelling injunction (Lacan 2006a, 650).

It is clear, in regard to the former requirement, that Sade's maxim has no immediate relation to sexual pleasure as it is usually understood. For instance, everyone recognises the violence that sex can represent, and the right to enjoyment does not demand any form of consent that might assure one, to the extent that such assurance is at all possible, that sex will be pleasurable or respectful. As such, compliance with the maxim *give yourself to whomsoever desires you, take from whomever you please* is undertaken not for the sake of pleasure, but for nothing but the duty explicit in the imperative mood.

In respect of the latter requirement of universality, Sade justifies himself through a parody of the notion of universal rights. In the pamphlet-within-a-book 'Yet Another Effort, Frenchmen, If You Would Become Republicans', for example, the anonymous author argues that women ought to be free to give themselves, unfettered by family and marriage, to whoever wants them – as is proper in the age of human rights, in which being treated as a family's or a husband's property violates the principle that each person is an end in themselves and never solely a means to something else (Sade 1965, 318–9; see also Lacan 2006a, 650). Thus, the imperative that one ought to give oneself to whoever wants to enjoy one's body or a part thereof is justified on the very same grounds upon which Kant bases his own categorical imperative, namely the universal dignity of humanity, or on the universally and rationally compelling grounds that no one can ever be the property of another.

Hence, the maxim *give yourself to whomsoever desires you, take from whomever you please* is not adopted for pathological interests, since not everyone wants to be treated as nothing but a sexual object; furthermore, it is universal in the sense that, like the prohibition that a human being be the property of another, it can conceivably compel rational assent universally and in every situation (so long as one foregoes one's pathological attachment to physical integrity). It therefore satisfies the criteria of Kantian morality. Sade, according to Lacan, even comes up with his own versions of the Kantian postulates of practical reason (besides that of freedom, which works for both): as Lacan argues in 'Kant *avec* Sade', for the God Kant uses as a prop for moral conscience, He whose actions cannot depart from the moral law and who can thereby serve as an example to be followed, Sade's Saint-Fond in *Juliette* (Sade 1968) substitutes God as the Being Supreme in Wickedness, and Nature as 'fundamental, metaphysical cruelty' (Benvenuto 2016, 82). For Kant's postulate on the immortality of the soul that is to perfect its virtue infinitely, Sade substitutes the physical immortality of his heroines, who suffer through hundreds of pages of sexual torment described in painstaking detail without losing any of their charms (Lacan 2006a, 654). However, Sade is more honest than Kant, because he recognises that the derisory world he conjures up in his novels would be a world with the highest degree of pain possible. If, for Kant, the pain of having our inclinations towards our good and others' contravened is the surest sign of the moral law, then the same holds for Sade, except that he recognises the perverse implication that the Highest Good and the Highest Evil (or, at least, the highest degree of pain) would therefore coincide in a truly virtuous (or truly wicked) world.

Thus Sade, in turning Kantian morality upside down, actually delivers the latter in a much more adequate form, at least to the extent that Sade's take on the categorical imperative shows how Kant's system only functions under the assumption that the Highest Good is the object of the moral law, and that it is both desirable and good – which, in turn, requires the entire paraphernalia of a well-meaning God, immortality, and freedom. Should one do away with that assumption, the opposite conclusion to Kant's becomes perfectly feasible, namely that the moral law may well be guiding those who hear its soft whisper towards something closer to the Highest Evil. A few questions might impose themselves at this point: is Lacan merely gesturing towards some notion of hedonism? Is he claiming that the ethics of psychoanalysis consists in proclaiming that the highest form of morality is the Sadean right to see one's desire satisfied at every turn, regardless of the consequences? Is he claiming, to the contrary, that the subject ought to content themselves with the ordinary, common sense, pathological (in the Kantian sense) good? He is very much not doing so. For Lacan, Freud had gone beyond the Kant-Sade deadlock by naming, in place of the God who alone might see the Highest Good or the Highest Evil accomplished, desire as such.

4 An Ethics of Desire

For Lacan, Kant had delineated a new ethical domain, but he could not have recognised in it that which Freud eventually would recognise. Kant's theory needed psychoanalysis as a means to let go of the fantasy-postulates which alone sustain the idea of the Highest Good (and which Sade adapts for his own purposes).

> Now we analysts are able to recognize [the place of Kant's *Thou Shalt*] as the place occupied by desire. Our experience gives rise to a reversal that locates in the center an incommensurable measure, an infinite measure, that is called desire ... If Kant had only designated this crucial point for us, everything would be fine, but one also sees that which the horizon of practical reason opens onto: to the respect and the admiration that the

starry heavens above and the moral law within inspires in him. One may wonder why. Respect and admiration suggest a personal relationship. That is where everything subsists in Kant, though in a demystified form ... there is no other articulatable meaning to give this divine presence except that which functions for us as a criterion of the subject, namely, the dimension of the signifier.

(Lacan 1992, 316)

For Lacan, Freud demonstrates that the Highest Good and its conceptual paraphernalia are nothing but religious reverie, but that the field Kant systematised in his account of morality is, in fact, occupied by desire and its articulation in the order of the signifier. Freud argued that religion found its origins in the demand of the infant for an omnipotent father, an argument that could very well be turned against Kant (Freud 1961). For Lacan, even if Kant is taken more seriously than Freud might have taken him, his argument would still rest on the respect he harboured for nature, on the one hand, and the moral law and the voice of conscience, on the other. Kant indeed seems to plead with his reader to accept that people entertain a sort of personal rapport with these transcendental forces (nature, morality), thus giving them a purchase and status that a scientific worldview cannot but contest.[2] The final lessons of *Seminar VII* claim that what one finds today in Kant's 'starry heavens' and 'Reason', or Sade's 'Nature', is the order of the signifier: the language in and through which desire is articulated. So, what appeared to Kant as the field structuring the rational necessity of morality appears to Lacan as 'the criterion of the subject, namely, the dimension of the signifier', such as it is demonstrated day in, day out, in an analytic itinerary.

If one accepts Lacan's proposition that psychoanalysis replaces the field of Kantian morality with the order of the signifier, it emerges that language is not merely the material with which a psychoanalyst works, but also the condition of possibility for a certain quantification, for the only moral judgement that psychoanalysis can pronounce. This latter judgement pertains to desire, and its form is an adaptation of the final judgement implied by Kant's concept of virtue, or the degree to which one has become more or less incapable of contravening the moral law. Kant's judgement as to whether one has become virtuous relies on the fantasy that God exists, that there is a subject who is capable of ascertaining whether our free, immortal souls have more or less complied with the moral law during their lifetime(s). Kant deemed this to be a necessary assumption, since otherwise mortals would never be able to form any well-founded judgements as to whether they have well and truly complied with the moral law. If, for Lacan, psychoanalysis does away with this Kantian requirement, it substitutes for it an unanswerable question: 'have you acted in conformity with the desire that is in you?' (Lacan 1992, 314).

Instead, then, of positing a final legislator who will decide whether the subject has acted morally and become virtuous, as Kant claims is necessary for practical reasons if it is to be appealing at all, Lacan displaces the question: ethics is not a matter of compliance with a law pronounced by an old bearded man in the sky, inscribed in the great Book of Nature, or inherent to the free use of reason. Rather, psychoanalysis speaks of ethics whenever the subject is faced with the matter of whether ultimately they have complied with that most particular law – the law articulated in the desire they have been bequeathed (for instance, by their earliest caretakers), even if that desire remains unconscious, inscrutable, veiled, and inscribed in the structure of language that each person will have been confronted with in a singular fashion. Desire, that most intimate of laws, is universal in that it exists in everyone, but is irreducible, though not unrelated, to the (paternal) law, to social dicta, or to what queer theorists call normativity. 'What the superego demands', finally, 'has nothing to do with that which we would be right in making the universal rule of our actions; such is the ABC of psychoanalytic truth' (Lacan 1992, 310). Thus, the instance of desire is not presented to us from some outside agency, in some hypothetical and ever-deferred future, but is intimately imbricated in everyday conduct and suffering. The psychoanalytic experience demonstrates that the subject can, and does, always measure their actions here and now against the final perspective of desire, even if this is only ever done unconsciously. So much so, that desire ignored or repressed cannot but insist, for instance, in the myriad ways analysands find to repeat certain situations in their personal lives, however painful they may be. As Lacan puts it, '[i]f analysis has a meaning, desire is nothing other than that which supports an unconscious theme, the very articulation of that which roots us in a particular destiny' (Lacan 1992, 319).

At the centre of Lacan's ethical thought lies the measure of desire, the measure of the extent to which the subject is engaged in 'something that is specifically [their] business'. The path of this 'something' can be followed, or one may stray from it, or indeed others may stand as obstacles to it, but it never ceases to be one's path, inscribed somewhere in the Other. Lacan's entire issue in this seminar is to confront the fact that '[a]nalysis is a judgment' (Lacan 1992, 291), that if analysis is to mean something it must allow a subject to evaluate and re-evaluate again and again whether they are or once were treading the path of their desire or otherwise, and to be given the choice to follow that path in spite of the costs that following it might entail (the judgement, in other words, allows them 'to know if he [*sic*] wants what he desires'; see Lacan 2006b, 571). However, this does not change the fact that the full unfolding of this desire will remain veiled to the subject, unconscious, and that it might simply be best to let it go if one wishes to live a comfortable or morally acceptable life.

This is why Lacan will make the fact that the psychoanalyst is terrified of their profession a cornerstone of his institutional thinking: fidelity to (discovering, reconstructing, interpreting) desire is at once fidelity to what is most inscrutable and, potentially, monstrous in the human. Yet Lacan is not an idealist for whom anything anyone might come to want is or should be made possible. Part of Lacan's point in demonstrating the link between Kant and Sade, and how Freud overcomes them, is to insist that the desire psychoanalysis recentres may well be, and most often is, antithetical to whatever is deemed to be for the common good. Desire often goes against the 'service of the goods', against the order of the state where places, hierarchies, and the distribution of goods are decided upon and enforced, ideally in the interest of all although not without much *malaise* (Zupančič 2023). I return to this point in the next part of this book. In addition to the outer limits societies are well within their right to impose on desire, it is also important to note that desire in *Seminar VII* is internally limited. At this stage in his thinking, Lacan identifies two intrinsic limits to desire: death, on the one hand, and satisfaction, on the other. Contextualising this point in relation to his wider theory of desire, Lacan teaches:

> It is precisely to the extent that the demand always under- or overshoots itself that, because it articulates itself through the signifier, it always demands something else ... desire is formed as something supporting this metonymy, namely, as something the demand means beyond whatever it is able to formulate. And that is why the question of the accomplishment [*réalisation*] of desire is necessarily formulated from the point of view of a Last Judgement.
>
> Try to imagine what 'to have realized one's desire' might mean, if it is not to have realized it, so to speak, in the end. It is this trespassing [*empiètement*] of death on life that gives its dynamism to any question that attempts to find a formulation for the subject of the realization of desire.
>
> (Lacan 1992, 294, translation modified)

Since desire refers to an object that is impossible – a mirage arising from the dialectic between need and demand described in Chapter 1 – it appears as nothing but the metonymy of all actually made demands. It is because I am never satisfied by the objects I can acquire that I can have a sense of desire as the very movement from one object to the next, a sense of my own rapport with lack as such, both the lack in myself and that which is lacking in all possible objects. There is, however, one moment in everyone's life when the movement of desire will inevitably come to a halt: the moment of death. I can imagine that, when I die, my life might appear to me as a finite series of events, as one observable and self-contained 'history' from the standpoint of which I may notionally know what it was that I was after all that time. So, what Lacan says here is that everyone is always constantly posing themselves the question: 'when I die, at the moment my life retrospectively becomes a finite series of accomplished events, will I be able to say that I have been true to my desire?' The problem is that the fact that one can pose this question without being on one's deathbed also makes the endpoint of desire present to oneself in the here and now. It is therefore not merely the eventuality of death itself that poses the problematic of desire, but also the fact that one can assume one's own death and develop a relationship with it, even if one will never experience it and can never really form a definite representation of it.

Lacan's theory of the analytic cure in this seminar, finally, is that the term of an analytic itinerary, and thus psychoanalysis's final ethical stake, coincides with an analysand's partial reconstruction of their unconscious desire, and with their confrontation with desire's internal limits – that is, with its constitutive relation to death, and with its structural insatiability.

> The question I ask is this: shouldn't the true termination of an analysis... confront the one who undergoes it with the reality of the human condition? ... The state in which man is in that relationship to himself which is his own death.
>
> (Lacan 1992, 303)

It is this confrontation that constitutes what Lacan calls the analyst's 'experienced desire' (*désir averti*) (Lacan 1992, 301), which in the closing lessons of *Seminar VII* he defines negatively. What the analyst cannot desire is for an analysand to attempt to live out and act out their instinctual drive in the most 'natural' manner possible – which emerges as a pseudo-Sadean fantasy of unbridled enjoyment, a kind of (im)moralistic hedonism. Conversely, what the analyst can want is for an analysand to be confronted with the imbrication of death in life called desire, and to construct an answer as to what it demands of them. Everything else is beside the (analytic) point.

5 A Politics of Desire?

A great many commentators, queer or otherwise (see, *inter alia*, Butler 2000; Edelman 2004, 2022; Stavrakakis 2007; Žižek 2016; Ruti 2012, 2017), have treated Lacan's ethical thought as being directly applicable to politics. There are many variations on this point, but I will allow myself a strawman for the purposes of exposition and suggest that there are two standard elements to the more famous applications of Lacan's ethical thought to politics: one, an interpretation of Lacan's motto that one can only be psychoanalytically guilty of giving ground to one's desire as a direct injunction to 'never give up' on the fulfilment of one's desire; and two, a consideration of Lacan's later concept of the psychoanalytic act, which is understood by analogy to a revolutionary moment capable of reconfiguring the entirety of a symbolic (political-institutional-cultural) universe retrospectively (Žižek's early reading of *Antigone* alongside Walter Benjamin is exemplary of this position; see Žižek 1989, 1997). In short, the ethics of psychoanalysis would be an ethics of the capital-E Event, an ethics of those moments (prototypically, revolutions and other forms of major social upheaval) when, through the relentless pursuit of the desire of a revolutionary subject, all social norms are suspended and wholly new social, political, and institutional systems are put in place.

Some psychoanalysts and scholars, unsettled by these political thinkers' tendency to (re)make Lacan into a revolutionary, have been attempting to oppose these readings, without much success, in cultural studies and other critical theoretical circles (see de Kesel 2009; Nobus 2022). As a matter of pure exegesis, it is difficult not to agree with the psychoanalysts. Lacan is quite explicit at various points in *Seminar VII* (and indeed throughout the *Seminar*) that he is speaking about the analytic experience, and not about politics, and the closing lecturers of the seminar are likewise explicitly pitched at the level of the question 'what are we analysts supposed to achieve with the suffering person on the couch, and why is my doctrine different to analytic orthodoxy?' Naturally, however, to restrict Lacan's ethical thought to the clinic is, in its own way, a misrecognition of what Lacan has to say, not only about ethics, but about subjectivity. For one, the psychoanalytic concepts of desire, the Oedipus complex, enjoyment, etc., are all obviously social, in that they come into being always already mediated by language and embedded in a wider political setting. Lacan also discusses the proper dimension of desire by reference, and in contrast, to the political order of the 'service of the goods', famously voiced by Creon in his reading of *Antigone*. The concluding remarks of *Seminar VII* are also tellingly about the political role of desire, and of the concept's apparent repression in the era of the social sciences.

Lacan's ethical thought is therefore also political. Let me venture a few paragraphs, in the remainder of this chapter, on the question of whether there is a sexual politics to Lacan's construal of desire and the ethics attached to that concept in *Seminar VII*. At this point it bears returning to the introduction to this chapter. The most famous interpretation of *Seminar VII* in queer theory is Lee Edelman's 2004 polemic, No *Future*. Edelman enlists Lacan into the antisocial thesis. An excellent early statement of what this thesis means can be found in French gay liberationist thinker Guy Hocquenghem's *Homosexual Desire*. Engaging orthodox Freudian explanations of, on the one hand, what a 'normal' genital-heterosexual sexuality ought to look like and, on the other, arguments about the aetiology of homosexuality, Hocquenghem argues that homosexual desire cannot but be seen as a developmental and social disaster, if one adopts a bourgeois-nuclear-familial moral yardstick:

> Homosexual desire is the ungenerating-ungenerated terror of the family, because it produces itself without reproducing. Every homosexual must thus see himself as the end of the species, the termination of a process for which he is not responsible and which must stop at himself ... The

homosexual can only be a degenerate, for he does not generate – he is only the artistic end to a species.

(Hocquenghem 1993, 107)

The antisocial thesis, then, sets off from the hypothesis that homosexuality, at least in heteronormative society's fantasy life, is directly associated with something like Evil, with the negation of every productive – and thereby good – social, moral, and political institution. The homosexual, in other words, is anti-family (they do not marry), anti-childhood (they do not reproduce, they are all pederasts), anti-work (they only make art), anti-human (they do not perpetuate the species), etc. To repeat Leo Bersani's claim, then, 'perhaps inherent in gay desire is a revolutionary inaptitude for heteroized sociality' (Bersani 1995, 6). Edelman accepts and radicalises this argument, enjoining those who are 'queered' by heteronormative society to actively pose as that society's downfall in strict compliance with the negative stereotypes ascribed them. To be Queer in *No Future*'s cosmos, in other words, is to fulfil a certain role in respect of the *summum bonum*, the Highest Good, aspired to by straight majority societies – that role being to embody and represent the negation of the (straight) Highest Good. Edelman calls the figure of the *summum bonum* in contemporary Western societies the Child, insofar as it can stand in for a far-off future in which the best possible state of affairs is realised. Every act in such societies must be judged according to the categorical imperative: so act that you preserve, reassert, etc., the Child that is the privileged image of the future.

For Edelman, finally, the special relevance of LGBT+ lives in the recent past has been to provisionally fulfil the role of Queer, of impediment to, the privileged image of the future that is the Child. This seemingly abstract point has very concrete coordinates. For example, Edelman zooms in on Christian conservatives' anti-abortion and homophobic discourse – clearly undertaken on behalf of an imaginary Child, such as it appears in various moral panics about 'grooming', pederasty, the moral 'corruption' of children, public hysteria over 'gender theory' being taught in schools, etc. – to suggest that non-heterosexuals cannot but take on the role of Queer when faced with these instances of far-right backlash. To persist in unproductive, debauched, and ultimately queer lives would finally also be to refuse to gauge the value of non-straight lives in accordance with the final measure of how much they have contributed to 'the future', as embodied in the Child. In Edelman's words:

Queers must respond to the violent force of such constant provocations not only by insisting on our equal right to the social order's prerogatives, not only by avowing our capacity to promote that order's coherence and integrity, but also by saying explicitly what Law and the Pope and the whole of the Symbolic order for which they stand hear anyway in each and every expression or manifestation of queer sexuality: Fuck the social order and the Child in whose name we're collectively terrorized.

(Edelman 2004, 29)

In sum, then, Edelman's is an argument for the refusal to assimilate. It is an argument for the reassertion of queer ways of being such as they are here-and-now, even as they fulfil a certain (stereotyped) role in heteronormative society's fantasy life, one that marks out queers for persecution and, tragically, even elimination. The alternatives to accepting such stereotypes have indeed proven unsatisfactory, to the extent that they have tended to accompany significant compromise. It is widely acknowledged today, for example, that gay activism in the wake of the AIDS crisis has focused on refashioning gayness into a viable rehash of the nuclear family (two monogamous same-gender parents and an adopted child), sweeping the distinctiveness of, say, queer sexual subcultures under the rug (certainly in respect of their notorious promiscuity), and leaving behind most of the LGBT+ acronym (most especially the 'T'). To be the Queer metaphor, then, is not solely a matter of negotiating stereotyping but also a moral calling, a duty that befalls those who cannot be recognised in and by societies structured around the reproductive imperatives condensed into the Child.

There are evidently a great many problems with this view. For example, critics are unanimous to the effect that Edelman's position requires that queers renounce politics as such, since politics is always in some sense or another about some notion of the common good, which will, in turn, always include some contextual diagnosis as well as an image of the future. (So, Mari Ruti argues that Edelman treats any reference to concrete social positions and workable political proposals – and accordingly the whole paraphernalia of social analysis, such as the notions of interest, struggle, access to goods and services, and concrete instances of social and sexual practice – as a loss of theoretical rigour; see Ruti 2017, 111). Edelman seems to confirm such critiques even in his most recent work (Edelman 2022). Here, I will confine myself to noting that, to my mind, Edelman's construal of the opposition pitting the Queer against the Child (which, he insists throughout *No Future*, is a structural one) can be dismantled with much the same tools as Lacan dismantles the purported opposition between Kant and Sade. In other words, it seems to me that Lacan's reading of Sade as delivering us the truth of Kant's system authorises the claim that the maxims 'act such that you uphold the Child' and 'act such that you refuse the Child (or, act as Queer)' are both compliant with (Lacan's take on) the categorical imperative (i.e. that a maxim be purged of pathological interest and universally, rationally compelling; see Lacan 2006a, 649). However, each also relies on the God-figure Edelman calls the Child, whether one is enjoined to reproduce the Child and its coherence or to envision its destruction as Queers. Each accordingly fails to give the Lacanian concept of desire its due – which means, at the level of *Seminar VII,* to confront the necessary prohibition of attaining enjoyment, as well as desire's internal limits in biological death and in the final settling of accounts that Lacan models after the Last Judgement – and remains at the level of what Lacan calls the superego. When Lacan speaks of the superego, one might hear the command of the father in whom, since Freud, one is authorised in seeing also the origin of the image of God (whether the Kantian God or the Sadean supremely evil being; see Lacan 2006a, 652). As Michael Snediker has suggested, in other words, 'it is difficult for me not to hear in the sheer absoluteness of Edelman's dicta something like a superego's militancy' (Snediker 2009, 22).

Finally, then, the ethics of desire cannot give rise to an absolute command such as that proposed by Edelman. Or, rephrased in queerer terms, an ethics of desire does not accommodate antinormativity – 'so act that you oppose heteronormativity' – the bread-and-butter of queer theory's politics, because antinormativity is nothing but another figure of the superego. That said, Lacan does provide an indication of the political side of the notion of desire in his concluding remarks to *Seminar VII.* There, Lacan poses himself the question of whether there can be a science of desire, a question he poses within the orbit of the social sciences, whether primarily statistical or structuralist in methodological persuasion. Answering in the negative, he tells us that

> the human sciences have in my eyes no other function than to form a branch of the service of goods ...
>
> the desire of man, which has been felt, anesthetized, put to sleep by moralists, domesticated by educators, betrayed by the academies, has quite simply taken refuge or been repressed in ... the passion for knowledge ...
>
> In other words, science is animated by some mysterious desire, but it doesn't know ... what that desire means.
>
> (Lacan 1992, 324–5)

Lacan advances three interrelated claims: first, there can be no science of desire conceived of in the mould of the social sciences; second, the social sciences (Lacan probably means structuralism as well as the broad array of work retrospectively grouped under 'cybernetics'; see Geoghegan 2023) are a means of repressing desire and channelling human effort into the proper channels of the 'service of goods'; third, as with any repressed desire, the desire repressed in and by the human sciences resurfaces elsewhere, namely in the natural scientist's passion for knowledge, and especially in the physicist's quest for ever-widening manipulation of the natural world (Lacan will go on to speak of Oppenheimer and the atomic bomb, for instance). The reason why Lacan seems to think it is desire that lies behind the adventure of scientific modernity – rather than, say, a belief in Reason or Progress – is partly that science has no substantive concept of the good towards which its machinations purportedly contribute. Lacan's reference to Oppenheimer is telling: science leads to advances in medicine just as well as it leads to the moon landing and to mutually assured destruction. Since science has no clear conception of the Good or the Evil towards which it supposedly tends, one might hypothesise it is regulated by nothing but its own inexorable march forward – or, its desire, inasmuch as it is unconscious. This is desire at its purest, employing the Kantian form of commandment (keep on knowing!) and buttressed by nothing but the final horizon of perfect compliance: virtue fully realised, for Kant, death for the Lacan of *Seminar VII*, or perfect control over the natural world, for the scientist (which is increasingly looking to coincide with death for humanity, anyway). The meaning of this final horizon of compliance, as is the case with any unconscious desire invested with a repressed meaning, is an open question until it isn't – and science is unlikely to find itself on the psychoanalytic couch.

These motifs are certainly not alien to queer theory. Lacan's argument that the human (or social) sciences had anesthetised, domesticated, put to sleep, etc., human desire agrees very well with the field's stance towards traditional social scientific inquiry (Love 2021). Queer theory's critical procedures also owe much to the presumption that a collective project as elevated as capital-S Science may be animated by a set of unconscious desires (and, of course, prejudices). More generally, Lacan anticipates here an important point that he will only make explicit much later, namely that every discourse must be considered not solely from the standpoint of its signifying coherence but also from the standpoint of its libidinal infrastructure: of how, in other words, discourse subjects not through overt repression, but through the channelling and administration of enjoyment (Chapter 4). This is, or could be taken as, a profound queer insight, suggesting a point of contact between the 'small' politics of everyday life and its libidinal renunciations or gratifications and the 'grand' politics of, say, the capitalist mode of production or capital-S Science (Sous 2017). In order to begin developing this insight, a detour through how psychoanalysts conceive of the rapport between their practice and their understanding of society is needed.

Notes

1 In *Seminar VII*, Lacan models the place of *jouissance* after the object of practical reason in Kant's *Critique of Practical Reason*. This means that what Kant calls the Highest Good, or the state of affairs corresponding to the conjunction of universal virtue and happiness in an endlessly deferred future, Lacan calls enjoyment or *jouissance*. This term is discussed further down.

2 For Lacan, science does away with 'nature' as a metaphysical entity, and transforms it into nothing but variables designating numerical values in equations meant to locally describe observable phenomena. There is no assumption that these phenomena add up to a harmonious whole. Rather, 'the world' in Lacan's view of modern physics is perfectly contingent, and its representation always fragmentary (see Milner 1995).

References

Aristotle. 2000. *Nicomachean Ethics*. Translated by Roger Crisp. 1st ed. Cambridge: Cambridge University Press.

Ashtor, Gila. 2021. *Homo Psyche: On Queer Theory and Erotophobia*. 1st ed. New York: Fordham University Press.

Benvenuto, Sergio. 2016. *What Are Perversions? Sexuality, Ethics, Psychoanalysis*. 1st ed. London: Karnac.

Bernini, Lorenzo. 2017. *Queer Apocalypses*. Translated by Julia Heim. 1st ed. Cham: Palgrave Macmillan.

Bersani, Leo. 1995. *Homos*. 1st ed. Cambridge, MA: Harvard University Press.

Blanchot, Maurice. 1965. 'Sade'. In *Justine: Philosophy in the Bedroom and Other Writings*, by The Marquis de Sade, 1st ed. New York: The Grove Press.

Butler, Judith. 2000. *Antigone's Claim*. 1st ed. New York: Columbia University Press.

Caserio, Robert, Lee Edelman, Jack Halberstam, Tim Dean, and José Esteban Muñoz. 2006. 'The Antisocial Thesis in Queer Theory'. *PMLA* 21 (3): 819–828.

De Kesel, Marc. 2009. *Eros and Ethics: Reading Jacques Lacan's Seminar VII*. Translated by Sigi Jöttkandt. 1st ed. New York: SUNY Press.

Dean, Tim. 2008. 'An Impossible Embrace: Queerness, Futurity, and the Death Drive'. In *A Time for the Humanities: Futurity and the Limits of Autonomy*, edited by Tim Dean, James Bono, and Ewa Plonowska Ziarek, 1st ed., 122–140. New York: Fordham University Press.

Deleuze, Gilles, and Didier Eribon. 1995. 'Life as a Work of Art'. In *Negotiations*, translated by Martin Joughin, 94–102. New York: Columbia University Press.

Edelman, Lee. 2004. *No Future: Queer Theory and the Death Drive*. 1st ed. Durham, NC and London: Duke University Press.

Edelman, Lee. 2022. *Bad Education: Why Queer Theory Teaches Us Nothing*. 1st ed. Durham, NC and London: Duke University Press.

Freccero, Carla. 2006. 'Fuck the Future'. *GLQ* 12 (2): 333–334.

Freud, Sigmund. 1961. 'The Future of an Illusion'. In *The Standard Edition of the Complete Psychological Works of Sigmund Freud*, vol. XXI, translated by James Strachey, 3–58. London: The Hogarth Press.

Geoghegan, Bernard Dionysius. 2023. *Code: From Information Theory to French Theory*. 1st ed. Durham, NC and London: Duke University Press.

Halberstam, Jack. 2011. *The Queer Art of Failure*. 1st ed. Durham, NC: Duke University Press.

Hocquenghem, Guy. 1993. *Homosexual Desire*. Translated by Daniella Dangoor. 1st ed. Durham, NC and London: Duke University Press.

Huffer, Lynne. 2013. *Are the Lips a Grave? A Queer Feminist on the Ethics of Sex*. 1st ed. New York: Columbia University Press.

Kant, Immanuel. 1996. 'Groundwork of the Metaphysics of Morals'. In *Practical Philosophy*, translated by Mary J. Gregor, 1st ed., 37–108. Cambridge: Cambridge University Press.

Kant, Immanuel. 2002. *Critique of Practical Reason*. Translated by Werner S. Pluhar. 1st ed. Cambridge: Hackett.

Kant, Immannuel. 2009. *Religion Within the Bounds of Bare Reason*. Translated by Werner S. Pluhar. 1st ed. Cambridge: Hackett.

Lacan, Jacques. 1992. *The Seminar of Jacques Lacan, Book VII: The Ethics of Psychoanalysis*. Translated by Dennis Porter. 1st ed. London: W.W. Norton.

Lacan, Jacques. 2001. 'Acte de fondation'. In *Autres écrits*, 1st ed., 229–242. Paris: Seuil.

Lacan, Jacques. 2006a. 'Kant with Sade'. In *Écrits*, translated by Bruce Fink, 1st ed., 645–670. New York: W.W. Norton.

Lacan, Jacques. 2006b. 'Remarks on Daniel Lagache's Presentation: "Psychoanalysis and Personality Structure"'. In *Écrits*, translated by Bruce Fink, 543–574. New York: W.W. Norton.

Love, Heather. 2021. *Underdogs: Social Deviance and Queer Theory*. 1st ed. Chicago: University of Chicago Press.

Milner, Jean-Claude. 1995. *L'Oeuvre claire*. 1st ed. Paris: Seuil.

Muñoz, José-Estéban. 2009. *Cruising Utopia: The Then and There of Queer Futurity*. 1st ed. New York: New York University Press.

Nash, Jennifer C. 2019. *Black Feminism Reimagined: After Intersectionality*. Durham, NC and London: Duke University Press.

Nobus, Dany. 2022. *Critique of Psychoanalytic Reason: Studies in Lacanian Theory and Practice*. 1st ed. London: Routledge.

Rao, Rahul. 2020. *Out of Time: The Queer Politics of Postcoloniality*. 1st ed. Oxford: Oxford University Press.

Roudinesco, Élisabeth. 1997. *Jacques Lacan*. Translated by Barbara Bray. New York: Columbia University Press.

Ruti, Mari. 2012. *The Singularity of Being*. 1st ed. New York: Fordham University Press.

Ruti, Mari. 2017. *The Ethics of Opting Out: Queer Theory's Defiant Subjects*. 1st ed. New York: Columbia University Press.

Schotten, Heike. 2018. *Queer Terror: Life, Death, and Desire in the Settler Colony*. 1st ed. New York: Columbia University Press.

Snediker, Michael. 2009. *Queer Optimism: Lyric Personhood and Other Felicitous Persuasions*. 1st ed. Minneapolis: University of Minnesota Press.

Sous, Jean-Louis. 2017. *Lacan et la politique: De la valeur*. 1st ed. Toulouse: Érès.

Stavrakakis, Yannis. 2007. *The Lacanian Left*. 1st ed. Edinburgh: Edinburgh University Press.

Sade, the Marquis de. 1965. *Justine: Philosophy in the Bedroom and Other Writings*. 1st ed. New York: The Grove Press.

Sade, the Marquis de. 1968. *Juliette*. Translated by Austryn Wainhouse. New York: The Grove Press.

Wiegman, Robyn. 2012. *Object Lessons*. 1st ed. Durham, NC and London: Duke University Press.

Wiegman, Robyn, and Elizabeth A. Wilson. 2015. 'Introduction: Antinormativity's Queer Conventions'. *Differences* 26 (1): 1–25.

Žižek, Slavoj. 1989. *The Sublime Object of Ideology*. 1st ed. London: Verso.

Žižek, Slavoj. 1997. *The Plague of Fantasies*. 1st ed. London: Verso.

Žižek, Slavoj. 1998. 'Kant and Sade: The Ideal Couple'. *Lacanian Ink* 13. https://www.lacan.com/zizlacan4.htm.

Žižek, Slavoj. 2016. *Antigone*. 1st ed. New York: Columbia University Press.

Zupančič, Alenka. 2000. *Ethics of the Real: Kant, Lacan*. 1st ed. London: Verso.

Zupančič, Alenka. 2023. *Let Them Rot: Antigone's Parallax*. 1st ed. New York: Fordham University Press.

Chapter 3

Lacanian Sexual Anthropology

Patro-phallocentrism and the Social
(1938–67)

1 On the Obsolescence of Psychoanalytic Categories

My previous chapters considered how Lacan's work has been received, interpreted, appropriated, and reappropriated by queer thinkers interested in psychoanalysis. While Butler and Edelman's two exemplary discussions adopt different stances towards Lacanian theory and practice – Butler is suspicious and Edelman enthusiastic – both have understood the value of Lacan's account of human sexuality. That these two stances, suspicion and enthusiastic appropriation, are understandable and defensible for thinkers concerned with queer theory and politics is quite interesting. These two stances towards psychoanalysis have always been both possible and defensible in light of the psychoanalytic theory of sexuality, which recognises a fundamental tension within its object: on the one hand, reproduction has long been thought to give us a clear-cut 'purpose' to sexuality, and therefore a ready-made standard of normality according to which to judge it; while, on the other hand, clinical (and personal) experience both demonstrate time and again that the ideal of an exclusively or even primarily reproductive purpose of sexuality is entirely absent in reality, appearing more often in the seemingly infinite ways people fail to achieve its norm than in our compliance with it.

Sexuality, in other words, is at once the locus of normalisation and what most clearly demonstrates the impossibility of normalisation. Psychoanalysis, in recognising this irreducible contradiction at the heart of its privileged object, has a conformist and a subversive sides. The question as to whether psychoanalysis tends more to the latter side or the former is fundamental in light of the current scientific mastery over the world and particularly over the human body. During the 20th century the increasing existence, availability, and visibility of various technologies with sexual, gendered, and reproductive uses and implications – hormonal birth control, artificial insemination, surrogacy, hormone replacement therapy, abortive technology, surgical and non-surgical forms of gender-affirming care, etc. – have irretrievably demonstrated the plasticity of the categories whereby people make sense of sex,

DOI: 10.4324/9781003424604-4

gender, and kinship. The very invention of the category of 'gender', owed partly to John Money's zeal to violently 'correct' intersex babies' sexual characteristics, may well be taken to be a core marker of our recognition of this plasticity. As Paul B. Preciado has argued in his reading of Money, the concept of gender, by implying that one's feeling of one's gender can be deliberately produced regardless of what markers of biological sex are present from birth, makes either category explicitly technical: gender, because it gets to be manipulated (more or less) at will; and sex, because bodies may not only fail to conform to their allegedly natural gendered morphology, but can also be surgically and hormonally 'corrected' to approximate it, according to certain criteria which are themselves gendered – including, for instance, the capacity to pee standing up or to penetrate a vagina with a penis (Preciado 2013; Fausto-Sterling 2000).

Relatedly, with the increasing recognition of the viability and diversity of non-straight sex lives and life worlds, the exclusive value historically accorded to the heterosexual, 'mum-dad-me' family feels not only anachronistic, but also actively damaging. Most people living in the West now recognise that homosexuals have a right to have sex with consenting adult peers, as was Freud's own opinion, and many governments as well as major international human rights organisations have made it clear that some recognition of homosexual relationships must be in place, even if not through the institution of marriage per se. The active and deliberate crossing of gender boundaries, whether or not it includes the remaking of the sexed body through surgical and hormonal interventions, has likewise become impossible to ignore – often receiving rather unfortunate attention, given the scapegoating of trans* people by various right-wing ideologues and retrograde feminisms, and by psychoanalysts themselves (Bassi and LaFleur 2022; Millot 1990; Miller 2021; Conclusion). Even in respect of the traditional heteronormative conceptual and social armature the cracks are too wide to ignore: for proof, one need only look at divorce rates during the 20th century and at the wave of misguided sociological malaise and nostalgia for the 'simpler times' they prompted (see Cooper 2017, 9).

In this sense, there is scope to wonder whether psychoanalysis can still help to make sense of the major historical changes shaping contemporary societies, and whether psychoanalysis is still relevant at all in light of these changes. One starting point for this discussion is the fact that the changes taking place in contemporary Western societies during the 20th century have not gone unnoticed by psychoanalytic commentators bent on diagnosing the new dysfunctions of the social order. The undoubtedly most prominent motif Lacanian thinkers use to make sense of this new dysfunction is that of the decline of the father (function). The general tenor of this thesis is that the changes observed in contemporary societies over the course of the 20th century were themselves surface symptoms of a deeper process whereby traditional modes of social and political authority – for which the purported decline of the role of the father in the family is often taken as an index – were on the wane. Thinkers across analytic orientations, and also beyond psycho-analysis, have espoused some version of this argument (for example, Lasch 1979; the corpus of the Frankfurt School). In the Lacanian field, Massimo Recalcati writes dramatically of an 'evaporation' of the father that is equivalent to the 'evaporation of the Law of the word', namely the disappearance of

> that which safeguards the possibility for humans to live together. The symptoms of this evaporation are clear for all to see and they do not only besiege the psychoanalyst's office (anxiety-ridden parents, lost chil-dren, families in a state of chaos) but run through the entire social body: a difficulty in instilling respect for institutions, the collapse of public morality.
>
> (Recalcati 2019)

Less apocalyptically, Colette Soler riffs on Zygmunt Bauman's 'liquidity' motif (Bauman 2000) and argues that the contemporary malaise is a result of the 'major experience in our societies' today, the threat of 'delinking', of the disappearance of the social tie: whether in respect of the precarity of work, or of relational and family instability, the contemporary analysand comes into the analyst's office under threat of a disintegrating atomisation (Soler 2016, 8, my translation). The major problem indexed by the new symptoms (anxiety, depression, addiction) would therefore be the subject's fear of being cast out of the social bond, losing their place in a human collective implicitly equated with traditional (whatever that means) forms of sociability. Elabor-ating upon a not dissimilar thesis, Slavoj Žižek has argued that people's rapport with symbolic authority today can be understood as an instance of the 'demise of symbolic efficiency', which Jodi Dean defines succinctly as 'the loss of shared symbols, of general ideas and norms, of a sense that we know what another means when they appeal to home, the common good, citizenship, the university, etc.' (Žižek 1999; Dean 2019, 332).

While these and similar theses have arguably become Lacanian truisms over the past 80-odd years, they should give us pause, if for no other reason than that they often rehearse well-known conservative anxieties about the decline of traditional familial institutions and the allegedly increasing law-lessness, disaffection, anomie, etc., brought about by contestations of the status quo. Whether psychoanalytic commentators are consciously aware that they may be reciting this other history of conservative protest is some-times unclear, but, in the conservative political field, at least, the background to these anxieties is less the subjective and social dynamics of the general-isation of capitalist socialist relations (the preferred explanatory motif for thinkers on the left) than the political mobilisation of oppressed groups attempting to address the social and economic conditions of their oppression. Conservatives are generally united in the thesis that part of the blame lies with the feminist movement, for example, or the gay and lesbian movements, anti-racist organising, and other social movements. What matters to us is that this conceptual repertoire can be, and has been, put to explicitly conservative, and often reactionary, usage – in Lacan and Lacanians' name, no less, and sometimes by them, too.

Some 30 years ago, French policymakers and conservative intellectuals were making explicit reference to Lacan's work so as to oppose the possibility that homosexual couples might be able to see their relationships recognised in France. Some 'experts' and policymakers claimed, during the debate over the recognition of homosexual relationships (the Pacte Civil de Solidarité was passed in 1999), that a child would need both a male (paternal) and a female (maternal) reference, lest they fail to accept sexual difference, and accordingly fall into psychosis, all in the name of a putative symbolic order so amazingly ignorant it could not even fathom homosexuals raising children (Butler 2002; Tort 2007; Carlson 2010; Robcis 2013). According to this view, to accept, for instance, that LGBT+ families could be families was at once to accept the very process whereby society was supposedly dissolving before one's eyes: to be complicit in what would appear, to the closeted or out homophobe, as nothing less than social apocalypse.

Some French Lacanians were seemingly on board with this rather grotesque form of reasoning (see Winter 2010; and Conclusion). Many other French Lacanians, however, have simply dismissed these arguments as having little to do with Lacan or Lacanian theory (notably Roudinesco 2002; Miller 2013). What I find most striking in this debate is less the diversity of positions taken by Lacanians – ranging from the rabidly homophobic to the near-libertarian – and more the remarkably low quality of all parties' reference to Lacan. While this is not at all unequivocally the case, unfortunately, as much as one would like to claim otherwise, what is at any rate clear, for anyone who is willing to read him, is that there is plenty of scope to read Lacan in terms sympathetic to such conservative, even reactionary protest, most certainly between the 1938 article on the 'Family Complexes' and the 1950 'A Theoretical Introduction to the Functions of Psychoanalysis in Criminology' (Zafiropoulos 2001), but also beyond these texts. Lacanians' responses to the charges of homophobia, sexism, and conservatism queer thinkers and more enlightened sociologists raised against them can only appear, in light of these texts, as a collective disavowal of the Master's failings, a failure to work through the traces of conservatism in Lacan's work, and to demonstrate how his work can still help us to think through the deadlocks of contemporary sexual life.

Take, for example, Lacan's first major psychoanalytic text, 'The Family Complexes'. In the space of fewer than six pages, Lacan deplores Western man's purported loss of virility; appears to decry Western woman's loss of her virginal ego-ideal; connects a purported decline of paternal authority to the appearance of neurotic disorders; 'explains' the West's political and cultural dynamism, as opposed to the alleged 'stagnation' of 'primitive' cultures, by reference to the West's patriarchalism and its dominant family forms; and exalts the role of severe paternal *imagos* in the making of 'great', as opposed to 'ordinary', men (Lacan 2001a, 55–61). These are not isolated arguments, nor are they confined to the earliest Lacan. Lacan returns to this motif in the 1947 text 'British Psychiatry and the War', where he appears to correlate the French capitulation in World War II to 'the degradation of the virile type' (Lacan 2001b, 112, my translation) supposedly evident in the traumatised French soldiers he saw as an army psychiatrist. In the 1950 'Criminology' paper, this one in the *Écrits*, he argues that the 'disintegration' of the Western family is partly to blame for criminality (Lacan 2006a, 111).

This is just a small sample, but these moments where the points of contact between Lacan's work and traditional conservative arguments become apparent could be multiplied *ad nauseam* by any attentive reader of his early work, and indeed of the *Seminar*. This has led commentators, such as Didier Eribon, to claim – not without reason – that Lacan's theory from start to finish is little but a rehash of psychiatric prejudice and Catholic dogma put in the service of a reactionary political agenda. Eribon writes that the problem with Lacan's theory was never his frequentation with Lévi-Straussian structuralism, which some claimed may have influenced Lacan's heteronormative bias (Carlson 2010), but rather that it 'was so profoundly fashioned by psychiatric ideology, and that this ideology was so politically close to the most retrograde Christian ideology: psychiatry (and psychoanalysis) is in cahoots with the familial order, just as Christian ideology is' (Eribon 2019, 218, my translation). Whether Lacanians are willing to recognise it or not, Eribon has a point, and Lacanians' refusal to grapple with the fact that interpretations such as Eribon's are both persuasive and often more textually grounded than their own is both deplorable and, one might add, unfaithful to Lacan's legacy.

Others have convincingly demonstrated the possibility, the value, and the dignity of queer kinship socially and theoretically (Butler 2002; Carlson 2010), such that I need not rehearse a point that is, at any rate, obvious here. What interests me in this chapter is the more exegetical question as to how it is that Lacan's work can lend support to such reactionary positions and yet also, I hope to suggest, help to disqualify them. My overarching argument in this chapter is twofold: the first, theoretical, point is that Lacan and Lacanians who wish to use such pivotal notions as father and phallus in their theory and practice simply cannot do without a theory of society. In fact, as I demonstrate in my consideration of Lacan's Lévi-Straussian moment, the notion of the father in Lacan's 1950s developmental theory means little but 'the operator of subjection to social structure', meaning that it is a largely empty concept in the absence of an explicit theory of the minimal set of rules that one must accept if one is to join society. If Lacanians do not have such a theory explicitly, whenever they mobilise their concepts, they have one implicitly, otherwise the concept of the father is vacuous. Furthermore, in the absence of explicit qualification on Lacanians' part, they defer to Lacan's implicit theory of society, which was, finally, conservative until at least May 1968, which interrupts *Seminar XV*. This is my second point: an exploration of Lacan's theory of the father demonstrates rather unambiguously that, before the events of May '68, Lacan had a conservative view of society, one that is quite obviously premised on an undue generalisation of male heterosexual fantasy.

2 The Man of the House (1938–50)

It is well known that Freud (1955) was a firm believer in the scientific myth he espoused in *Totem and Taboo* to the effect that the basis of all social institutions – morality, law, religion, etc. – issued from the prehistoric event of the murder of the father by the band formed by his sons, who were jealous of the father's monopoly over the women of the primal horde. Freud's anthropological fable is particularly ambitious, since it purports to offer us no less than an account of the origin of culture and society – in brief, of the social bond. For Freud, the origin of culture is a foundational act: a crime against nature, and one that must be psychically recapitulated by each new aspiring member of society in their own overcoming of their Oedipus complex. Freud, in this sense, comes up with a justification for the purported universality of the Oedipus complex that manages to sidestep a biological explanation, which would have overtaken the legitimate boundaries of psychoanalytic reasoning. There are cultural universals – the prohibitions of murder and incest – and, whenever a child is called upon to join culture and society, there the Oedipus complex will be, as the recapitulation of the transgression that made those universals possible, the criminal act by which culture came into the world at nature's expense.

Lacan was not originally an orthodox Freudian. He rejected the Freudian presumption that the Oedipus complex, with its attendant patro- and phallocentrism, was universal, just as he rejected the post-Freudian proposition that the Oedipus complex was, in any sense, biological. Rather, as Markos Zafiropoulos has convincingly demonstrated (Zafiropoulos 2001, 2010), Lacan's early work is in constant dialogue with the French sociological tradition, especially that of Émile Durkheim and Marcel Mauss, and therefore had a culturalist and relativist (read: not universalist or structuralist) orientation towards the father and the phallus. In brief, the earliest Lacan considered that a set of social circumstances, especially the dominant family form in a given culture, represented the 'infrastructure' or the Oedipus complex, or rather, as he would put it in 1950, the 'social conditions of Oedipalism' (Lacan 2006a, 111). Lacan places quite a lot of faith in this proposition. He goes so far as to suggest that the psychic pathologies characteristic of mid-20th-century Western Europe could only be explained by reference to these social conditions, and indeed that the very discovery of psychoanalysis was only possible on the basis of changes to the Western family form and the coexistence of various such forms in turn-of-the-century Vienna. The familial conditions of late-19th-century Vienna would, in this view, have presented Freud with the pathologies characteristic of societies where the power of the father was on the wane, juxtaposed to family forms that were not so affected, and therefore would have given him the material he needed to observe the symptoms of the degradation of the paternal *imago* (an image as causative of psychic effects).

Lacan was not original in this view of the family. Worries and anxieties about the family, paternal authority, and their purported decline were a prominent motif of French political and social debate from at least the late 18th century (Robcis 2013). The general contours of the thesis Lacan appears to accept at this stage are simple. In a text Zafiropoulos (2001) locates as one of Lacan's core sources into the issue of the European sociology of the family, Émile Durkheim (1921) proceeds on the assumption that the conjugal family enshrined in the 1804 French Civil Code is exemplary of the Western European family. This family model consisted of a household comprising a husband and wife and their minor children. In it, the father was tasked with feeding and educating the children, who had rights but no responsibility for themselves or their property until they reached marriageable age, whereupon their dependency was dissolved, and they went on to constitute households of their own. For Durkheim, this model differed from a prior historical model he called the 'paternal' family (as opposed to the Roman patriarchal family), which consisted in a larger household comprising a husband and wife and all generations issuing from them, minus the marriageable daughters, who would have been given away to other, similar households. For Durkheim, the conjugal family had broken apart a prior family communism, or the presumption that the family unit was the relevant juridical personality as opposed to the individuals that make it up (so, for instance, it was the family that held rights over property, rather than any of the individuals that compose it). In the conjugal family, to the contrary, each individual was their own person and had their own rights, even if the children were dependent until they reached their majority. The conjugal family was also, Durkheim goes on, entirely disciplined by the state: the 1804 Civil Code, for instance, forbade that a child might be fully disinherited, and provided strictly marital definitions of filiation, which left little room for the juridical recognition of empirical and even biological forms of kinship (for instance, a child born out of wedlock would have a mother but not a father, and the biological children of various fathers would be children of the birthing woman's husband, with some exceptions; see Robcis 2013).

Accepting the broad contours of Durkheim's thesis, Lacan purported to account for how the Oedipus complex, and its pathological forms in early

20th-century Central and Western Europe, were a function of this newly dominant, reduced family form. Lacan writes in 1950:

> Most, if not all, of the psychopathological effects in which the tensions stemming from Oedipalism are revealed, along with the historical coordinates that imposed these effects on Freud's investigative genius, lead us to believe that these effects express a *dehiscence of the family unit at the heart of society*. This conception – *which is justified by the ever greater reduction of this unit to its conjugal form and by the ever more exclusive formative role it consequently plays in the child's first identifications and early discipline* – explains why the family unit's power to captivate the individual has waxed as the family's social power has waned.
>
> (Lacan 2006a, 108, emphasis added)

The concentration of the family into its conjugal form therefore limited the child's repertoire of social relations by largely reducing it to their rapport with their parents (rather than with their parents and siblings as well as with various generations of cohabiting uncles and their own wives and children, as would be the case under the Durkheimian paternal family), even as the importance of the family as a unit (represented by the father) was decreasing in favour of the rights of individuals within families. So, the family monopolised the child's affective life more and more, all the while it became less and less powerful in society. Lacan is therefore clear to the effect that the Freudian Oedipus, with its patriarchal, phallocentric bias, is conditioned by a set of social factors, chief among which the dominant shape of households and family units and the autonomy granted the family and its head by the law. This thesis ramifies into a correlation Lacan draws between the West's cultural and technological achievement and its characteristic family form. Lacan salutes, in 1938, the conjugal family for concentrating both a repressive and a sublimatory functions in the *imago* of the father, who provides the basis of both the superego (repressive) and of the gendered ego-ideal (the idealising or sublimatory motor whereby ordinary men become 'virile' and perhaps 'great', and ordinary women become 'virginal'). The (male) child, by both resenting the paternal prohibition of the mother and idealising his father's image as an ego-ideal, was led to strive to become better than his father by sublimating his repressed anger and desire into great cultural achievements. The problem, as Lacan explains, is that the historical process of familial contraction giving rise to this greater Oedipal tension and to its sublimatory resolution has also been accompanied by a degradation of the paternal *imago*:

> We are not of the kind to despair over an alleged loosening of the familial bond.[1] Is it not significant that the family has been reduced to its biological grouping at the same time as it integrated [*intégrait*] the

highest cultural progresses? But a great number of psychological effects appear to us to have to do with *a social decline of the paternal imago*. A decline conditioned by the turning upon the individual of the extreme effects of social progress, and a decline that can be seen today most especially in the groups most affected by them: economic concentration [*concentration économique*], political catastrophes … A decline most intimately connected to the *dialectic of the conjugal family*, since it takes place through the relative increase, very clear, for example, in American life, of matrimonial obligations …

Whatever its future, this decline constitutes a psychological crisis

(Lacan 2001a, 60–1, my translation, emphasis added)

As argued by Lucchelli (2018; see also Dews 1995), it is likely that Lacan is reciting a diagnostic from Max Horkheimer's 1936 'Authority and the Family' (it is cited in the original bibliography to 'The Family Complexes'). For Horkheimer, the family was an indispensable institution of bourgeois society, whereby 'authority-oriented types of character' bent on reproducing the *status quo* were created, and therefore it was pivotal in ensuring the social stability of modern society, so much so that every conservative movement had sought to 'strengthen the family and all its social presuppositions', for instance through 'the outlawing of extra-marital sexual relations, propaganda for having and rearing children, and the restricting of women to the domestic sphere' (Horkheimer 1975, 112). The pivotal term in the process whereby the family assured the child's submission, Horkheimer argued following conservative sociologist Le Play, was the father. However, the material basis of the father's authority was being eroded by capitalist social relations, particularly due to the greater precarisation of labour (the availability of work being increasingly subject to market forces). This was a great problem, for if the 'authority-promoting effects of the family depend essentially on the man having the decisive role he does, and [if] his domestic power depends in turn on his being the provider', then the father's role ultimately depends on how highly he is regarded by his family members. Furthermore, if he is, for instance, unemployed, if 'he ceases to earn or possess money, if he loses his social position, [then] his prestige within the family is endangered' (Horkheimer 1975, 122). A father thus 'humiliated', 'pathetic' (Lacan 2006d, 482), could not instil a healthy deference to authority within his children. In this sense, they might turn to authoritarian strongmen to compensate for their lack of autonomy, itself a function of the absence of strong fathers capable of instilling a strong sense of morality.

To Horkheimer's analysis Lacan adds little but a nod to a 'dialectic of the conjugal family' and the alleged 'increase' in matrimonial obligations (Lucchelli 2018). For Lacan, it was therefore the curtailing of the father's absolute power – his defeat by the forces of 'progress', including his authority's limitation before the rights of other family members – that led to

psychological malaise, and indeed to psychoanalysis. However, Lacan's analysis also obviously falls short of Horkheimer's, to the extent that Lacan
refuses to call capitalism capitalism; rather, what is at issue is the even vaguer
notion of 'social progress', the meaning of which is never explained explicitly
except in the cryptic reference to the 'dialectic of the conjugal family', supposedly plain to see in North Americans' conjugal lives, that operates
through the 'increase in matrimonial obligations' (probably a reference to the
role of the state in regulating family life or to the increasing recognition of
the need for mutual emotional fulfilment in a conjugal context). This, finally,
makes it reasonable to suggest that the net result of Lacan's discussion is to
identify the motor of the decline of paternal authority with the rise in
importance of the conjugal family as defined by the modern, liberal state,
pivot and administrator of modern individualism (which, finally, is the
Durkheimian moralising theme *par excellence*; Zafiropoulos 2001, 73–9).

In this regard, however much Lacan and contemporary Lacanians might
wish to deny Lacan's investment in a traditional image of paternal authority,
his argument at this stage can be very easily read as relying on a set of conservative ideological tropes that require exactly such an image. On the ideological front, it is difficult to contest that Lacan's thesis here can be quite
reasonably read as a reactionary nostalgia for a deceptive image of the 'good
old days': a time in which a benign patriarch is presumed to have ruled over
a large, multigenerational household with largely unregulated authority,
deplorably disrupted by the ravages of modernity, its push towards a reduction of the family form and corresponding curtailing of the father's authority, and its delusions of equality and individual rights (it is well known that
Lacan frequented for a short time the far-right group Action Française,
whose ideologue Charles Maurras professed a sort of Catholic anti-revolu-
tionary monarchism; Roudinesco 1990, 104). This is obviously problematic,
if for no other reason than that it fails even to acknowledge the brutal violence that this ideology legitimises, certainly against women and children,
and of course sexual minorities. It should not be forgotten that Lacan wrote
'Family Complexes' at a time when women could not even vote in France. As
Michel Tort (2007) correctly points out, in other words, Lacan's reasoning,
whatever else it might do, invites a rather grotesque idealisation of terribly
unequal and violent social relations under the guise of something like order
and progress.

One might try and salvage the argument by pointing out that ideological
preference does not override empirical study – if Lacan's diagnostic is
empirically arguable, that should be enough. On the empirical front, however, contemporary historians of the family have demonstrated that, for
many centuries now, there was never any trace of the idealised past the conservatives Lacan probably read pointed to as the 'good old days' of large,
multigenerational, patriarchal ('paternal' in the Durkheimian sense) households in much of Western and Central Europe, at any rate not in the last

1,000 years. As Josef Ehmer puts it, '[a]mong the lasting achievements of family history in the 1960s and 1970s are that the myth of a universal pre-industrial large and multigenerational family was deconstructed, and that the long historical continuity of nuclear family households was revealed' (Ehmer 2021, 146; Zafiropoulos 2001, 145–72). The reduced, conjugal family form, in other words, which Lacan claims is partly responsible for Oedipal pathology, has been a prominent feature of European social life since the Middle Ages. Which means that his gripe is probably not with changes to the family form, but more likely with the greater influence of the state and of liberal individualism in it, much as it had been for Durkheim. All of which might reasonably lead one to think that the problem for Lacan is not quite the form of the family and its subjective effects, in other words, but primarily the increasingly fair distribution of juridical prerogatives among its members, and therefore the demise of patriarchal authority, taken as a symptom of disintegrating modern individualism.

3 The Condition of Exchange (1955–9)

Lacan's sociological reference would soon shift from the sociology of the family to structuralist anthropology. An explanation of Lacan's second concept of the father requires a preliminary excursion into two themes in anthropology: magic and exchange. In 1950, Claude Lévi-Strauss published an introductory essay to a collection of Marcel Mauss's writings. There, Lévi-Strauss discussed Mauss's theory of magic and of the gift, the first of which in relation to the native concept of *mana*. Mauss writes that 'the word [*mana*] covers a host of ideas which we would designate by phrases such as a sorcerer's power, the magical quality of an object, a magical object, to be magical, to possess magical powers, to be under a spell, to act magically' (Mauss 1972, 108). The word, Mauss goes on, is a general designator for efficaciousness, for the ability to generate magical effects, to stand as the cause of something, just as its apportionment – the question as to who or what has or yields *mana* – is intrinsically bound up with the process whereby a society ascribes differential value to someone or something.

> It is really mana which gives things and people value, not only magical religious values, but social value as well. An individual's social status depends directly on the strength of his mana, and this applies particularly to roles in secret societies. The importance and inviolability of property taboos depend on the mana of the individual who imposes them. Wealth is believed to be the result of mana. On some islands mana is the word for money.
>
> (Mauss 1972, 109)

Mana is, in a sense, a general principle of causality: it accounts for the power of the sorcerer to generate magical effects but also for the power of mana-bearing people and objects; it provides for an individual's authorisation to hold wealth and to fulfil a certain elevated social or religious role, but also for the fear of women and their association with dark magic. Mauss purports to account for the capaciousness of the notion of *mana* by suggesting that it is the 'translation', so to speak, of 'the status or rank attributed to [a thing or person] by all-powerful public opinion, by its prejudices', and concludes that *mana* and similar ideas are 'nothing more than a kind of category of collective thinking which is the foundation for our judgments and which imposes a classification on things' (Mauss 1972, 120–1). The cultures Mauss considers, in other words, resort to *mana* when they need to make conscious a judgement that has already been made for them in the way their society is affectively and effectively organised: it is because there is no rational, consciously available explanation as to why the shaman is capable of curing, for example, that *mana* is needed to acknowledge those judgements public opinion has always already made to the effect that the shaman is indeed, and purely because he is socially designated as 'shaman', capable of curing.

Lévi-Strauss, picking up on Mauss's insight, considers the notion of *mana* to be a general linguistic function, analogous to that of 'algebraic symbols' used to 'represent an indeterminate value of signification' (Lévi-Strauss 1987, 55). This function exists even in societies that seemingly ascribe it no institutional place: Lévi-Strauss likens it to indeterminate words, such as the English 'stuff' or the French *truc* and *machin* – placeholding signifiers to an unknown content, the assigned place for a signification one does not have at hand, if ever it is available. This function is relevant even to the sphere of desire and love: 'what attracted you to him, specifically?' 'oh, there was just something about him'. So, for example, whether I end up with this partner, rather than with that other one, can be explained by reference to an indeterminate notion not entirely unlike *mana*: I cannot explain what circumstances impelled me to select this person over any other, and so I defer the task of explaining those circumstances to some third entity in which the 'something about him' is known, as when one says: 'God knows'. This third entity who knows, for Mauss and Lévi-Strauss, is, in fact, the social world, inasmuch as it contains a series of judgements that have been made independently of any individual living in them.

Unlike Mauss, Lévi-Strauss considers *mana* and similar notions not as the observable effects of a set of implicit moral consensuses, but as expressions of a fundamental problem posed by humanity's capacity for symbolic thinking, namely that its material basis, language, always already implies a sort of surplus-signification *in potentia*, more signifiers than a speaker can possibly know what to do with. Lévi-Strauss writes:

Things cannot have begun to signify gradually ... [In the history of humanity,] a shift occurred from a stage when nothing had a meaning to another stage when everything had meaning. Actually, that apparently banal remark is important, because that radical change has no counterpart in the field of knowledge, which develops slowly and progressively.

(Lévi-Strauss 1987, 59–60)

Lévi-Strauss is frankly on speculative ground: his suggestion is that there was a moment in humanity's evolutionary history when it suddenly separated from every other animal species because it acquired the capacity for meaning. However, the capacity for meaning marks out a radical before and after: if one accepts Lévi-Strauss's reasoning, there was first a world without any meaning whatsoever (definitionally, since only humans are capable of meaning and there were not yet humans), and then a world where quite literally anything that could be seen, felt, said, thought, done, etc., became meaningful. However, this enormous field of non-articulated meaning did not find an appropriate counterpart in anyone's conscious knowledge of it, nor can it ever do so: there will always be more unspoken than actual meaning, such that pragmatic, everyday speech has always needed tools to discipline that excess meaning, to mark out the places where conscious knowledge fails to grasp things as they are, whether in the natural or social worlds. This is one role of *mana* and other notions: they provide a conscious representation of the insufficiency of knowledge, of the fact that no social group can apportion the available stock of signifiers to the available stock of signifieds in a way descriptive of the (social or natural) world. This insufficiency, finally, is threatening to the entire edifice of language and, with it, to subjectivity and social life. This is because, if Saussure's account of language is followed to its last consequences (Chapter 1), meaning cannot arise as such unless each speaker takes into account every existing signifier in its difference to every other existing signifier, and then do the same for every signified, and then to every sign, and so on. Obviously, no individual or collective thinker could consciously do this, such that any speech act necessitates a *mana*-like notion so it can acknowledge: 'I believe there is a totality of signification which, if it were known, would make this utterance meaningful; you believe this, too, which is why you and I can agree provisionally that what I am saying is meaningful, even if neither of us, if prompted to explain why, would be able to'. Lévi-Strauss thus writes:

I believe that notions of the *mana* type ... represent nothing more or less than that floating signifier which is the disability of all finite thought ...

I see in *mana, wakan, orenda,* and other notions of the same type, the conscious expression of a semantic function, whose role is to enable symbolic thinking to operate ...

In the system of symbols which makes up any cosmology, [*mana*] would just be a zero symbolic value, that is, a sign marking the necessity of a supplementary symbolic content.

(Lévi-Strauss 1987, 63–4)

Mana-type notions, in this sense, mark out the place *x* of a sign that is yet to be consciously constructed there where no particular signifier has been fitted to a particular signified, in such a way as to explain away a part of the total existing signification that is not consciously available. They substitute an opaque signifier for what would be a knowledge, and in so doing mark out, cordon off, a place within the existing knowledge structure where understanding of the world, whether the physical or the social world, is lacking. Lévi-Strauss's explanation therefore relies on a disjunction between knowledge and the 'total' meaningfulness of the world born with the irruption of language. His point with this discussion is partly to disqualify too-sharp distinctions between 'primitive' kinds of magical thinking and modern scientific thinking: even if science is a more orderly way of fitting signifier to signified in a way appropriate to the world, it is no less partial than the 'magical' thinking earlier anthropologists had disparaged, since the 'total' meaningfulness of the world can only be grasp from a God-like perspective capable of grasping the totality of possible meanings.

There is an important link between this epistemological problematic and social life, a link Lévi-Strauss establishes through Mauss's discussion of the gift. In his famous essay 'The Gift', Mauss paraphrases a Maori informant's account of a practice of reciprocal gift-giving, in which the valuable thing exchanged (the *taonga*, or 'everything that makes one rich, powerful, and influential'; Mauss 1990, 13) has a quality or an attribute (*hau*) that forces the recipient to return it to the giver after passing through a circuit, on pain of death and misfortune:

> The *taonga* and all goods termed strictly personal possess a *hau*, a spiritual power. You give me one of them, and I pass it on to a third party; he gives another to me in turn, because he is impelled to do so by the *hau* my present possesses. I, for my part, am obliged to give you that thing because I must return to you what is in reality the effect of the *hau* of your *taonga*.
>
> (Mauss 1990, 15)

For Mauss, the closely related obligations to give, accept, and reciprocate, seen in a great deal of societies documented by anthropologists and missionaries, take on the importance of the elementary fact of social morality, 'the very principle of normal social life' (Mauss 1990, 88). Mauss has good empirical reason to claim that the exchange of gifts is a 'total' social phenomenon, since the forms of economic prestation Mauss analyses in 'The

Gift' cut across all arenas of social life, 'religious, juridical, and moral, which relate to both politics and the family; likewise economic ones, which suppose special forms of production and consumption' (Mauss 1990, 3). Lévi-Strauss will follow through on this intuition. Picking up on the theme of exchange, Lévi-Strauss disagrees with Mauss's insistence in disaggregating the phenomenon of exchange into a threefold obligation. Rather, Lévi-Strauss wishes to see in this core social institution not primarily a phenomenon taking place in time, through the initiative of a conscious agent, and according to a temporal sequence of events (give, accept, give back), but as the observable aspect of a network of reciprocal duties and obligations isolatable at any given point in time as an autonomous, coherent social structure, binding each node (each person, family, clan, etc.) to all the others through the obligations they contract to one another. Giving, accepting, and giving back are thus like speech, in that they are the observable, time-bound aspect of a wider network of reciprocities which is, in turn, like language: a coherent and consistent system with its own operative rules determining what can and cannot, what must and must not, be 'said' (given, taken, given back) and to whom. In this respect, for Lévi-Strauss, there is a deep kinship between *hau* and *mana*:

> [L]ike *hau, mana* is no more than the subjective reflection of the need to supply an unperceived totality. Exchange is not a complex edifice built on the obligations of giving, receiving and returning, with the help of some emotional-mystical cement. It is a synthesis immediately given to, and given by, symbolic thought, which, in exchange as in any other form of communication, surmounts the contradiction inherent in it.
>
> (Lévi-Strauss 1987, 58)

The obligations to give, accept, and return, then, are not three moments in a contingent chain freely initiated by the original gift-giver, but merely some of the observable aspects of a system of reciprocal duties that, at any given time, binds each member of a social group to the others. This system of reciprocal duties exists regardless of the fact that none of the individuals implicated in it would be able to draw a chart detailing what is owed to whom and for what reason, in the same way that everyone buys groceries without thinking about the state of the global commodities market, or speaks without formal knowledge of grammar: its existence is objective, to the extent that it imposes duties on its participants, who acknowledge it and act accordingly even when they do not have perfect knowledge of it. In this sense, the existence of the system is a matter for the (implicit, even unconscious) belief of each of the exchanging parties that such a system exists and must be respected. It is precisely this belief that the concept of *hau* manages to bring into consciousness. This is why Lévi-Strauss can argue that *hau* and *mana* alike are 'the subjective reflection of the need to supply an unperceived totality': the full network of gift-acceptance-counter-gift that binds together a culture cannot be appropriately made into an object of knowledge by any of its participants, but the fact that it is perceived as obligatory by all those involved suggests that, regardless of its irrepresentability, it exists as a meaningful and orderly structure.

Finally, then, *mana*- and *hau*-type concepts are local instances of a general operator that allows for two things: one, it allows for the appearance of meaning in a situation where the 'fit' between signifier, signified, and reality is not and cannot be immediately given in our knowledge; and, two, it allows for individuals to insert themselves into a wider network of reciprocal duties and obligations that is more or less explicitly seen as the elementary basis of human sociability, the condition for the communicative structure that society (allegedly) is. In this sense, the acceptance of *mana*- and *hau*-type notions is not merely a matter of linguistic convenience, though it is also that, but more importantly the sign that an individual has become well and truly integrated in their culture, that they accept the categories whereby the exchanges constituting their society assure that society's continued existence through each of the individuals that comprise it. Moreover, it is known where this reasoning leads in Lévi-Strauss's work: as discussed in Chapter 1, Lévi-Strauss is developing his *Elementary Structures of Kinship* argument that the prohibition of incest is the fundamentally humanising operation, and that the exchange of women is the elementary social fact, into a wider structuralist research programme capable of subsuming every social institution under the rubric of symbolic exchange. The problem is that Lévi-Strauss reduces the Maussian gift to its logical form only to make it all too concrete once more: read in conjunction with *The Elementary Structures*, the argument in the Introduction to the Work of Marcel Mauss is not a matter of exchange per se but of the exchange of women specifically, which is supposedly exceptional among those systems embodying the necessity of exchange. *The Elementary Structures* argues, rather bluntly, that '[t]he emergence of symbolic thought *must* have required that women, like words, should be things that were exchanged' (Lévi-Strauss 1969, 496, emphasis added).

This is precisely the point at which Lacan enters this problematic. Lacan's concept of the Name-of-the-Father, introduced in *Seminar III* as the famous *point de capiton* (typically translated as quilting point), is modelled after the Lévi-Straussian reading of *hau* and *mana* (Zafiropoulos 2010). This second avatar of the father in Lacan's work is an incredibly abstract function, having little in principle (although a lot in practice) to do with any empirical father. Elaborating upon what the quilting point is meant to do in *Seminar III*, Lacan defines it as 'the point of convergence that enables everything that happens in this discourse to be situated retroactively and prospectively' (Lacan 1993, 268). The quilting point is what makes a discourse, made up of a series of heterogenous propositions, make sense retrospectively: it gives a signifier such that an interlocutor might think 'so that's what that was about' *ex post facto.* Lacan makes Oedipus the prime psychoanalytic instance of quilting, the means by which the child tethers a mass of signifiers to an unruly flow of signifieds in such a way that they stick together with enough heuristic value to make sense of a life.

> Why does this minimal schema of human experience which Freud gave us in the Oedipus complex retain its irreducible and yet enigmatic value for us? And why privilege the Oedipus complex? Why does Freud always want to find it everywhere, with such insistence? Why do we have here a knot that seems so essential to him that he is unable to abandon it in the slightest particular observation – unless it's because the notion of father, closely related to that of the fear of God [a reference to Lacan's discussion of Jean Racine's *Athalie*], gives him the most palpable element in experience of what I've called the quilting point between the signifier and the signified?
>
> (Lacan 1993, 268)

To return to the Lévi-Straussian example, then: if *mana* is what is invoked by a 'native' to explain the successful shamanistic cure or why women are both desirable objects and malevolent witches, from a psychoanalytic vantage, the father is what will be invoked so one might explain, for example, what it is that makes a woman-who-is-not-the-mother desirable (the shaman-father explains: women are the phallus); or a man who is capable of giving one a child (penises and children are the phallus). Similarly, the father can be appealed to in those moments when a subject must situate themselves in relation to a symbolic mandate: when someone goes from being a child to a man or woman, to a husband or wife, to a father or mother, etc. – that is, when they change their position in the network of places and exchanges that makes up culture and society. If the Name-of-the-Father is there, comfortably installed, the subject will have less trouble in these major symbolic transitions (they will 'have what it takes'), when, as Lacan put it in respect of Schreber, something 'solicits a renewing integration' from them, when their symbolic status changes and their subject-position must change accordingly (Lacan 1993, 321). That this concept is introduced in the seminar-year dedicated to the psychoses is interesting in itself: for Lacan, Schreber, Freud's paradigmatic case of psychosis, does not have the signifier 'being a father' that would allow him to make sense of what he himself might be, when he is called upon to become one (and what sets off Schreber's crisis is precisely his appointment to an elevated judicial office, a sudden call to join a 'society of fathers'). It all takes place because he could not, for whatever reason, countenance the binding force of his culture and language in and through the *mana-hau-*(Name-of-the-)Father and model his speech accordingly.

In Lacan's work, the psychotic proves that the signifier to the father is a guarantor of stable, shared meaning and predictable sociability, which already makes him into something that no mere empirical father could conceivably provide. However, the father is also called upon to play a central normalising role, inasmuch as he signals, being a *mana-hau*-type notion, the subject's unconscious assent to the binding force of the culture they inhabit. Lacan's ideas in this regard will be elaborated upon, for the more typical case of the neurotic, in *Seminars IV* and *V*. In these seminars, Lacan's derealisation of the father becomes not only amazingly explicit, but also explicitly integrated into a social reflection. Lacan declares, for example, that 'an Oedipus complex could very well constitute itself even when the father isn't there' (Lacan 2017, 151, translation modified); that the father's empirical role in the family was a separate question to his normalising efficiency (meaning that there is no immediate correspondence between the father's social standing and his capacity to make his child into a cisgendered heterosexual neurotic); and that the empirical father's 'normality' or 'pathology' have no *a priori* connection to the outcome of the normalising process he is called on to participate in, in respect of his child (Lacan 2017, 151–3). The signs of a successful assent to the father will become irreducibly cultural, and therefore variable. In *Seminar V*, Lacan explicitly claims that there are no universal signs of successful normalisation but, at most, preferential achievements societies ascribe to the Oedipal situation, which will give the clinician evidence to pronounce on the success or otherwise of the father's normalising thrust in respect of a given analysand.

> The Name-of-the-Father's position as such, the attribution of father as procreator, is something that is located at the symbolic level. *It can be brought about in various cultural forms, but as such it does not depend on its cultural form.* It is a requirement of the signifying chain. Merely by virtue of the fact that you institute a symbolic order, something corresponds to, or does not correspond to, the function defined as the Name-of-the-Father. And within this function you place significations that may be different according to the case, but which in no case depend on any other necessity than the necessity of the father's function, to which the Name-of-the-Father corresponds in the signifying chain.
>
> (Lacan 2017, 165, emphasis added)

The Name-of-the-Father, understood as normalising instance (in the abstract, as it were) is universal; whatever criteria can be used to determine whether the normalisation the father imposed was successful, concretely, in a given society, for a given individual, is not. Therefore, the Freudian Oedipus that generates manly boys who are afraid of castration and feminine girls who are resentful of having been castrated, but are willing to settle for a child, is a regional instance of a wider universe of possible quilting-points, one iteration of a process taking place wherever a human being is called upon to alienate themselves unto a community. Several consequences follow, first and foremost that there is not one Name-of-the-Father but as many ones as there are possible ways to become subjectively integrated into a social group. As Zafiropoulos (2010) argues convincingly, the very fact that the axis of Lacan's exploration across *Seminars III* to *V* shifts towards the question of how subjects compensate for insufficiently established Names-of-the-Father – for instance through the phobic object, the neurotic symptom, and the psychotic delirium, all of which are attempts to make up for the father there where he was missing or weak – is enough to say that the Name-of-the-Father was always plural, always Names-of-the-Father. Even the symptom, in other words, to the extent that it lends itself to interpretation, is in and of itself a private version of the Name, since it compensates for the Name's absence or weakness.

The point remains, however, that at the height of Lacan's elaboration of his classical Oedipus, he still conceived of the normalisation the complex occasions (at least in the West) as a process allowing a subject to consent to heteronormativity, which he therefore thought of, like Lévi-Strauss, as the minimal basis of society. Lacan does not even mean heterosexuality exclusively, as the 'appropriate' mode of object-choice, but quite precisely heteronormativity, inasmuch as the child must not only come to desire people of the other gender but also to identify with the ideals associated with their own, as ego-ideals, through the intermediary of the father – that is, the boy must resolve his Oedipus complex by becoming manly and woman-loving like him, and the girl, womanly and male-loving as he wanted his objects.

> While analytic theory ascribes a normalising function to the Oedipus complex, we should recall that our experience teaches us that this normalising function is not enough to culminate in the fact of the subject making an object-choice … after the Oedipus complex, the subject, boy or girl, must not only arrive at heterosexuality but also reach it in such a way as to situate him- or herself in the proper manner in relation to the function of the father.
>
> (Lacan 2020, 193)

> Virility and feminization are the two terms that translate what is essentially the function of the Oedipus complex. Here we find ourselves at the level at which the Oedipus complex is directly tied to the function of the ego-ideal – it has no other meaning.
>
> (Lacan 2017, 150)

Finally, then, even if Lacan dematerialises the father to such an extent that he becomes, theoretically, little but the pivot of the subject's inclusion into their linguistic, cultural, and juridical worlds, in a heteronormative society the relevant norms of belonging are themselves heteronormative. Thus, the father in Western societies must be identified with, or in relation to, specifically as the bearer of the insignias of one's gender, those attributes that are socially valorised as those of a man or those of a woman. Perhaps ironically, Lacan anticipates a point that queer thinkers such as Judith Butler will leverage against him: sex, gender, and sexuality are all principles of intelligibility whereby someone becomes amenable to social recognition (read: normal enough to take their place in the apportionment of social places), which is why the result of Oedipus is and must be an intelligible (read: cisgendered, heterosexual) subject.

4 Enjoyment in the Kinship Machine (1959–66)

Soon after Lacan's canonical account of the Oedipus complex in *Seminar V*, he will start to complexify his reflection on Oedipal normalisation. The first appearance of this theme comes in the form of the well-known aphorism 'There is no Other of the Other', from *Seminar VI* (Lacan 2019, 298), which Lacan introduces as a way to mark out the disjunction between some hypothesised, extralinguistic life force (a concept that was once closely associated with that of 'need', and one that will soon morph into enjoyment) and the organism deadened by the impact of the signifier. In Lacan's first explanation of this motto, he claims that, there where the subject hopes to find life put into words, so to speak, there where the subject expects to find the sign compensating for the libido they sacrificed to language and society, they find only the signifier marking out the place of the lack of any such thing. The major index of the disjunction between life and word, Lacan argues, is the phallus, 'the very symbol of the life that the subject makes signifying', which nevertheless 'cannot in any way guarantee the signification of the Other's discourse'. Subjection to the Other, as disciplined by the father and his dicta, in other words, does not restore the life paid for that subjection, does not adequately compensate the subject for their loss: 'regardless of how much he may have sacrificed his life, it is not given back to him by the Other. The Other replies: S($\bar{A}$) [the signifier S of the incomplete Other $\bar{A}$]' (Lacan 2019, 300).

Lacan's *Seminar VI* elaboration of the S($\bar{A}$) and of the Other's incompleteness is truly momentous, even if he will not draw out all of its consequences immediately. It amounts to a recognition that the function of the father, who Lacan had hitherto treated as a sort of external, guaranteeing instance of the meaningfulness of language and of the coherence of society, is not transcendental to those signifying systems, but is immanent to them. This marks out an important difference to Lévi-Strauss. For Lévi-Strauss, *mana-hau*-type notions were conscious representations of the signifier authorising the existence and the binding force of a social system, such that the one (the sum of propositions in which *mana-hau* might be evoked) was merely a nod to the other (of the really existing total social system). In this sense, the meaningfulness of such sentences was only assured by each interlocutor's assent to the totality of the signifying system they inhabited. Lacan agreed with Lévi-

Strauss in *Seminar V*: 'within the signifying system the Name-of-the-Father has the function of signifying the entire system of signifiers, authorizing its existence, making it law' (Lacan 2017, 223). Any proposition relying on *mana, hau*, and father was, in other words, an acknowledgement of the partiality of one's knowledge of a greater whole called society, language, etc., and its continued use was the means through which that society made 'puppets' out of each of its members (Godelier 2004). However, Lacan questions this point in 'Subversion of the Subject', and critiques Lévi-Strauss and, through him, his own earlier Lévi-Straussian theory of the father:

> I had to situate here [in S($\cancel{A}$)] the dead Father in the Freudian myth ... Claude Lévi-Strauss ... no doubt wishes to see in mana the effect of a zero symbol. But it seems that what we are dealing with in our case is rather the signifier of the lack of this zero symbol.
>
> (Lacan 2006e, 693–5)

For the Lacan of *Seminar VI* onwards, a piece of the puzzle was missing in the Lévi-Straussian account of symbolic exchange: enjoyment, inasmuch as it occupied the place of the lack of the zero symbol evoked by *mana-hau*.

The proposition that there is a signifier to the lack of a zero-symbol entails a radical relativisation of the father: he no longer guarantees, as does whatever *mana-hau*-type notions refer to, the *sine qua non* of human sociality. Rather, he is sustained in, by, and through our libidinal implication in his maintenance. To pursue a political analogy, S($\cancel{A}$) is Lacan's near-Thatcherite proclamation that 'society does not exist', but that something nevertheless causes us to behave as if it did through a complex economy in which everyone ends up contributing to society – not because it exists, pure and simple, but because everyone has a libidinal interest in keeping up the pretence that it does. The cause and support of the exchanges that sustain the social bond, in other words, is no longer the law as spoken by the father, but the pursuit of the very enjoyment renounced in castration. In hopes of retrieving an enjoyment presumed lost, individuals build up their lives according to the social scripts provided them: they study, marry heterosexually, get jobs, etc., running after the proverbial carrot. In the process, babies are made, homes mortgaged, friendships formed, value created for an employer, all of which ends up thickening, so to speak, the bonds between them and others (marriage, mortgages, Facebook groups, work contracts), and thereby reinforcing the coherence of society. There is some pleasure to be found in this way, but never the enjoyment the subject presumes that they have lost – and there really is no alternative. There is no presumption that one can simply open one's eyes to the ideological nature of social reality and become truly free by an act of sheer will. There may well be different ways to renounce enjoyment and hope to get it back, for instance through less repressive fictions than that of private property, but there is no way to keep it entirely without refusing both society and language (a Lacanian version of Marx's fetishism of the commodity; see Žižek 1989).

It will be a while before Lacan recognises the full implications of the contention that the subject hopes to find the life they renounced to the world of signifiers in the world of signifiers, and that it is through the 'recirculation', so to speak, of this enjoyment that society is given the force of a binding fiction. I would suggest that the reason for this delay is, at least partly, the fact that Lacan's insight cannot be comfortably accommodated in a Lévi-Straussian theoretical frame, which, like anthropology generally, tends to speak of kinship precisely in order not to have to speak about sex (David-Ménard 2023). Just as Lacan had to abandon his prior sociological reference points so that he could follow through on his transference to Lévi-Strauss and structuralism, he will be prompted to abandon the Lévi-Straussian reference and shift conceptual universes once more – this time, towards Marxian political economy, through which he will start to speak of a political economy of enjoyment. This contention will propel us into the next chapter. For now, I will content myself with noting that, it seems to me, Lacan will realise the need for this further shift in conceptual universes when he reaches the height of his phallocentrism, which comes, somewhat contradictorily, at a point where the notion of the father has all but disappeared in his work. The rigour of Lacan's exploration of phallocentrism in the mid-1960s, which he quite comically pursues to its last consequences, can even be seen as a sort of self-parody.

By the 1960s, the Lacanian problematic will have decisively shifted towards enjoyment. *Seminar XIV* presents an interesting account of how (male) enjoyment gets renounced and recirculated in a kinship system, which is conceived of as an enjoyment market. The father's authority is no longer seen as an external imposition – specifically, the subject's assent to the authority of the social – and the phallus comes to take its place as the natural consequence of the fact that the subject, in renouncing their enjoyment, will purport to find it once more through their engagement with a community of speakers. In this way, each subject who has renounced their enjoyment so that they might speak will have a libidinal stake in the maintenance of the social (because they hope to retrieve that renounced enjoyment from and within the social). In one of the final lessons of *Seminar XIV*, which presents the most complete account of the rapport between enjoyment and kinship, Lacan returns to a topic he had approached much earlier in his work, and presents a new theory as to why, in Lévi-Strauss's theory, it is women who end up being exchanged among men, and not men who are exchanged among women. He had broached the topic with Lévi-Strauss in the 1950s, who replied that the fact that women are exchanged among men, rather than the reverse, could only be explained by man's holding of political power (Chapter 1). Seemingly dissatisfied with Lévi-Strauss's explanation, Lacan attempts to justify the affinity between phallus and man not politically, but by means of some characteristics of the penis, which would supposedly make men especially suited for the subtraction and symbolisation of enjoyment Lacan calls castration, and therefore make it so that the stakes of society are always already male, since men are the ones who renounced enjoyment so that there might be society in the first place.

Lacan starts out in this lesson from a simple proposition, namely that psychoanalysis demonstrates, indeed is centred around, the fact that there are inherent difficulties for the human species in the sexual act. Lacan traces this difficulty to the fact that, an act being defined as the 'constitution, in action, of a signifier' (Lacan 2023, 372, my translation), any act must call up not merely the signifier it itself produces but also its opposite. The grounding signifier of the sexual – whether one starts with 'man' or 'woman' – does not, however, have such an opposite, Lacan claims. There are two senses to this proposition. On the one hand, 'woman' is not man's opposite as 'light' opposes 'dark', as 'raw' opposes 'cooked', etc. Rather, Lacan argues that, when one speaks of a man or a woman, one speaks of beings who are simply different to one another, and are not defined a priori by a relationship – opposition, complementarity – to the other. As Freud had already argued, the definitions of 'masculine' and 'feminine' had no meaning but for the proxies through which they are observable, notably in the psychoanalytic lexicon, passivity and activity (Freud 1953, 219). On the other hand, 'man' and 'woman' are also categories that denote the meeting point between the subject and the body. They are, in other words, modes of enjoyment, categories purporting to name the incommunicable experience (although the word 'experience' is already inadequate) of embodiment. The phallus provides a solution to both of these problems: it helps to reduce the radical heterogeneity between the modes of enjoyment called 'man' and 'woman' to the opposition 'has it' and 'does not', and therefore founds something resembling a rapport between the two; and it provides a signifier acknowledging, disciplining, and deadening at least one, out of at least two, modes of enjoyment that would otherwise remain inscrutable. This operation, Lacan goes on, comes at a cost to both parties. On the one hand, the currency in which this cost is paid is male enjoyment, and this enjoyment has to go somewhere; and, on the other hand, this operation leaves open the question as to whether, within a value-system disciplined by the basic opposition 'has it' and 'does not', women, who do not have the phallus, get to retain an enjoyment that is moreover different to phallic enjoyment.

> We do not know whether woman's body is well and truly what the male says it is – and he does nothing but *say* that it is – in his *You are my wife* [*Tu es ma femme*, recalling a prior discussion of marriage], namely that the woman's body is his enjoyment [*sa jouissance à lui*].

Effectively, it is not just the couple at stake in the sexual act. As other structuralists working in other fields have reminded us, the rapport between man and woman is subject to exchange functions, which, by that token, implies the existence of an exchange value. To constitute this exchange value as such, needs must that the place where something is of habitual usage [*soit d'usage*, an expression meaning something that is of habitual, even traditional usage, but the wordplay, in context, refers to the Marxist use-value] be struck by the necessary negativation. Here, for reasons taken from the natural constitution of the function of copulation, the part necessary to the constitution of exchange-value is taken from masculine enjoyment, inasmuch as we know where it is – well, we believe so. There is a small organ that can be grabbed. That's what the baby boy does immediately, and with great ease.

(Lacan 2023, 379, my translation)

At this point, Lacan launches into an aside concerning a 19th-century book about the evils of masturbation he had found himself in possession of. He notes that it has nothing to do with what he is saying – although what he has to say will easily disabuse us of this notion, as it is obvious that the digression is integral to his argument. He continues:

The exchange of women, I am not telling you that it can be easily translated into an exchange of phalluses … It is the exchange of phalluses, yes, but insofar as the phallus is the symbol of an enjoyment subtracted as such – that is to say, not the penis, but this negativized part of the body we call the phallus, precisely to distinguish it from the penis. That's a new metaphor, which takes the place of the penis – just as woman becomes the metaphor of enjoyment …

In other terms, something is instituted, another process, the process of social exchange, founded upon the material, so to speak, destined to the sexual act – but this still leaves in suspense what this external element, social exchange, allows us to situate in respect of woman in her function as a metaphor in relation to an enjoyment passed over to the function of a value.

(Lacan 2023, 380, my translation)

There are several blanks in this quotation that need to be filled in to make sense of Lacan's novel account of the libidinal infrastructure of the exchange of women. I suggest that they ought to be filled thus. Lacan argues that the enjoyment of the male body would be (a) easily locatable in the penis, which would make the male organ and its enjoyment apprehensible as a tool or instrument of sorts, perhaps even as something with which to accomplish something else (for instance, an alliance with another family); and (b) that man's enjoyment would be intrinsically limited by the habitual coincidence of orgasm, ejaculation, detumescence, and the disappearance of arousal (its function in specifically human copulation), which would furnish man with an intuition of the intrinsic limits to enjoyment (as if the coincidence between the 'loss' of the erect penis and the highest point of pleasure, orgasm, were saying 'there is a limit you cannot cross, but must acknowledge symbolically on pain of anxiety'; see Lacan 2014, 238–9). These factors would give man an innate intuition of the need to renounce the use of his organ (for instance, in masturbation, but also in any other 'asocial' sense, including homosexual sex), such as to subject enjoyment to the exigencies of social intercourse, and such as to limit, and thus civilise, the satisfaction man might derive from unlimited use of their penis (or wife). Furthermore, because women suppo- sedly cannot localise their enjoyment in similar fashion (it is unclear why, since psychoanalysts have always fussed over the clitoris in their debates, although Lacan does comment on female orgasm as 'unplaceable'[2] elsewhere, so he may well be referring to this particular cliché; see Lacan 2014, 265; for a critique, Leader 2021), they do not have an innate intuition of castration, and therefore it may never have occurred to them to make a symbol out of an enjoyment they have never lost. The process would therefore follow this course:

1   From men's intrinsic understanding of the need to renounce asocial use of their penises, which are naturally the loci of their enjoyment, arises the need to acknowledge socially the enjoyment they thereby renounced.
2   The symbol of this renounced male enjoyment is the phallus.
3   The phallus is embodied in women.
4   Women, since they are, after step 3, made into a symbol of male castra- tion, can be circulated among men as a deceptive equivalent to the enjoyment renounced to human sociality.

Hence, from a couple of particularities of the subjective experience of having a penis, Lacan appears to derive ultimate justification for the 'world histor- ical defeat of woman' (Rubin 1975, 176). At risk of repeating myself, I want to be clear about the implications of this view. Lacan's claim is that, because men derive the highest pleasure available to them from their penises and their penile orgasms, and because this pleasure habitually leads to the loss of their erections, it is men who first intuited an enjoyment beyond detumescence and made a metaphor out of it, collectively blackmailing women into becoming that metaphor for them. There is therefore a causal relationship between the age-old political, social, sexual, etc., subordination of women and the fact that boys are afraid they might masturbate (or masturbate each other) to death. I hope any reader will agree that this is quite obviously an elucubra- tion on male fantasy: a man's scary dream that he might masturbate himself or his buddies until he starves becomes a fantasy that his pleasure is 'asocial' or 'destructive', which fantasy must be defused by the notion that to truly enjoy is to enjoy a woman's body, but that that enjoyment, too, must be limited by a social convention, marriage (*you are my wife*), which finally provides the juridical infrastructure for the 'give a woman, take a woman' which constitutes the alleged basis of society (see Lacan 2023, 342–3, 379–80).

Where, in conclusion, is the father in this perspective? Seemingly he is nowhere and everywhere, since he is nothing but the psychoanalytic version of the myth accounting for the appearance of the system whereby men renounce their enjoyment such as to exchange women as symbols of that renunciation and form bonds among each other on that basis. There are several other such myths, including the one in Genesis, which Lacan had quoted in a previous lesson (Lacan 2023, 345–6), and certainly also the pseudo-historical one about the invention of paternity he had elucubrated in the closing lesson of *Seminar III* (Lacan 1993; see also Chapter 1). Lacan even suggests that, given the fact that women analysts had nothing to say that particularised women's enjoyment enough to distinguish it from men's, psychoanalysis only really had one thing to say about good sex:

> What can be formulated of the sexual act today is the dimension of that which, in another register, we call good intentions [*la bonne intention*]. Good intentions in respect of the sexual act, here is what we reasonably can, indeed must, say the psychoanalysts, be content with ...
>
> When the original Father is said to enjoy all the women, does that mean that the women enjoy even a little bit?
>
> (Lacan 2023, 344, my translation)

Not much, then.

5 Towards a Political Economy of Enjoyment

What emerges from Lacan's trajectory is a clear tendency towards a dematerialisation of the father, and eventually to the near disappearance of that concept. The mid- to late 1960s Lacan conceives of the father as a myth purporting to explain away the origin and cause of the exchange of women and its gendered and sexual paraphernalia. The subjective assumption of this myth will be quite enough to carry one through a satisfactory resolution to the Oedipus complex. This, in turn, is a process in which the child will prepare to exercise their role in the social structure by accepting the need to transmute their enjoyment into an operative symbol – the phallus – that allows them to desire a socially legitimate object and to love their peers with a sublimated passion. The concrete shape this process has taken in most societies, Lacan suggests, is due to a restricted number of characteristics of male sexual experience, largely reducible to the fact of detumescence and the intense interest (and anxiety) boys experience in relation to their penises. In this process, the disjunction of desire and enjoyment will be named at its place, desire and enjoyment will be normalised, and their normalisation will find juridical expression in a social institution disciplining the rapport of man with woman – in most societies, marriage, which is the pact whereby a man asserts property rights over a woman's body and the products thereof, and therefore what constitutes the precondition for the exchange of women.

I hope that I have reiterated sufficiently that Lacan's reflection on these issues is at times rather difficult to countenance for a feminist or queer thinker, and this for several reasons. For one, it naturalises the fact that it is women who are circulated as objects, by claiming that something about the penis makes it especially suitable for becoming the imaginary material for a man-made metaphor for renounced enjoyment (the phallus). It is conspicuous, in addition, that it has little to say about forms of sexual activity and self-designation that are not reducible to the rather ridiculous picture of heterosexuality (the bit about 'good intentions' is particularly deplorable in light of the contemporary awareness of sexual violence) Lacan offers in *Seminar XIV*, which leads one to think that any kind of, say, homosexuality must be taken to be a perversion, regardless of gays and lesbians' obvious aptitude for leading plainly unexceptional social and sexual lives. As an aside, whenever Lacan broaches the subject, he is quite openly homophobic. He voices surprise that more homosexuals are not 'cured' in *Seminar V* (the context and wording in the French leave no doubt that he means curing homosexuals of their homosexuality;[3] see Lacan 1998a, 207; Lacan 2017, 190–1); he describes Plato's *Symposium* in *Seminar VIII* as 'a gathering of aging fairies, as people call them' (Lacan 2015, 41); he claims that homosexuality is just as much a perversion today as it was in ancient Greece, because whether something is a perversion or not is not a cultural question – the sole difference being that today gay men have to go looking for their objects in 'dark alleys or in the gutter' (Lacan 2015, 31). He even suggests that all sexuality is heterosexuality in *Seminar XIX*, in which it is explicitly stated that what is at issue for the subject, regardless of what gender they prefer and of how they have sex, is always the other sex (Lacan 2018, 134). In other words, even for a gay man, what is at stake in sexuality is the non-rapport with woman (as would be the case too for a lesbian[4]).

Gay thinkers have suggested that all this means that Lacan's theory is homophobic all the way down (Eribon 2019), and one can also certainly see why it could be considered problematic for a feminist programme (Chapter 1). However, one can also see why the knee-jerk queer and feminist reactions might be wrong, or at least premature. In response, one could choose, for example, to rehearse the now-classic argument that Lacan's account of the Oedipal machine and its paternal pivot is a diagnosis and critique of heteronormative societies, and not an endorsement of them (see, for instance, Rubin 1975; Mitchell 2000). When Lacan claims that what is at issue for the subject is always the Other sex, for example, he does not mean simply that men are from Mars, women are from Venus. He means that the neurotic or perverted subject, whether they see themselves as a man or a woman or anything else, is always and necessarily subject to a signifying apparatus that is driven, by its own internal necessity, to pose the question as to 'what is it like to not be castrated?' In a phallocentric social order, a society-wide game in which participants become participants by dint of being Oedipalised as men who are subjects and women who are objects to be circulated among men, this question can be rephrased as the classical hysterical question, 'what is woman?' (Lacan 2006d, 181). This is because woman is only castrated if she is implicated in man's fantasy that she, like him, is subject to the subtraction of enjoyment (castration), a fantasy he harbours, says the Lacan of *Seminar XIV*, because he assumes that her experience is the same as the one determined by the apprehensibility of his own renounced enjoyment (that is, the fact that he can grasp it, with masturbation physical or mental, which allegedly she cannot do to the same extent).

If one takes the view that Lacan is critical of heteronormative society, then, one arrives at the classical French feminist position: woman is only castrated if she is understood by analogy to man, who supposedly has an innate understanding that he is, indeed, castrated, regardless of whether he got to keep his little appendage or not. It is easy to dismiss this position as essentialist, but at minimum it does give woman her due: Lacan's account of gender, finally, consists in that man sees himself castrated in woman, and in that woman is only woman to the extent that she sees herself in what he sees in her – all the while, in the real, she is not deprived of anything, therefore not castrated, therefore the Other sex, object of the perennial question of the mythical subject of enjoyment.[5] So, Lacan will call men and women '*l'homme-elle*' and '*l'homme-il*', 'she-man' and 'he-man', to designate that Oedipal men and women are both produced by the same phallocentric social machine (Lacan 2023, 268, English in the original). From this point, it is but one step for us to arrive at the feminist and queer position, which consists simply in saying that society can be changed into a non- or less phallocentric machine.

On the other hand, one might continue to follow the thread of Lacan's thought and attend to how he himself would come to question the basis of his long return to Freud. Soon after the *Seminar XIV* account of enjoyment in the kinship machine, in *Seminar XVII*, Lacan will argue that the Freudian Oedipus he quite desperately tried to put on a scientific footing through his decade-long Lévi-Straussian detour ought to be interpreted as Freud's dream, just as he had earlier qualified it as a remnant of Freud's 'patriarchal civility', and just as he would later call it Freud's misguided attempt to 'save the father' (respectively, Lacan 2007, 117; Lacan 1992, 177; Lacan 1998b, 108). At the same time, Lacan will start speaking of politics in a brief but consistent interlocution with Marx and Marxist thinkers such as Louis Althusser. What will arise from Lacan's work at this stage is a complexification of the political economy of sex and sexuality, or rather a sexualisation of political economy. Instead of a rudimentary sexual anthropology premised on the binary alternative 'yes' or 'no' father, inside or outside the kinship machine, '+' or '–' phallus, etc., Lacan will begin to see the subject as an entity determined by multiple simultaneous discourses, the sum total of which fails to cohere into a whole, eventually arriving at his famous theory of discourses whereby the form of the social link is operationalised according to a restricted number of permutations between functions, relations, and terms. Discourse will be conceived not only as the sum of possible utterances within a given social and cultural field, but also as an apparatus of enjoyment, a means through which the subject convinces themselves that they can regain what they lost in speaking and produces a surplus in the process. One might hypothesise that this shift in Lacan's work was very much brought about by his realisation of the limits to his prior, phallocentric views. *Seminars III–XIV* work through the phallocentric hypothesis consistently and thoroughly, and it is, I think, quite clear by the time of *Seminar XVI* that Lacan deems his prior model to be irredeemably partial, so much so that the axis of Lacan's discourse shifts completely: the theoretical matrix of the *Seminar* between 1968 and 1970 is Marxian political economy, not functionalist sociology (as it had been prior to the 1950s), structural linguistics and anthropology (as it was from 1953 to the 1960s; see Zafiropoulos 2001, 2010), nor finally formal logic (which it partly was during the 1960s and will return to in the 1970s).

Lacan's language is perhaps the most obvious indicator of the fundamental change *Seminars XVI* and *XVII* signal in his work. No longer does he speak of father and phallus, but of a 'swarm' of master signifiers, S_1 (Lacan 2007, 35), and the knowledges they refer to, S_2; there is little to no talk of kinship and the exchange of women, terms replaced with (a renamed) *objet a* and an Other conceived of as a market; later, the very notion of 'discourse' will be defined as 'a form of social link' (Lacan 1998b, 82), in which can be read the very important, if rather obvious, acknowledgement that kinship is not the elementary form of human togetherness but that various relational forms are always and necessarily active and synchronous within any really existing society, all of which contribute to the thickness, so to speak, of the social link, and which can only be separated out from that bundle of relational forms by a methodological sleight of hand (Godelier 2004). There can, in other words, be no presumption that kinship is the total or indeed the pre-eminent social institution, which was most certainly an assumption Lacan held whenever he broached anything concrete in respect of the rapports between men and women. From this point onward, the 'traditional' Oedipal solution (neurotic heterosexuality via identification with the father or his object, depending on whether one has or has not a penis, and submission to the law) will become one solution among others to the threat of an excess of unsymbolised enjoyment (on the idea of the paternal as a 'solution', see Tort 2007).

While this theoretical move would appear to completely destabilise the proper 'field' of psychoanalysis – it certainly has the salutary effect of allowing for a psychoanalytically informed social analysis, with the 'master's' seal of approval, as it were – Lacan will keep the boundaries of his reflection in check by focusing on two macrohistorical processes he appears to consider the defining forces of Western modernity: science and the capitalist mode of production (with religion assuming greater importance soon after, although typically outside the *Seminar* or the major published writing collections). What is most distinctive about Lacan's subsequent reflections is that he will not treat these major discursive formations – science and capitalism – as phenomena impinging upon an otherwise autonomous sexual arena. Lacan does not speak of how capitalism thwarts the realisation of the exchange of women, for example, or of how science destroys an otherwise idyllic patriarchal social order. Rather, he consistently aims at the libidinal aspects of capitalism and science, for instance in his claim that capitalism offers us commodities as if they were equivalent to *objet a*, those bodily objects the subject gives away so they can accede to fantasy; or his longstanding concern with the desire animating modern science. In this sense, Lacan's subsequent theory is not a political economy of sex, as has been called for before (Rubin 1975), but rather a sexualisation of political economy. It is to this contention that I now turn.

Notes

1   Éric Laurent (2005, 137) has claimed that this sentence makes it clear that Lacan bore no idyllic illusions in respect of traditional family forms. I think it is perfectly arguable, quite to the contrary, that Lacan is only hedging an obviously and self-consciously conservative argument, since this piece was to end up in an encyclopaedia and should therefore not look too partisan.

2   Compare the English and French published transcriptions of *Seminar X* (Lacan 2004, 307; Lacan 2014, 265).

3   I invite the reader to read the passage in question, which also provides a very interesting theory of homosexuality as a fully accomplished, but inverted, Oedipus complex, in which the mother becomes the agent of the law rather than the father. What is missed in the English translation is that Lacan uses the words *guérir* and *soigner*, that are entirely alien to analytic work, which Lacan mostly describes as a '*cure*'. Although '*cure*' is sometimes translated as 'treatment' in English (Bruce Fink translates the *écrit* '*Direction de la Cure*' as 'Direction of the Treatment', for instance), it has a very different connotation to *guérir* and *soigner*. The latter are not technical concepts and mean something closer to 'to heal' and 'to care for'. Given the context and wording, Lacan is unequivocally saying 'it is surprising that we do not heal more homosexuals, who are sick with their homosexuality, despite the fact that they are eminently healable of that condition'.

4   'Castration cannot be deduced from development alone, since it presupposes the subjectivity of the Other as the locus of its law. The alterity of sex is denatured by this alienation. A man serves here as a relay so that a woman becomes this Other to herself, as she is to him' (Lacan 2006b, 616, translation modified).

5   For instance, Irigaray will always insist on the autoeroticism of women's bodies, their uncastrated self-relatedness: 'Woman "touches herself" all the time, and moreover no one can forbid her to do so, for her genitals are formed of two lips in

continuous contact', etc. (Irigaray 1985, 24). The implication that women are always and uninterruptedly masturbating, and therefore get to keep their auto-erotic enjoyment, is not a critique of Lacan but an instance of the strictest Lacanism.

References

Bassi, Serena, and Greta LaFleur. 2022. 'Introduction: TERFs, Gender-Critical Movements, and Postfascist Feminisms'. *Transgender Studies Quarterly* 9 (3): 311–333.

Bauman, Zygmunt. 2000. *Liquid Modernity.* Cambridge: Polity.

Butler, Judith. 2002. 'Is Kinship Always Already Heterosexual?' *Differences* 13 (1): 14–44.

Carlson, Shanna T. 2010. 'In Defense of Queer Kinships'. *Subjectivity* 3 (3): 263–281.

Cooper, Melinda. 2017. *Family Values: Between Neoliberalism and the New Social Conservatism.* 1st ed. New York: Zone Books.

David-Ménard, Monique. 2023. 'Does the Anthropology of Kinship Talk about Sex?' In *Psychoanalysis, Gender, and Sexualities: From Feminism to Trans*,* edited by Patricia Gherovici and Manya Steinkoler, 1st ed. London: Routledge.

Dean, Jodi. 2019. 'Communicative Capitalism and Revolutionary Form'. *Millennium* 47 (3): 326–340.

Dews, Peter. 1995. 'The Crisis of Oedipal Identity: The Early Lacan and the Frankfurt School'. In *Psychoanalysis in Contexts,* edited by Anthony Elliott and Stephen Frosh, 53–71. London: Routledge.

Durkheim, Émile. 1921. 'La Famille Conjugale'. *Revue Philosophique de La France et de l'Étranger* 91 (1): 1–14.

Ehmer, Josef. 2021. 'A Historical Perspective on Family Change in Europe'. In *Research Handbook on the Sociology of the Family,* edited by Norbert Schneider and Michaela Kreyenfeld, 143–162. Cheltenham: Edward Elgar.

Eribon, Didier. 2019. *Écrits sur la psychanalyse.* 1st ed. Paris: Fayard.

Fausto-Sterling, Anne. 2000. *Sexing the Body: Gender Politics and the Construction of Sexuality.* 1st ed. New York: Basic Books.

Freud, Sigmund. 1953. 'Three Essays on the Theory of Sexuality'. In *The Standard Edition of the Complete Psychological Works of Sigmund Freud,* vol. VII, translated by James Strachey, 1st ed., 125–243. London: The Hogarth Press.

Freud, Sigmund. 1955. 'Totem and Taboo'. In *The Standard Edition of the Complete Psychological Works of Sigmund Freud,* vol. XIII, translated by James Strachey, 1st ed., 1–164. London: The Hogarth Press.

Godelier, Maurice. 2004. *The Metamorphoses of Kinship.* Translated by Nora Scott. 1st ed. London: Verso.

Horkheimer, Max. 1975. 'Authority and the Family'. In *Critical Theory: Selected Essays,* translated by Michael O'Connell, 47–128. New York: Continuum.

Irigaray, Luce. 1985. *This Sex Which Is Not One.* Translated by Catherine Porter. Ithaca, NY: Cornell University Press.

Janssens, Angélique. 1997. 'The Rise and Decline of the Male-Breadwinner Family? An Overview'. *International Review of Social History* 42: 1–23.

Lacan, Jacques. 1978. *The Seminar of Jacques Lacan, Book XI: The Four Fundamental Concepts of Psychoanalysis.* Translated by Alan Sheridan. 1st ed. New York: W.W. Norton.

Lacan, Jacques. 1992. *The Seminar of Jacques Lacan, Book VII: The Ethics of Psychoanalysis*. Translated by Dennis Porter. 1st ed. London: W.W. Norton.

Lacan, Jacques. 1993. *The Seminar of Jacques Lacan, Book III: The Psychoses*. Translated by Russell Grigg. 1st ed. New York: W.W. Norton.

Lacan, Jacques. 1998a. *Le Séminaire de Jacques Lacan, Livre V: Les Formations de l'Inconscient*. Paris: Seuil.

Lacan, Jacques. 1998b. *The Seminar of Jacques Lacan, Book XX: Encore*. Translated by Bruce Fink. New York: W.W. Norton.

Lacan, Jacques. 2001a. 'La psychiatrie anglaise et la guerre'. In *Autres écrits*, 1st ed., 101–120. Paris: Seuil.

Lacan, Jacques. 2001b. 'Les complexes familiaux dans la formation de l'individu'. In *Autres Écrits*, 1st ed., 23–84. Paris: Seuil.

Lacan, Jacques. 2004. *Le Séminaire de Jacques Lacan, Livre X: L'Angoisse*. Paris: Seuil.

Lacan, Jacques. 2006a. 'A Theoretical Introduction to the Functions of Psycho-analysis in Criminology'. In *Écrits*, translated by Bruce Fink, 1st ed., 102–122. New York: W.W. Norton.

Lacan, Jacques. 2006b. 'Guiding Remarks for a Convention on Female Sexuality'. In *Écrits*, translated by Bruce Fink, 1st ed., 610–622. New York: W.W. Norton.

Lacan, Jacques. 2006c. 'On a Question Prior to Any Treatment of Psychosis'. In *Écrits*, translated by Bruce Fink, 1st ed., 445–488. New York: W.W. Norton.

Lacan, Jacques. 2006d. 'Presentation on Transference'. In *Écrits*, translated by Bruce Fink, 1st ed., 176–187. New York: W.W. Norton.

Lacan, Jacques. 2006e. 'The Subversion of the Subject and the Dialectic of Desire in the Freudian Unconscious'. In *Écrits*, translated by Bruce Fink, 1st ed., 671–702. New York: W.W. Norton.

Lacan, Jacques. 2007. *The Seminar of Jacques Lacan, Book XVII: The Other Side of Psychoanalysis*. Translated by Russell Grigg. 1st ed. New York: W.W. Norton.

Lacan, Jacques. 2014. *The Seminar of Jacques Lacan, Book X: Anxiety*. Translated by A.R. Price. Cambridge: Polity.

Lacan, Jacques. 2015. *The Seminar of Jacques Lacan, Book VIII: Transference*. Translated by Bruce Fink. Cambridge: Polity.

Lacan, Jacques. 2017. *The Seminar of Jacques Lacan, Book V: Formations of the Unconscious*. Translated by Russell Grigg. 1st ed. Cambridge: Polity.

Lacan, Jacques. 2018. *The Seminar of Jacques Lacan, Book XIX: …Or Worse*. Translated by A.R. Price. 1st ed. Cambridge: Polity.

Lacan, Jacques. 2019. *The Seminar of Jacques Lacan, Book VI: Desire and Its Interpretation*. Translated by Bruce Fink. 1st ed. Cambridge: Polity.

Lacan, Jacques. 2020. *The Seminar of Jacques Lacan, Book IV: The Object Relation*. Translated by A.R. Price. 1st ed. Cambridge: Polity.

Lacan, Jacques. 2023. *Le Séminaire de Jacques Lacan, Livre XIV: La logique du fantasme*. 1st ed. Paris: Seuil.

Lasch, Christopher. 1979. *The Culture of Narcissism: American Life in an Age of Diminishing Expectations*. 1st ed. New York: W.W. Norton.

Laurent, Éric. 2005. 'Le Nom-Du-Père entre réalisme et nominalisme'. *La Cause Freudienne* 60 (2): 131–149.

Leader, Darian. 2021. *Jouissance: Sexuality, Suffering, and Satisfaction*. 1st ed. Cambridge: Polity.

Lévi-Strauss, Claude. 1969. *The Elementary Structures of Kinship*. Translated by James Harle Bell, John von Sturmer, and Rodney Needham. 1st ed. Boston, MA: Beacon Press.

Lévi-Strauss, Claude. 1987. *Introduction to the Work of Marcel Mauss*. Translated by Felicity Baker. 1st ed. London: Routledge.

Lucchelli, Juan Pablo. 2018. 'Lacan, Horkheimer et le déclin du père'. *Psychanalyse YETU* 42 (2): 139–151.

Mauss, Marcel. 1972. *A General Theory of Magic*. Translated by Robert Brain. London and Boston, MA: Routledge and Kegan Paul.

Mauss, Marcel. 1990. *The Gift: The Form and Reason for Exchange in Archaic Societies*. Translated by W.D. Halls. London: Routledge.

Miller, Jacques-Alain. 2013. 'Non, la psychanalyse n'est pas contre le mariage gay'. *Le Point* (blog). 14 January. https://www.lepoint.fr/invites-du-point/jacques-alain-miller/non-la-psychanalyse-n-est-pas-contre-le-mariage-gay-14-01-2013-1614461_1450.php#11.

Miller, Jacques-Alain. 2021. 'Docile to Trans'. *Lacanian Review Online*. https://www.thelacanianreviews.com/docile-to-trans/.

Millot, Catherine. 1990. *Horsexe*. Translated by Kenneth Hylton. New York: Autonomedia.

Mitchell, Juliet. 2000. *Psychoanalysis and Feminism*. 2nd ed. London: Penguin.

Preciado, Paul B. 2013. *Testo Junkie: Sex, Drugs, and Biopolitics in the Pharmaco-pornographic Era*. Translated by Bruce Benderson. New York: Feminist Press.

Recalcati, Massimo. 2019. *The Telemachus Complex: Parents and Children after the Decline of the Father*. Translated by Alice Kilgarriff. 1st ed. Cambridge: Polity.

Robcis, Camille. 2013. *The Law of Kinship: Anthropology, Psychoanalysis, and the Family in France*. 1st ed. Ithaca, NY: Cornell University Press.

Roudinesco, Élisabeth. 1990. *Jacques Lacan & Co.* Translated by Jeffrey Mehlman. 1st ed. Chicago: University of Chicago Press.

Roudinesco, Élisabeth. 2002. 'Psychanalyse et homosexualité'. *Cliniques Méditerranéennes* 65 (1): 7–34.

Rubin, Gayle. 1975. 'The Traffic in Women: Notes on the Political Economy of Sex'. In *Toward an Anthropology of Women*, edited by Rayna Reiter, 1st ed., 157–210. New York: Monthly Review Press.

Soler, Colette. 2016. *O que faz Laço?* Translated by Elisabeth Saporiti. São Paulo: Escuta.

Spillers, Hortense J. 1987. 'Mama's Baby, Papa's Maybe: An American Grammar Book'. *Diacritics* 17 (2): 64–81.

Tort, Michel. 2007. *La fin du dogme paternel*. 1st ed. Paris: Flammarion.

Winter, Jean-Pierre. 2010. 'Homoparentalité et refus du réel.' 412 (5): 607–615.

Zafiropoulos, Markos. 2001. *Lacan et les sciences sociales: Le déclin du père*. 1st ed. Paris: Presses Universitaires de France.

Zafiropoulos, Markos. 2010. *Lacan and Lévi-Strauss or the Return to Freud (1951–1957)*. Translated by John Holland. 1st ed. London: Karnac.

Žižek, Slavoj. 1989. *The Sublime Object of Ideology*. 1st ed. London: Verso.

Žižek, Slavoj. 1999. *The Ticklish Subject: The Absent Center of Political Ontology*. 1st ed. London: Verso.

Chapter 4

Marx *avec* Lacan

Concepts for a Libidinal Economy (1968–74)

1 Was Lacan a Conservative?

My previous chapter concerned itself with Lacan's theory of the father, which, under its different forms, is a theory of how a subject assents to the authority of the social so as to come into being in the first place. For a while, Lacan conceived of the function of the father in the West as premised fundamentally on the set of institutions that constitute and regulate heteronormative kinship. As I noted in the conclusion to Chapter 3, however, Lacan's views on this issue start to change in the 1958–9 *Seminar VI*, and more explicitly when his reflections turn properly political. This move on Lacan's part engages an intractable problematic that is as old as psychoanalysis itself, namely its rapport with politics and the social. The first thing to note on this issue is the most obvious one: it should come as no surprise that, however much psychoanalysis might necessitate a reflection on collective life – if for no other reason than the fact that there is more than one psychoanalyst, that the analytic situation takes two, that both parties to the analytic encounter are immersed in historical time, etc. – it is not itself politics. While certain ethical tenets and theoretical claims Lacan makes might help us to conceptualise the issues posed to a thinker of the limits and possibilities of sexual politics, a claim I hope to have substantiated in my previous chapters, Lacan was keenly aware that psychoanalysis has no privileged interpretive claim whatsoever over the political world. Let us consider two fragments, one from a 1957 interview, and another from the 1966 'Responses to Philosophy Students':

> I will not be made to say that I think universal analysis is the spring of the resolution of all antinomies, that if all human beings were analysed there would no longer be war, no more class struggle; indeed, I formally say the opposite. All that may be thought is that such dramas would perhaps be less confused.
>
> (Lacan and Chapsal 1957, my translation)

DOI: 10.4324/9781003424604-5

Know that I hold psychoanalysis to have no right to interpret revolutionary practice ... but that revolutionary theory would do well to hold itself responsible for leaving vacant the function of truth as cause, even as this [that is, leaving vacant the function of truth as cause] is the first prerequisite of its efficaciousness.

(Lacan 2001d, 208, my translation)

The gist of what Lacan has to say about the relationship between psychoanalysis and politics is captured in the first quotation shown above: fundamental political phenomena such as class struggle would at best be clarified by universal analysis. If everyone were analysed, everyone would have arrived at a sufficiently satisfactory enunciation of their unconscious desire and the field that structures it – yet this enunciation, and its effects in respect of, for instance, facilitating everyone's rapport with satisfaction, would leave the antagonisms subtending political-economic life entirely intact. The reason for this contention, at least until Lacan's later theory of discourse, is that politics delineates a different order of reality than the psychic reality psychoanalysis describes. Put cursorily, no predicate attaching to individual psychology, however universal, can determine the course of political phenomena, such that one could predict the outcome of a political process on the basis of some psychological trait.[1] Accordingly, acting upon the psychoanalytic subject would not change the dynamics proper to the political field, which retain their autonomy – object, axioms, conventions – in respect of the analytic subject and of analytic practice.

All that psychoanalysis can teach those engaged in politics, according to the second quotation shown above, is that the place of truth should remain vacant. Or, that no knowledge ought to elevate itself to the rank of what Freud once called a *Weltanschauung*, a worldview buttressed by an overriding hypothesis capable of explaining everything away (Freud 1964, 158), so as to arrest the movement of thought and practice. Put simply, people can only work on behalf of a truth if they do not yet fully know what that truth entails. Leaving the place of truth vacant, in this sense, amounts to the assumption that there are still new propositions to be derived from a practice. If a truth presents itself as a knowledge, as something fully accomplished, no work needs to be done to maintain it – it is already there, complete. As such, revolutionary practice is only worth pursuing if the place of its corresponding truth is vacant.

Lacan is even more explicit about the autonomy of politics in respect of psychoanalysis when he wonders, in a *Seminar XV* lesson held on 15 May 1968 in the midst of student protests and factory occupations, about a meeting of his school in which the question 'what does the revolution expect of psychoanalysis?' was posed to an unnamed 1968 militant (according to Jean-Michel Rabaté, this was Daniel Cohn-Bendit; see Rabaté 2009). Lacan suggests that the only reasonable answer on the militant's part would have been 'what we expect from you at the moment is to help us to throw paving stones [at the police]!' In brief, revolution wants nothing from the psychoanalyst but that they act as a revolutionary, and not as a psychoanalyst. For Lacan, in fact, it was 'the psychoanalysts who should expect something of the insurrection' (Lacan 2024, 279, my translation), and not the other way round.

Despite the apparent enthusiasm of these remarks, Lacan's position would soon shift as the May '68 upheavals subsided. Already in 1969, he would infamously tell student revolutionaries that 'what you aspire to as revolutionaries is a master. You will get one' (Lacan 2007a, 207). As Lacan explicitly claims on this occasion, however, his intent is not to disqualify politics but to 'enable', through the 'progress' of psychoanalytic discourse, student revolutionaries 'to locate what it is exactly that you are rebelling against – which doesn't stop it [that against which you are rebelling] from continuing on incredibly well' (Lacan 2007a, 208, translation modified). Finally, Lacan suggests that his own reflection might help students to see how they themselves, and indeed their demands, are implicated in what they denounced: 'The regime is putting you on display. It says, "Look at them enjoy [jouir]!"' (Lacan 2007a, 208). Although these are certainly harsh words, it seems hasty to suggest that Lacan's wild interpretation of revolutionaries' desire is at once a dismissal of the autonomy of politics in respect of psychoanalytic interpretation. Rather, read in conjunction with what Lacan was saying in his 16th and 17th seminars, the shifting Lacanian take on revolutionary politics may actually be seen as a systematic recognition that politics – and here one ought to understand 'political economy' in the Marxist sense – while it is and will remain autonomous in respect of psychoanalysis and any psychological or psychiatric discipline, can also be conducted through the very stuff that makes up psychoanalysis.

In other words, Lacan recognises that there is a political economy of things such as desire, enjoyment, and fantasy, and that politics (specifically, the discourse of the master), as he put it in the title to one of his most famous seminars, constitutes the obverse or reverse [l'envers], not merely an 'Other Side', of psychoanalysis. At this point, one might turn to queer theory's archive and politics. Even if Lacan allows for the proposition that there is a political economy of sex, he and other thinkers of May '68 and gay liberation are also clear to the effect that the reverse is not true: there may well be a political economy that acts upon, and even determines sexuality and the categories through which it is spoken of (desire, fantasy, pleasure, etc.), but the existence of a political economy of sex does not necessarily authorise the proposition that sexuality might directly amount to a political intervention. Writing in 1973, still under the sway of the 'hangover' of May '68 and chronicling the then-obvious demise of the gay liberationist Front Homosexuel d'Action Révolutionnaire (FHAR – Homosexual Revolutionary Action Front), Guy Hocquenghem argued:

There is a multinational power of sex as stateless as capital but also as nonchalantly oppressive and sure of itself, whose dividends are measured in cock thrusts. Here, too, we get caught willingly, as if the whole journey since May could be summarized in the move from the world of slaves to the world of libertinized masters ... Sade and the French Revolution – these two ruptures – and many others meet here.

(Hocquenghem 2022, 116, translation modified)

Hocquenghem's argument here may well have been taken directly from Lacan's 'Kant *avec* Sade'. For Hocquenghem, there has always been a transnational market for sexual 'deviance' – not only for homosexuality, but also many other things psychoanalysts might qualify as 'perverse', such as necrophilia or coprophilia. Hocquenghem's impression at the time was that French student activism, as well as the gay and lesbian activism of '68 and of the immediate post-'68 period could be understood in retrospect as a mere demand for the democratisation of this market, and democratisation does not change anything like a 'structure' but only ever degrees of access to a fundamentally flawed playing field. Perversion, for Hocquenghem, is therefore not per se political in capitalist modernity: the gravest offences to a moral-sexual order can perfectly well be integrated into a supple enough economic system like capitalism, and certainly also in a flexible enough political and moral system, such as liberal democracy. In this sense, the generalisation of the right to enjoyment, pleasure, consumption, etc., does not represent an escape from capitalist political economy, but a reaffirmation of its obscene, perverse underside.

If Hocquenghem's argument here might strike one as odd in light of the better-known *Homosexual Desire* (Hocquenghem 1993), which advances the proposition that desublimated (anal) eroticism has untapped political potential, one might imagine that it is because his experience after the publication of that book confirmed the simple fact that sexuality, however outrageous, is not political in and of itself. The FHAR general assembly meetings, for example, have been said to have quickly become little more than cruising grounds for gay men rather than more or less serious gatherings where a coherent political programme might be discussed (Sibalis 2010); and, indeed, in retrospect, commentators have tended to agree that the FHAR's historical merit, besides facilitating cruising, was to make homosexuality a topic of debate (Marshall 1996). Hocquenghem's question to his comrades, in this context, amounts to something like this: is this all we want? Is what queers expect from the bringing in of (homo)sexuality into the political field no more than to become equal to the masterly figure of the libertine? Is the goal of gay politics a democratisation of perversion and therefore political passivity? His question, at least in respect of its preferred terminology, is posed not in terms of the cultural politics of sexuality, but of the material reality within which it is concretely lived and practiced. Hocquenghem's talk of cock thrusts as dividends and capital is meant to be interpreted literally: something of the structure of capitalist production and its subjective paraphernalia creeps into even that most intimate stranger called (sexual) desire and remakes the subject in its image. The professional pervert's pleasure, exquisite or execrable, presupposes and accepts the productive system and its ongoing violence, and therefore does not and cannot question it.

What I want to take from Hocquenghem at this stage is the rather more modest point that there is such a thing as an intersection of political economy and sexuality, and indeed a political economy of sexuality. I mean this in two different senses. The first sense, as clear to Hocquenghem in 1973 as it was to Lacan in 1970, as it had been to radical psychoanalysts such as Wilhelm Reich and others much earlier (Reich 2012), is that political-economic conditions furnish the background against which sexuality takes place (for queer work that proceeds on a similar assumption, see d'Emilio 1996; Morton 1996; Hennessy 1996; Penney 2014; Lewis 2016; Chitty 2020). So, for example, Wilhelm Reich argued in the early 20th century that poverty and inequality precluded young people from living independently of their parents, which in turn inhibited their sexuality, since they did not or could not have sex under their parents' roof. Queer theorists have acknowledged this basic fact and theorised it, for instance in Lisa Duggan's call for queers to become 'literate in economic policy' (Duggan 2012) and her analysis of neoliberalism and the gay movement (Duggan 2003). However, queer work that acknowledges this basic fact tends to reduce its scope to chronicling the systematic impoverishment of (non-white, at times non-first world sections of) LGBT+ people under the neoliberal hegemony of the past 50-odd years, or to the growing conservativeness of gay and lesbian rights politics after the routinisation of the HIV/AIDS crisis. In this sense, what many queer theorists who want to bring political economy back in the picture are concerned with is not capitalism as a social structure, but mostly its effects on, to put it bluntly, LGBT+ people's income.

The acknowledgement of the deleterious effects of capitalism and the neoliberal sect upon queer and non-queer lives, while certainly very important, does not go very far in thinking about how capitalism defines and institutes a libidinal reality that is simply inescapable for anyone alive today. This is the second sense in which I understand the proposition that there is a political economy of sexuality. The Marxist critique of political economy, which inspired some gay liberationist accounts of gender, sexuality, and social reproduction, as well as the Lacanian reading of the imbrication of modern science and capital, both reject the proposition that the deleterious effect of the universalisation of capitalist social relations is merely the unequal distribution of resources. Rather, for both traditions, there are subjective consequences arising from this universalisation – that is, there are definite and definable modes of desire, fantasy, and enjoyment imposed upon everyone by virtue of their inhabiting such a system, including but not limited to the compulsion to (over)work and (over)consume – and these consequences have yet to be systematically worked through by queer theorists in respect of the limits and possibilities of a politics of sexuality. The Lacanian 'libidinal economy', as Tomšič calls it, borrowing from Jean-François Lyotard, is also a critique of a 'damaged subjectivity' (Tomšič 2019) which subsists at once by virtue of, and in spite of, the damaging social relations that capitalism fosters (on this claim see also Bruno 2010; Tomšič 2015; Vighi and Feldner 2015; McGowan 2016). Some queer work has taken this kind of proposition seriously, especially Lauren Berlant's *Cruel Optimism* analyses of precarity and overconsumption (Berlant 2011). However, Berlant's work stands generally alone in the field – and, although it is in conversation with some post-Lacanian work, it does not itself refer to Lacan or Lacanian theory systematically. This chapter proposes to remedy this gap and to set up a queer Lacanian theoretical framework for working through the libidinal consequences of capitalist, scientific modernity.

2 Lacan's Marx: The Proletariat as Symptom

The first volume of Marx's *Capital* opens to a commonplace definition of wealth in general: that it presents itself originally as an immense collection of commodities, a set of things that can be bought and sold. This hoard, however, will be shown to be full of philosophical finesse. Marx proceeds to show that the commodity houses a certain difference, namely that between use-value – a thing which, by its thingness, satisfies a human want, irrespective of whether the latter arises from the belly or the mind – and exchange-value – a use-value that, by some property it can be presumed to bear, is liable to being expressed as equivalent to some quantity of another use-value and to change hands on that basis (Marx 1976, 125). Pursuant to this common attribute, commodities at first relate to one another one to one, such that their value is always expressed in their relation to some other definite commodity (in Marx's classical example, x yards of linen $= y$ coats). Marx then proceeds to analyse the process whereby, through a series of abstract operations, one such commodity attains the status of a universal equivalent. The presupposition to the universal equivalent is a totalisation; the general form whereby value is represented as quantities of one and only one commodity 'can only arise as the joint contribution of the whole world of commodities' (Marx 1976, 159). The process through which a commodity is elevated to the rank of universal equivalent, moreover, is simultaneously a removal of that commodity from the ranks of all the other commodities. Henceforth, I can no longer directly exchange a few cows for a plot of land, but can only sell them for a set amount of the universal equivalent (currency) with which I may buy land later.

As Lucio Coletti puts it, it is not a thinker who undertakes this operation of abstraction; rather, this operation takes place 'within the machinery of the

social order, in reality' (Coletti 1992, 37). This is a hefty doing that is impu-
ted to a seemingly fully automated social order: not only does it impose a
fictitious uniformity upon very different things so that they may be exchanged (answering seemingly outlandish questions such as 'how are x kilograms
of carrots the same as y litres of jet fuel?'), it also posits a refined conceptual
apparatus including the notion of a totality, the idea that there is such a
thing as a whole world of commodities, in order that a single commodity
might come to represent the value of all the other ones ('how is currency like
every single product of human industry?'). However, capitalist social relations go even further, and this is (according to Lacan's Marx) their uniqueness. They posit that the thing from which other useful-and-exchangeable
things arise, human labour, in time is itself a commodity. Under capitalism,
in other words, human expenditure in time counts as merchandise.

The inclusion of labour, the source of commodities, in the set of commodities is a momentous achievement. It is the condition for what Marx
calls surplus-value. For Marx, surplus-value does not come about through
the capitalist's faculties – for instance, by virtue of his capacity to bargain for
better prices on the market, or by virtue of the superior quality of his products, etc. – but through workers' expropriation. The *locus classicus* of this
expropriation is the labour contract, which involves a worker giving up a set
amount of their life, quantified in labour time, as well as all the products
thereof, in exchange for a wage. The catch, of course, is that a wage need
only reach a high enough magnitude to reproduce the workforce considered
in toto, meaning that the capitalist class can take possession of a large chunk
of the value effectively produced by the working class, and only pay them
whatever is needed for enough of them to survive to an arbitrary standard.
For instance, the average worker in a given sector of the economy may produce enough to pay for their basic daily necessities in four hours, yet they are
contracted for eight. So, the capitalist pays the worker for four hours' worth
of productive labour, knowing that he is entitled to all the surplus the worker
produced in the remaining four hours, and knowing that the worker has no
choice but to sell their time – if for no other reason than that, if they take
issue with the terms of the contract, there are plenty of others to hire (see
Marx 1969).

None of this is a matter of each individual labourer's skills or productivity
taken in isolation, but a matter of what Marx calls socially necessary labour
time – that is, the average time an average labourer will take to produce a
given amount of a commodity, assuming access to average-quality means of
production ('under the conditions of production normal for a given society';
see Marx 1976, 129). Regardless, then, of the individual outcomes of the
production process (for instance, if it makes a capitalist even richer or desti-
tute and disgraced, if it allows a worker to save money and open a small
business, etc.), the gears of the socioeconomic order keep running in the
same direction: those who have the means of production collectively exploit

those who have nothing to sell but their labour-power; and, so long as the two classes' relationship remains so defined, there will be (increasingly small, depending on the technological advancement) surplus to be extracted. The 'origin' of the system's obvious injustice lies, then, not in some intrinsic inequality among its agents, but in the unequal hand they were (always already, in Althusser's parlance; see Althusser 2001) dealt from the start, by virtue of having had no choice but to occupy a place within a pre-existing productive structure that allows for the creation of surplus-value.

It is in the space between bourgeois economics and Marx's critical inter-vention, indexed in the concept of surplus-value, that Lacan locates the novelty of Marxism. As Lacan puts it in *Seminar XVI*:

> We pay for labour with money, since we are in the market. We pay its full price, such as it is defined in the market by the function of exchange-value. There is, however, unpaid value in what appears as the product of labour, for the true price of that product is in its use-value. This unpaid labour, no matter how justly it has been priced in regard to the con-sistency of the market in the functioning of the capitalist subject, is surplus-value.
>
> Surplus-value is therefore the product of the means of articulation that constitute capitalist discourse. It is what results from capitalist logic.
>
> Well, articulated in this fashion, this discourse entails a certain posi-tion of the *I* [that is, the 'ego', not the subject] in the system. When this *I* is at the place of the worker, which is more and more the case, said position includes a demand concerning the 'frustration' of the worker.
>
> (Lacan 2006, 37, my translation)

For Lacan, who follows Marx in emphasising structure over individuals, the worker's immiseration is not a function of 'theft' or 'inequality'; it does not arise from the fact that the capitalist robs the worker of the products of their labour, to which they would be naturally entitled were they the true subjects of capitalist social relations. This view assumes that capitalist and worker are fully constituted individuals endowed with rights and prerogatives prior to their encounter with the social position they will occupy. As capitalist social relations have it, however, the worker has always already been robbed, not of the products of their labour, but of the means of producing without selling themselves to a capitalist, just as the capitalist has been robbed of the possi-bility of acting ethically by virtue of being subject to the laws of competition, etc. Counterintuitively, capitalist social relations, however much they have historically been accompanied or preceded by various forms of direct dom-ination (for instance, chattel slavery, marriage, vagrancy laws, the ongoing deprivation of the working class, etc.), are intrinsically egalitarian, in the sense that they presuppose that the exchanging parties are qualitatively equal, that they could swap places in any given exchange procedure without

altering its outcome (quite unlike, for instance, the Greek polis, which pre-
supposed and could not exist without the various distinctions of citizen,
slave, wife, etc., in which an individual was effectively the property of another
by virtue of some personal characteristic they could typically not change; see
Žižek 1989). Exploitation arises not directly out of any intrinsic inequality
between the exchanging parties but from the place they occupy in the
arrangement of the terms that constitute capitalism as a system, and it does
not, in principle (although naturally it does in practice), matter who occupies
what place.

Lacan's Marx proclaims that capitalist social relations contain a truth
indexed in the concept – and not per se in the set of empirically locatable
people – of the 'worker':

> Without a doubt, the worker is the sacred place of this conflictual ele-
> ment that is the truth of the system, which emerges when a knowledge,
> one that holds itself together all the more perfectly by being identical to
> its own perception in being [*perçu dans l'être*], tears itself apart
> somewhere.
>
> (Lacan 2006, 39, my translation)

The 'knowledge' Lacan refers to is the full network of equivalencies established in each commodity's value expressed in money, and the rapport they
each establish with the rest of the world of commodities through money. It is,
in other words, the entire universe of exchange-values at any given point in
time, to the extent that labour is counted in it. This knowledge is 'identical to
its own perception' because it is but a series of equivalences: it does not
represent anything aside from a quantitative determination issuing from a
relationship between two or more commodities mediated by a universal
equivalent, since everything that is, from the perspective of the market, is a
value-bearing commodity. Finally, truth in political economy is 'conflictual'
for a simple reason: the knowledge embodied in capitalist social relations is
inconsistent, for it cannot recognise the dual face of labour-power, namely
that it is purchased for its fair market value, and that its use-value is to
create more value than was paid for it in the first place, and that this implies
an irreducible opposition between the interests of workers and capitalists.

There is therefore a conflictual truth concealed by the surface fairness of
capitalist social relations, and this truth is conflictual because it must be
maintained by force over and against the opposition of the core participants
of the system – the proletariat. The effect of this 'conflictual' truth is that, by
the normal operation of capitalist social relations and quite independently of
any given actor's identity or indeed of their consciousness of their own role
within them, the basic circuit through which capitalist social relations reproduce themselves seemingly miraculously produces more (exchange-)value
than the market contained from the outset. Each time the circuit of

production-distribution-consumption buckles itself up with the involvement of labour-power, then, there is a surplus that is not paid for, that does not figure in the structured network of knowledges making that circuit possible, since the true exchange-value of labour-power is less than the value obtained through the conversion of its use-value into exchange-value. Thus, the knowledge embodied in capitalist social relations 'tears itself apart' each time surplus-value realises itself. It is as if the market enunciated contradictory propositions: as if it said, 'the value of labour-power is x_1 value', while also saying 'the use-value of labour-power is to create $x_1 + x_2$ value', and the coexistence of these two contradictory propositions that allows for the end-less process of valorisation. The catch is that the endless surplus enabled by this contradictory knowledge embodied in capitalist social relations entails a certain position for those subjected to it. At the place of the working I, in other words, a demand will inevitably arise for the spoils of exploitation – that is, for equality of access to the goods the workers themselves produce.

Psychoanalysis is acquainted with this form of contradiction. Freud had already approached it through the concept 'symptom', a compromise 'between the repressed sexual instincts and the repressing ego instincts; [which] represents a wish-fulfilment for both partners to the conflict simul-taneously, but one which is incomplete for each of them' (Freud 1955, 247). While psychoanalysis' bread and butter is the unveiling of the contradictory propositions embodied in the symptom, Lacan will not hesitate to claim that the critical concept of the symptom Freud seemed to have inaugurated is actually due to Marx. The truth of contradiction comes out, Marx demon-strates, in the *dramatis persona* of the worker. If 'the (exchange-)value of labour-power is x_1', and 'the (use-)value of labour-power is $x_1 + x_2$ (exchange-)value' cannot be logically true simultaneously, they give rise to a compromise, such as: 'workers are owners of the commodity labour-power, and they willingly and fairly exchange it for a fair wage as free and rational individuals. If, in reality, most of them only get poorer and poorer, it is their own fault'. This latter proposition reduces the cause of surplus-value to the consciousness and freedom of the worker: it is through the worker's con-scious design and effort that more value is produced than that which existed before the worker sold their time to the capitalist, and not through the self-contradictory character of the knowledge materialised in capitalist social relations, which allows for the creation of value seemingly out of nowhere (but actually, it is known after Marx, out of exploitation). A compromise-formation (workers are free and equal to the bourgeois) endowed with a hidden truth (workers are exploited, since the value created through their labour is more than what they are paid for) and determining the creation of a substitutive enjoyment that did not exist before the contradiction was in place (surplus-value), is a symptom. Therefore, as Alenka Zupančič has put it, 'the proletariat is not the sum of all workers, it is the concept that names the symptomatic point of this system, its disavowed and exploited negativity'

(Zupančič 2018, 34). The Marxist critique of political economy amounts to an unveiling of this truth, and prophesises the resolution of that symptom through revolution. The psychoanalytic critique of libidinal economy, a term to which I will return, makes use of the structure of the Marxist critique of political economy, but claims that its own discovery is located at a more basic level: that of the infrastructure of enjoyment and its renunciation.

3 Is there a Homology between Marx and Freud?

The core proposition from my previous section is that the proletariat, insofar as Lacan's Marx is concerned, is not immediately reducible to an empirical social group (to an *I*, a set of egos, as Lacan had put it; see Lacan 2006, 37). Rather, the proletariat is an effect of capitalist social relations considered as a totality. It is because there exists a market economy in which labour is represented as a commodity, and because there is no aspect of contemporary human life that can be reasonably said to be indifferent to this economy, that there are proletarians. 'The proletariat' is therefore not a fixed set of people, but denotes a contradiction within the knowledge embodied in capitalist social relations, which serves as the material support of a supplementary satisfaction, of a surplus. For Lacan, in other words, there is a sort of hole in the logic embodied in capitalist social relations, signalled by the concept of the 'proletariat', which allows for the seemingly miraculous creation of surplus-value, which, finally, 'satisfies' the system and fuels further production and consumption. While Lacan's point may appear a bit esoteric, it is certainly not spurious. 'Opening up', so to speak, the concept of the proletariat, such that it is not immediately identifiable to the industrial workforce, but appears as the rather more formal idea of 'truth to the capitalist system', is indeed important to navigating times when production has been globalised and made precarious to such an extent that there is no longer a sufficiently articulate industrial workforce on whom to deposit any serious political hopes (see, for a model that takes this problem seriously, Laclau and Mouffe 2000). It is also an important means to dispel erroneous notions that Marxists or post-Marxists consider, implicitly or explicitly, the 'proletariat' to be a presumptively white and male workforce to the exclusion of all other workers (Ferguson 2003). That said, Lacan himself is not a political economist, nor is he primarily concerned with the fate of the labouring masses, nor indeed could he have been interested in the contemporary vagaries of identitarian or anti-identitarian critical theory. Lacan is concerned with the novelty that psychoanalytic discourse has brought into being. For this reason, Lacan shifts the object of Marx's claims by suggesting that this surplus(-value), this 'extra' value not counted within the set of commodities, is a local instance of a more general process that psychoanalysis brings into view.

Surplus-value, Lacan will go on to claim, allows us to locate a more primary phenomenon having to do with the renunciation of enjoyment, which is a condition of symbolisation as such, and not just a particularity of the capitalist mode of production (although the capitalist mode of production does have a particular way of putting this renunciation to work). Lacan's thesis begins with the postulate that the constitution of any knowledge, conscious or unconscious, presumes a renunciation of enjoyment – castration – and causes some work to be performed. This work, finally, will be appropriated and made useful by the system that knowledge defines, including by producing some substitutive satisfaction for the subject. The renunciation of enjoyment, in other words, is made useful by a system that recaptures and recirculates it according to a conscious or unconscious knowledge, such that the form of the social bond becomes saturated with lost-and-refound enjoyment. This point is easy to illustrate in respect of the structuralist account of social systems: in the case of the classical Oedipal narrative, for instance, castration makes it known to a boy that he must find a mother-replacement and occupy a place in the web of kinship relations, forcing him to do some kind of work (establish an alliance between families through marriage, for instance) on behalf, as it were, of the collective – but at least he gets a wife, who, as a woman, is enjoyed as a body and as a symbol of the enjoyment he renounced to join the system in the first place, and children, who will further 'feed' the system by becoming men and women, etc. Under capitalism, the worker's expropriation forces them to sell their labour and produce a surplus, but at least they get a monetary wage, which is likewise a symbol (money) of what they renounced to become sellers of labour-power in the first place. And so on, presumably for many other kinds of social systems, so long as they demand the renunciation of one's enjoyment (which, certainly in the worker's case, amounts to a renunciation of much of their lives).

Drawing out the implications of this view, Lacan claims in *Seminar XVII* that 'what psychoanalysis enables us to conceptualize is nothing other than this, which is in line with what Marxism has opened up, namely that discourse is bound up with the interests of the subject' (Lacan 2007a, 92). This means, quite simply, that the persistence of a discourse is a function of its capability of capturing and recirculating enjoyment, in the same way as the capitalist captures and recirculates the worker's enjoyment by reinvesting the value he creates by exploiting him, and in the same way as kinship captures and recirculates male enjoyment by making women and children its representatives. Every discourse, Lacan postulates, produces a surplus-enjoyment in this fashion. Each time someone places themselves within a discourse rather than any other, then, the explanation for that choice is not to be sought in the persuasiveness, the reasonableness, or even the apparent necessity of that discourse, but in the enjoyment that choice procures, all the while inclusion into any discourse will be seen to presuppose the renunciation of enjoyment. It follows that surplus-value, inasmuch as it presumes the alienation of the worker's enjoyment of the fruits of their labour, is at once the cause and the effect of capitalist discourse (it is what motivates capitalist social relations, and what they produce), just as it follows that penile-centric copulation leading to reproduction, inasmuch as it presumes the alienation of man's full enjoyment of his body, is at once the cause and effect of the kinship machine (it is what motivates heterosexual relations, and what they hope to produce). It follows too that 'beneath' the systems these logics delineate – capitalism, kinship – there lie the means whereby a subject is capable of enjoying their imbrication in a discourse: the line manager's approving gaze or the father's, the drink after work or the contentment of the child at the breast, etc. As Jean-Louis Sous argues, then, '[t]he deconstruction of every fictional entity' – society, the economy, the family – 'would pass through its reduction to the drive apparatuses [*dispositifs pulsionnels*] that organise the interest of its usage [*l'intérêt de son usage*]' (Sous 2017, 52, my translation).

Lacan's argument implies that there is a formal equivalence between Marx's description of the capitalist system and Freud's description of the psyche: that, despite the fact that the psyche is obviously a different kind of system to capitalism, they can be described with a similar logic. Of course, this argument is somewhat facetious in the sense that it grossly simplifies what Marx and Freud actually do over the three volumes of *Capital* or the 24 of the *Standard Edition*, and I will not dwell on the legitimacy of Lacan's gesture. What I do want to highlight, however, is that there is a special kind of difference between the objects of desire, in the case of the psyche as it is constituted in relation to the 'deep' structure of kinship in the Lacanian account, and of production, in the case of capitalism. On the one hand, it is plainly clear that, under capitalism, the act of exchange does not cement any kind of alliance. A buyer and seller only really exist to one another in the moment of the transaction, and not before or after. No tie of reciprocity is created on the basis of buying and selling, and therefore no social link in the Lacanian sense. At best, contractual relations take the place of implicit reciprocal obligations, but they also clearly lay down each party's responsibilities as guaranteed by the state, which likewise means that the contract does not create an alliance-like pact but merely a temporally bound quid pro quo. On the other hand, the exchange of women in the kinship systems foregrounded by Lévi-Strauss and put to work in Lacan's phallocentric models (see Chapter 3) represented a qualitative, so to speak, gift – whereas commodities only change hands as quantitative equivalents, implicating therefore the intermediary of the universal equivalent, money. Capitalism, in this sense, introduces a fundamental difference to phallocentric kinship in the form of its capacity to count. What is circulated in the capitalist market is not a set of women-phalluses-gifts but a series of exchange-values, or simply numerical equivalences (which has led some to claim that the phallus is 'sexual money'; see Goux 1990, 24). Lacan was well aware of these differences, and indeed made them a cornerstone of his extremely brief account of the birth of capitalism:

Something changed in the master's discourse at a certain point in history. We are not going to break our backs finding out if it was because of Luther, or Calvin, or some unknown traffic of ships around Genoa, or in the Mediterranean Sea, or anywhere else, for the important point is that on a certain day surplus *jouissance* [enjoyment] became calculable, could be counted, totalized. This is where what is called the accumulation of capital begins ...

[From that point on, s]urplus value combines with capital – not a problem, they are homogeneous, we are in the field of values.

(Lacan 2007a, 177–8)

There is therefore a fundamental difference between the basis of the social ties as described in the Freud-Lévi-Strauss-Lacan series and as described in the Marx-Freud-Lacan series, between the elementary bases of society seen from *Totem and Taboo* and from the concept of the proletariat-symptom. Women, as much as they are also exchanged for things in various societies, are understood 'qualitatively' as gifts buttressing a social bond in the Oedipal, phallocentric model, whereas commodities are exchanged 'quantitatively' as commodities bearing exchange-value, and therefore do not embody a promise or determine a social link. If this is the case, and if capitalism represents a definite change in the dominant form of the social bond in Western societies (and, through colonialism and globalisation, also to all other societies that are thereby Westernised; see Sous 2017; Lacan 2023, 317), what does Lacan think capitalism means for the normalisation of desire? What kinds of objects does it offer to our desire, and what kind of social link can it buttress among us? (I take the form of these two questions from the helpful Declercq 2006.) For convenience, I will discuss Lacan's answers under two headings, respectively: the destruction of those traditional semblances structuring the social bond, and the infinitisation of demand implied by the commodity-form.

4 The Asocial Bond

The first point I will discuss relates to the difference between the social bond determined by the semblance of the phallus and that determined by whatever it is that binds us to each other under capitalism. Lacan establishes a somewhat allusive theory to the effect that capitalism destroys traditional modes of the social bond in scattered pronouncements of the first half of the 1970s. In the 1974 talk 'La Troisième', Lacan returns to the theme of the proletariat as a social symptom. He argues that psychoanalysis should not be seen as a social symptom, even if he had been elaborating the thesis, during the 1960s, that psychoanalysis was only conceivable as a sort of respondent to modern science (which might reasonably lead one to think that psychoanalysis is science's symptom). Rather, Lacan makes clear that, if there is a modern social symptom, it is the proletarian, though not necessarily the Marxian one:

There is but one social symptom – each individual is really a proletarian, that is to say, they have no discourse out of which to make a social link, otherwise stated, to make believe [*'faire lien social, autrement dit, semblant'* – *'faire semblant'* means 'to act as if', 'to make believe', but could also be translated more technically as 'to make a semblance' at the cost of Lacan's wordplay]. This is what Marx compensated for, and incredibly so. Said and done. What he proposed [*émis*] implies that there is nothing to change. Which is why, by the by, everything continues as before.

(Lacan 2011, my translation)

Let us begin with Lacan's first argument. Lacan defines the proletarian as someone who suffers from the absence of a discourse out of which to form a social link. Or, which amounts to the same for him, someone who suffers from a lack of material out of which they might fashion a semblance. Lacan defines a semblance in *Seminar XVIII* as 'the proper object through which the economy of discourse regulates itself' (Lacan 2007b, 18, my translation). The paradigmatic example of a semblance so defined is precisely the phallus: men make believe that they have it, women make believe that they are it, and the 'economy' of heteronormative discourse regulates itself on the basis of this mutual pretending. Lacan speaks of a discourse such as heterosexual parading as having an 'economy', in this sense, because it of necessity implicates the Freudian libido, enjoyment: there is a dynamism to the whole theatre of gender, which can only hold together to the extent that each party to it gets (or expects to get) some form of satisfaction out of it. Men find women and women find men, in other words, by force of this make-believe, which means that participating in it is a precondition for them to obtain some enjoyment. It is accordingly the case that '[t]he phallus is quite precisely sexual enjoyment insofar as it is coordinated to a semblance' (Lacan 2007b, 34, my translation).

Lacan's remark therefore implies that whatever it is that assured the pertinence of semblances such as the phallus for the subject in the past – and Lacan ascribed this role to the father – becomes increasingly inoperative as soon as something like a proletarian appears on the historical stage. The appearance of capitalist social relations, which alone create proletarians, therefore eclipses something in the role of the father. In 'Radiophonie', Lacan argues that workers owe their exploitation less to any individual capitalist, or indeed to the capitalist class, than to the very form the commodity takes under the capitalist mode of production. As Lacan parodies Hamlet's speech to Horatio,[2] there are 'other ways to make a subject than the objects dreamt of in your understanding [*connaissance*]' (Lacan 2001b, 415, my translation). If it is the case that the commodity can 'make a subject', as Lacan puts it, it follows that he believes the notion of the father to have lost its monopoly over what might be called 'subjectivation' in capitalist modernity. In other words, because labour-power is a commodity under capitalism, and (presumably) because it is exceptional among commodities in that it purports to coincide with the subject (I cannot sell my labour without selling myself for a set time), it is the capitalist system that takes over the task of subjectification once ascribed to the father.

If the father is understood as the castrating instance in the Oedipal drama, and capitalism overcomes him, Lacan can argue that capitalist social relations are exceptional in that they refuse to acknowledge anything of the various forms of lack to which the father gives meaning. For example, in the 1972 'Télévision', Lacan claims that the first logical step of capitalism is 'getting rid of [sex]' (Lacan 2001d, 532, my translation), while, that same year, in the parallel sessions of *Seminar XIX*, he argues:

> What differentiates the discourse of capitalism is *Verwerfung*, the fact of rejecting, outside all the fields of the symbolic … What does it reject? Well, castration. Any order, any discourse that aligns itself with capitalism, sweeps to one side what we may simply call, my fine friends, matters of love. You see, it's a mere nothing.
>
> (Lacan 2017, 91)

One might very well wonder in what world Lacan is living when he suggests that capitalism sets aside castration, when it was none other than Freud's nephew Eddie Bernays who put that concept to work for capitalism in birthing modern marketing. Capitalism most certainly does not set aside castration; if anything, it is the economic system that has the keenest grasp of its importance and usefulness, at least when it comes to refashioning human desire so as to ensure pointless consumption. The key to Lacan's argument here is not the argument about castration, which, combined with the reference to the psychotic mechanism of *Verwerfung*, has led Lacanians to argue (far too hastily) that science and capitalism push us towards psychosis (Miller 2024). Rather, the most important interpretive key to this fragment is the notion that capitalism disallows 'matters of love'. I hasten to note that I do not think that this is Lacan's version of the endlessly reiterated motif of 'liquidity' in modernity, although it can, of course, be uninterestingly read as such (Soler 2016). It is an argument about the nature of the social bond in Western capitalist societies. For Freud as for Lacan, the heteronormative social bond is not premised on the love of a man for a woman, which admits of direct satisfaction in penetrative coitus and might even lead a couple to social isolation, but the sublimated love of a man for another, which the gift of a woman helps to keep sublimated. Lacan is explicit about this in *Seminar X*, and he follows this reasoning to its last consequences in *Seminar XIV* (see Chapter 3): 'The homosexuality that is placed at the root of social adhesion in our theory, Freudian theory, is the male's privilege … This libidinal adhesion of the social bond … is especially allotted to the male due to the fact of castration' (Lacan 2014, 269). If, as Lacan defines it, love is the gift of one's lack ('to love is to give what one hasn't got'; Lacan 2014, 108), then every man who gives away a woman in the anthropological circuits of Lévi-Straussian kinship *ipso facto* loves the man who marries that woman, since a woman embodies the phallus, which is a metaphor for a man's castration (his renounced enjoyment), and therefore a symbol of his lack. The conclusion imposes itself: the gift of a woman is the gift of one's lack, which is love, such that every handshake cementing the alliance between two families is also a sort of sublimated handjob.

If capitalism disallows 'matters of love', then, it also disallows the kind of male-centric eroticism that heterosexual marriage ensures will remain sublimated, and therewith the libidinal basis of the social. In this sense, the universalisation of capitalist social relations would destroy the implicit power of the exchange of women to bind man to man. Part of a justification as to why Lacan makes this claim, I think, has to do with the dominance of contractual fictions in our societies, which presumes that an individual is identical to their will, inasmuch as it can be expressed in a voluntary and legally binding promise. In this sense, liberal individualism presumes that each person (not the father) is a master in and of themselves, and the master is defined by 'this ultrareduced myth of being identical with his own signifier' (Lacan 2007a, 90). One may well view the signature of one's name to a contract as the major empirical index of this myth:[3] I sign a binding document so as to ensure that my transcendental will was present at the time of making that promise, as it were, in the eyes of the state. However, the difficulties of keeping the boundaries of this generalised contractualism in check are reasonably clear, since arguably any and all social relations have the potential to be conceived of as contractual. Paul B. Preciado, for example, has parodied this idea in his argument that a radicalisation of liberal contractualism into the sexual arena could further erode the heteronormative institutions that stubbornly regulate sexual activity and identity. Proposing a countersexual contract as a new basis for a renewed sexual life, Preciado writes that

> countersexuality aims to replace this social contract we refer to as 'nature' with a countersexual contract. Within the framework of the countersexual contract, bodies recognize themselves and each other not as men or women but as speaking bodies. They recognize in themselves the possibility of acceding, as subjects, to every signifying practice and to every position of enunciation that history has established as masculine, feminine, trans, intersex, or perverse.
>
> (Preciado 2018, translation modified)

One interesting example of the generalised contractualism Preciado suggests here is not so much the queer practices he suggests in his book, and more the contemporary discussions of sexual consent, which have been highlighting the odd consequences of 'overcontractualising' social relations. A recent BBC

Radio 4 series, for example, interviewed teenage boys who were so afraid of being accused of sexual violence against their partners that they had them record a kind of video contract listing the sexual acts they consented to beforehand. What emerges from this notion seems to be precisely that the contractual fiction assuages anxiety on much the same terms as, *pace* Lacan, the inheritance of the phallic prerogative would historically have done for a boy in respect of sex. At any rate, if even sexual activity, probably the paradigmatically private activity according to traditional liberal political theories, can be refashioned into a contract, it follows that it is not entirely inconceivable that contractual relations might subsume all other forms of the social bond. It is certainly the case for marriage, which, lest conservative psychoanalysts enamoured with anthropological universals forget, has been defined as a contract, a voluntary promise intended to create legal obligations between contracting parties, for centuries or even millennia in the West (Donahue 2016).

In sum, then, Lacan argues that the central fiction ('semblance') organising enjoyment in capitalist social relations is no longer the one psychoanalysis, aided by ethnology, ascertained to be father and phallus in premodern societies. Rather, what takes the place of that fiction is generalised contractualism and its liberal individualist presupposition: the legal person who is identical to their will and capable of expressing that will contractually. This might help us to explain the less defensible remainder of Lacan's argument, to the effect that 'Marx compensated for' the destruction of traditional semblances – so much so that '[w]hat he proposed [*émis*] implies that there is nothing to change' (Lacan 2011, my translation). What Marx did, in this argument, was to compensate, through the discovery of surplus-value and the naming and rallying of the proletariat around the exploitation it indexes, for the disappearance of the basis of sublimated male homosexual love once assured by the exchange of women. After Marx's call for workers of the world to unite, men got to love each other platonically as workers, rather than as bearers of a phallus they got to traffic in in the form of women. Instead of a right to a woman, finally, workers can band together to claim their right to their fair share of the value they produce, and in so doing love each other as a group of fellow men.

As a final note, the motif of the overcoming of the father function by capitalist social relations may be one reason why Lacan preconised a greater part played by segregation in contemporary societies. If there is no traditional father function assuring us that the coherence of the social is premised entirely on the exchanges that allow men to form group effects at the expense of women, the field is clear for the appearance of any number of groups that might, like Marx's newly declared proletariat, manage to constitute themselves as groups without reference to a pre-existing, transcendental principle of sociability. The controlling instance for the legitimacy or otherwise of these groups will be, one might surmise, less and less their compliance with the heteronormative dicta that determined the basic criteria for social belonging in the past, but simply their capacity to assert themselves as such, in the same way that homosexuals have successfully established the dignity and viability of their lives so as to join 'mainstream' society. Lacan relates something like this process to the greater domination of knowledge in Western societies, a growing faith in the benevolence of technocracy (knowledge as a principle of governance), which is 'desegregational [*déségrégatif*]', even if it 'carries' the master's arbitrary injunction, since it 'liberates' the master from his truth (Lacan 2001a, 396, my translation). Or, to put it more simply, technocracy is potentially desegregational; for example, it allows for the constitution and social integration of the homosexual community because it cannot forcibly separate the 'desirables' from the 'undesirables' in someone's name, for instance in the name of the king or queen, or indeed of the father. However, technocracy also liberates political power from its subjective truth, which is always the arbitrariness of a desire, whether the king's or the father's: the technocrat cannot countenance the exercise of political power in someone's name, except if a knowledge authorises it. This is why institutions such as prisons, asylums, and even concentration camps become so important in our modernity: they are ways to enforce segregation in no one's name, and with no acknowledgement of the political basis of that segregation, but under the alibi of some knowledge or other. The counterpart to the erosion of authority exercised in the name of some transcendental principle, such as those embodied in the heteronormative basis of sociality that might see political authority as paternal authority, is the proliferation of those other, 'softer' modes of confinement that Michel Foucault analysed under the heading of disciplinary power, and which are still important, for instance, in the vertiginous boom of the U.S. prison population (Foucault 1978).

5 The Commodity-Gadget

If the social link determined by capitalism can be described as a kind of asocial link, to the extent that it is premised on the erosion of traditional semblances, it is reasonable to expect that the objects through which it makes the renunciation of enjoyment useful will have their own specificity. Lacan gives pride of place in this respect to the technical objects science makes possible and capitalism generalises as consumer goods. Speaking of castration and science in *Seminar XVI*, Lacan argues that:

> There is certainly a rapport between these two points that appear so distant from each other. [This rapport] is, on the one hand, this damming up that makes it so that sex ... far from taking a single step in the direction of any possible solution in the field of the erotic, becomes increasingly obscure, highlighting the insufficiency of our traditional landmarks [*de nos repères*]. On the other hand, what is at issue are these

effects of our knowledge, [effects] that I call 'widespread' – that is to say, the prodigious surge [*déferlement*] of our rapport to *objet a*, of which our mass media are no more than the return to presence [*retour à la présentification*].

(Lacan 2006, 277, my translation)

This fragment proposes that, whatever science may have to say about human sexuality, in respect of 'the erotic' it has done nothing but highlight how insufficient, perhaps even futile, knowledge in this area ultimately is. In other words, try as it might, science cannot get rid of castration, nor can it get rid of the discontent generated by the parasitism of language and of linguistic categories upon the living body. Something, therefore, remains opaque in the field of the human, even if one might try to saturate it with scientific knowledge. This is a theme that Lacan had been struggling with for some time. He concluded *Seminar XV*, for instance, with a programmatic statement regarding the point of *Seminar XVI*:

> At the level of the Other, there has never been anything truer than prophecy.
> All the same, it is at the level of the Other that science totalises itself, that is to say that, in relation to the subject, it alienates itself thoroughly.
> What is at issue is to know where, at the level of the subject, something of the order of prophecy might still reside.

(Lacan 2024, 299, my translation)

The problematic of the immediately following *Seminar XVI*, then, will be precisely the limits of knowledge, predictability, etc., to which is to be counterposed everything that is 'of the order of prophecy': for the subject, in brief, sex and sexuality. One need only read the enormous profusion of sexual advice available online, and its patent ineffectiveness, to know that Lacan may well have a prescient point. Contemporary queer work on orgasm, for example, has demonstrated that the shift from subjective to biological reasoning in trying to 'locate' sexual enjoyment has done little to help us to access it more reliably and equitably (Jagose 2012; Frith 2015). Even the presumption that orgasm is and should be available to everyone on the same terms might even be experienced as a superego injunction ('what does it say about me if I can't have one?'). Even if scientific knowledge might fail to fully saturate the field of sexuality, installing in it an order of perfect predictability, however, Lacan holds that scientific knowledge does have direct and observable effects on desire and subjectivity. For instance, it makes possible a set of substitutive objects seemingly capable of producing desire: those objects Lacan would call 'gadgets' (Lacan 2011, 32), which are a subset of the commodity, and which purport to offer a compensation for the problem of sexuality in the speaking being.

Mass media are one of Lacan's recurring examples of 'gadgets', which he defines as technical objects allowing for the 'prodigious surge' of *objet a*, inasmuch as they make present the functions of voice and gaze – pillars of the superego and of fantasy – at no less than a planetary scale. Lacan would elaborate upon this thesis further in 'La Troisième', in which he claims that the gadgets science makes possible give us 'something to sink our teeth into' there where something is lacking in our rapport to knowledge [*connaissance*],[4] that is, in respect of sexuality. Gadgets in a wider sense, such as 'television, the journey to the moon [rather, the space shuttle?]' and 'automobiles' (Lacan 2011, 32, my translation), then, all attempt to 'plug up', as it were, the deficiency in our knowledge of the sexual. Lacan is still more direct on this point when he humorously claims that 'it is quite certain that people have cars [that function as] false women [*comme une fausse femme*]' (Lacan 2011, 32, my translation). The gadgets that scientific knowledge generates therefore stand in for something that is missing at the purportedly deeper level into which psychoanalytic work delves, that of castration or the foundational renunciation of enjoyment. They can intervene at the level of desire and fantasy, just as they can pose as the voice of a global superego. Television tells us to enjoy; automobiles compensate for a small penis; and the moon landing is a symbol of phallic omnipotence. A paradigmatic contemporary example may well be the smartphone and social media, premised on a generalised counting not of attention – since people are rarely aware of what they are staring at on a smartphone screen for hours on end – but, rather, of the enjoyment of looking. As Isabel Millar puts it:

> Whilst [Lacan] may not have imagined that we would have a smartphone in our pockets capable of giving us instant access to encyclopaedic information, global news, or even sex with strangers, Lacan was alluding to the suspicion that science would soon have a means of harvesting and registering these objects of desire in such an efficient way as to completely change our way of pursuing them … [Such devices] may be thought of as a function which attempts to drain *jouissance* from the body, or perhaps more accurately, regulate and administer it.
>
> (Millar 2021, 53–4)

In this sense, the notion of 'gadget' as a subset of the commodity points to a historically novel form whereby the socius captures the renunciation of enjoyment, prompting desire, and makes it productive – one arising directly out of the technical expertise embodied in a product. As I discuss above, Lacan argues in 'Radiophonie' that workers owe their exploitation more to the commodity-form than to their bosses. In this sense, the exploitation that capitalism occasions is also a result of the system itself, and not exclusively of the oppressive class relations that structure it (although, of course, these are indispensable to it). There is a further side to this argument, in that the commodity, for Lacan, is not merely the index of the specificity of capitalist social relations but also something that is offered to each of us as consumers and therefore something that must appear enticing to us. The commodity must be capable of prompting desire, as marketers have known since the beginning of their craft. In this sense, it must also represent the subject's lack back to them, in the same way as Lacan's *objets a* do (classically, these objects are the breast, the faeces, the voice, and the gaze). In this sense, the gadget is another index of the decline of the tradition that, to slightly decontextualise one of Lacan's more cryptic comments in *Seminar XVII*, 'man' plays 'the spokesman of God in order to believe that he forms a union with a woman' (Lacan 2007a, 162).

Although the commodity would appear to be directly capable of capturing desire in Lacan's account, it retains a certain peculiarity in respect of his classical list of objects, including the missing phallic object ('missing' because it is a signifier, not an object). This difference has to do with the parasitism of exchange-value upon the commodity – the fact that, as Marx demonstrated, whatever physiochemical properties a commodity might bear, it is always subsumed under a quantitative determination. Lacan's account would seem to lead us to the suggestion that capitalism offers a substitute object-cause of desire in the form of the commodity, assigning it with a quantitative determination, which finally also amounts to something like a denial of castration. The subject renounces their being by 'becoming' their labour-power in the market, and the main systemic result of that renunciation – surplus-value – gets circulated, reintegrated, and reinvested into the system. 'Surplus value combines with capital – not a problem, they are homogeneous, we are in the field of values' (Lacan 2007a, 178). As a result, the renunciation of enjoyment can be made to reappear in the market as something of the same order of the commodity (since they can both be expressed as a quantity), such that the irretrievable loss Lacanians place at the origin of subjectivity is, as it were, 'covered over' by the idea that 'I can feel better if only I could have this or that other commodity', or 'if only I could get more money', unrestrained consumerism and hoarding being two opposite expressions of the perversion of capitalist modernity. After all, what the worker renounced so they could get paid a wage is, through the intermediary of money, qualitatively the same as the stuff they get to buy with their wage. The capitalist mode of production therefore 'infinitises' the demand for commodities, which henceforth stand in for what the subject renounced in becoming subject to capitalist social relations in the first place, and accordingly allows them to pursue the fantasy of not being castrated through the continuous purchase of commodities or the endless accumulation of money. While this fantasy will, of course, be inflected along class lines, as with most other things under capitalism, the implications here are reasonably clear. As Lyotard colourfully puts it in *Libidinal Economy*, a book he later denounced as 'evil':

And here is the question: Why, political intellectuals, do you incline towards the proletariat? In commiseration for what? I realize that a proletarian would hate you, you have no hatred because you are bourgeois, privileged smooth-skinned types, but also because you dare not say the only important thing there is to say, that one can enjoy swallowing the shit of capital, its materials, its metal bars, its polystyrene, its books, its sausage pâtés, swallowing tonnes of it till you burst ... We abhor therapeutics and its vaseline, we prefer to burst under the quantitative excesses that you judge the most stupid.

(Lyotard 1993, 115–16)

In sum, then, Lacan provides a sort of catalogue of how capitalist social relations and their logical corollary – the presumptive commodification of every object of human interest – capture human desire and remake social bonds in their image. In this sense, Lacan also construes the libidinal logic of capitalism as a mode of domination through enjoyment, rather than solely through its renunciation. One of the most important arguments in *Seminar XVII* is that, under capitalism, the signs of domination become ever more diffuse, 'unassailable', in part because they cannot be isolated through the language of subjective responsibility, in part because they implicate us into the system as if 'directly', by capturing desire and providing a series of substitutive enjoyments, without the need for overt repression. If responsibility for the wrongs the economic system subjects us to can only be laid at the feet of some abstract entity called 'capitalism', 'the system', 'money', 'greed', 'the commodity form', etc., what is left for us labouring subjects can only ever be 'more or less tolerable exploitation' (Lacan 2007a, 178) – the exploitation that, when all is said and done, we can live with, since there is at any rate no one privileged embodiment of societal malaise, but only a thorough libidinalisation of the social field through the commodification of everything. Surreptitiously, desire ends up thoroughly captured by the commodity-form, which is at once the embodiment of the capitalist mode of production as such.

6 Queerness as Commodity

What, then, does Lacan's proposed libidinal economy amount to, in terms of a politics of sexuality? First, Lacan's thesis is that Marx and Freud start from the concept of the signifier, even though they did not possess the language to recognise it as such. From this starting point, furthermore, both insist on the centrality of the symptom as the ciphered expression of an underlying contradiction or conflict in the knowledge structuring an economic or subjective system. This expression allows for a sort of paradoxical satisfaction, one that is in excess of the subject's needs, and gets to be captured and recirculated by the systems they find themselves implicated in, whether the capitalism mode production, or the species (for example) in respect of the reproduction that sometimes accompanies sexuality. If Marx can dream of the resolution of the symptom in a revolutionary act, however – a dream Lacan suggests ended up reifying the proletariat and postponing our confrontation with the unbearable truth of generalised proletarisation – Freud would remain content with notions like 'working through' or indeed with the 'common unhappiness' issuing from the subjective acceptance of castration.

For Lacan, as may well be expected from a psychoanalyst, Freud is in the right both at the level of analytic practice and at the level of politics. If Freud is in the right, however, there is an ineradicable malaise that comes with the mere fact that, there where there are humans, there is society. Capitalism, in Lacan's discussion of the Marxist critique, is one way of putting this malaise to work, of appropriating it and making it useful. Capitalist logic, for Lacan, consists fundamentally in the 'counting-as-a-commodity' of that which the subject renounced in order to come into being in the first place, that is, in the commodification of that of which the worker and subject will always have been dispossessed, namely enjoyment. This 'counting-as-a-commodity' is simultaneously a denial of the fact that some irretrievable and irreparable loss was, at any rate, incurred upon our accession to social life; and a recognition of the productive potential of this loss. Capitalism attempts to make good on this loss by offering back to the subject a series of 'gadgets' – technical objects, in a broad sense – ever more divorced from what may legitimately be called a need, which stand in for the lost objects in relation to which the subject's desire will have been positioned. In so doing, capitalism gets to capture the subject's loss and put it to work for the production of surplus.

Lacan's is a general description of the libidinal underpinnings of a capitalist economy, and so it falls to us, his contemporary readers, to work through its particular consequences. At this stage, since Lacan's interrogation of these issues is framed by the events of May '68 and their aftermath, it may be productive to return to Guy Hocquenghem's quotation from the beginning of this chapter, now slightly expanded. It is my contention that this fragment contains an important, almost Lacanian, argument about how contemporary sexual identity is always at risk of mimicking capitalist social relations. Prophesising the end of the homosexual movement, and putting forward a case for what might come next, Hocquenghem proclaims:

> Let's not fool ourselves: 'gender' is no more the grand signifier than anything else. And for that matter, sex can and should be challenged with violence, with art … The desiring fascism that marks the annals of the great libertines of the Western world is also the great big sense of being in one's place, dressed up to look like the most absolute radicalism and revolutionary apoliticism. Those who enjoy the most advanced perversions, lavish necrophiles of New York, or connoisseurs of

Amsterdam's saunas and all of Europe's parks, terrify me in their perverse professionalism, having the power to rebuild everywhere (with the
help of credit cards and the grand hotels) their territory from which any
event is excluded ahead of time. There is a multinational power of sex as
stateless as capital but also as nonchalantly oppressive and sure of itself,
whose dividends are measured in cock thrusts. Here, too, we get caught
willingly, as if the whole journey since May could be summarized in the
move from the world of slaves to the world of libertinized masters. But,
breakthrough, we want to cut up the world of masters with the world of
slaves, just like we want to cut up the world of slave territories pains-
takingly defended by narrow morals with the stateless *jouissances* of the
world of masters.

Sade and the French Revolution – these two ruptures – and many
others meet here.

The great upending imagines stronger emotions, more intense joys,
deeper fractures, than the incomes of some perversions – fags, motor-
cycles, leather, drugs – whose capital is as off-limits as a big bank's.

(Hocquenghem 2022, 116, translation modified)

Let us follow Hocquenghem's text. First, neither 'gender' nor 'sex' are 'the
grand signifier' – here, a sort of metaphor for what would count as the
Central Struggle, a place once occupied by labour, and later colonised by the
various agendas of the new social movements. Hocquenghem was, of course,
vindicated by the later history of these movements: feminist theorists, for
instance, have demonstrated repeatedly that 'gender' is not as central a political category as one could once have believed it was, since it is co-con-
stituted by other axes of social difference (see, for instance, Crenshaw 1989).
The same goes for a sex and sexuality that, contrary to what some queer
theorists have advanced (Chapter 2), is neither the central axis of political
analysis, nor in any sense revolutionary, however antinormative, antisocial,
or simply useless (that is, sidestepping the heteronormative imperative to
procreate) some forms of it might be. Indeed, Hocquenghem demonstrates a
keen awareness in this fragment that the great perverts of the Western imagination were not revolutionary underdogs, but rather aristocrats – certainly
those kept alive by their elevation into diagnostic categories, such as Sade
and Sacher-Masoch. Perversion, from this point of view, is an aristocratic
form: a far cry from the queer abject, which is always presumed to be the
refuse of the social order (Edelman 2004). The new aristocracy of perversion,
Hocquenghem suggests, consists in these great professional perverts, 'lavish
necrophiles of New York' and 'connoisseurs of Amsterdam's saunas', (men)
acquainted with 'all of Europe's parks', whose presence and power brings even
the ineradicable contingency of the world under the sway of their enjoyment.
There where these new 'capitaloperverts', so to speak, assert their influence,
'any event is excluded ahead of time'. One always knows, in other words,

what is going to happen, indeed all that could possibly happen, when such perversions are at play, since they count their pleasures as one counts currency: all that can happen is one more fuck, one more instance of whatever gets them off.

The goals of the homosexual movement, Hocquenghem goes on, can accordingly not ever be merely to democratise perversion or generalise hedonism. The homosexual's political import is not to demonstrate that there is a viable life in the figure of the 'libertinised master'. Despite the general tenor of Hocquenghem's argument, for instance, in the better-known *Homosexual Desire*, the libertinised master appears here as little but the logic of capital transposed to, and embodied in, interpersonal, sexual relations. Indeed, to live out a perversion of this kind is at once to reproduce the procedures of capital: if the market proclaims that 'anything (up to and including human life materialised in labour) is a commodity', a proclamation of which Lacan's reading of Marx draws out some implications, the libertine master proclaims that 'anyone (or anything) is an object to be enjoyed'. The sole difference is that the dividends extracted from the capitalopervert's sex life are measured in 'cock thrusts', in a surplus-enjoyment adequate to the world-market of libertinised masters, rather than in money. One moves from surplus-value to some sort of enjoyment-value – with a market-Other happily enthroned in either case, for it should not be forgotten that Sade's libertines always refer to some figure of the Other, whether God as the Being-Supreme-in-Wickedness or Nature as a pure will to destruction.

Hocquenghem's figure of capitalist perversion is thus not so far removed from the command in which Lacan would later embody the superego: *Enjoy!* (Lacan 1998, 3), and certainly not at all removed from Lacan's exploration of Sade's perversion in its rapprochement to Kant. In *Seminar IX*, for instance, Lacan claims Sade diligently counted his orgasms by carving small notches onto his nightstand, commemorating not quite the irruption of pleasure but merely the fact of bodily expenditure, the 'one more', $n + 1$. Elaborating upon the similarity between this alleged Sadean procedure and that of the prehistoric hunter who records his kills on a bone, Lacan notes: 'I've killed one, it's an adventure. I've killed another, it's a second adventure, which I can distinguish by some traits … At the twentieth, how is it that I can find my bearings again? Do I even know if there's really been twenty?' (Lacan 1962, session of 6 December 1961, my translation). At the tail end of repetition, in other words, whatever is inscribed or recorded loses all meaning, ceases to bear any reference to anything outside itself: the kill for no other purpose than to kill, the purchase for no other purpose than to purchase, the sex for no other purpose than to have had it (as opposed, for instance, to it having been pleasurable).

Note that this position is emphatically not the same as that which Foucault would go on to espouse a few years later in his famous *History of Sexuality*. Hocquenghem's text points to a different problematic, in which

what is at issue is not to oppose a putative repressive hypothesis by advocating for the free expression of a 'natural' sexuality – and therefore to fully
historicise sexuality – but rather to critique a sexual imaginary that does little
but transpose the basic tenets of economic hedonism onto a sexual arena.
The shift from *homo economicus* to his erotic counterpart, one way in which
some of the demands advanced in May '68 may be understood, is not a shift
at all for Hocquenghem, but merely a further step in capitalism's colonisation of every lifeworld, an extension of capitalism's particular commodifying
of human expenditure in time into the most radically private domains and
onto the most radically heterogenous objects.

As Lacan had already noticed (in relation to Sade; see Lacan 1992, 78),
this transposition and generalisation of the imperative of counting ends up
quite simply in boredom. Reading Sade's painstaking descriptions of sex and
torture, interspersed with philosophical digressions on the virtues of evil,
debauchery, destruction, etc., eventually does seem to lead to a mood of
intense boredom, one that might be produced today by browsing the Netflix
catalogue, online shopping on Amazon, or cruising on Grindr. The same
may justifiably be said of some recent queer writing, especially writing
centred on the gay male lifeworld, for instance Guillaume Dustan's *Dans ma
chambre*, which drily describes the protagonist's colourful (perhaps compul-
sive, as Dustan himself admits in the title of another novel, *Plus fort que moi*
[*Stronger than I*]) sex life down to the smallest minutiae (Dustan 2013).
Dustan's descriptions of sexual encounters read like a spreadsheet: what did
the sex consist of, what was the quality of parties' erections, which toys were
used, who bottomed and who topped, which drugs were used, etc. The net
result of his dry, descriptive style is, strangely enough, to thoroughly desex-
ualise sex itself, which becomes a nihilistic exercise in consumption. Dustan's
writing stages gay sex as a description of the repetitive motions of an
assembly line, or indeed of a streaming service's catalogue. This is, of course,
not some moralistic fable, but an instance of concrete social analysis. For
Lawrence Schehr, Dustan's is a reflection on the colonisation of the gay male
lifeworld by the form of capitalist social relations and the accompanying U.S.
cultural paraphernalia. Schehr writes:

> For Dustan, a series of spaces, objects, and pleasures relates to a repre-
> sentation and expansion of gay sexuality. They combine in the Holly-
> woodization of male homosexuality as a commodity; spaces –
> nightclubs, bars, backrooms, sex clubs, and the like – are publically
> marked either for sex or for encounters ... The images of this world are
> translated through a move toward a universalization of Western homo-
> sexuality, declined à *l'américaine* ... It is, after all, the McDonaldization
> of gay sex ...
>
> Dustan opines that counting becomes a natural thing in this world in
> which the exact image of the self must conform to the projected image

for that self as a sexual being ... [Counting is a matter of becoming irresistible, a 'machine of seduction':] he then gives a detailed description of his daily toilette, including the exact length to which he cuts his pubic hair.

(Schehr 2009, 21, 26)

The commodification of sex becomes the truth of the gay male lifeworld, and the commodification of self, the truth of the gay male subject: both trans-mutations carefully constructed to return to the subject an adulterated form of that enjoyment they have renounced in becoming a subject in the first place. Unsurprisingly, this restitution is done through consumerism, so thoroughly embraced that the subject comes to present themselves as commodity (incidentally, one way in which Lacan describes masochism; Lacan 2019, 123). In light of these reflections, I would not purport to suggest that Lacan in any way points the way forward – certainly not in respect of a queer lifeworld he was patently unfamiliar with, and probably also unsympathetic to. It is probably the case that he did not even think such a way might exist, since it is reasonably clear he mostly shared Freud's political pessimism. Rather, I want merely to suggest that reckoning with the subjective effects of capitalism and of scientific discourse's destabilising of traditional justifications of authority, and the seeming kinship of capitalism's injunction to a deceptive hedonism and its reduction of enjoyment to its counting-as-a-commodity, could become problems for queer theorists after the thrill of the 1990s wave of deconstruction has now decisively waned. This may allow us to establish a more honest and productive interlocution with Marxism (and psychoanalysis) than has hitherto been the case.

Notes

1 There is at least one exception to this claim, namely that psychoanalysis (rightly) proposes that politics and psychology or subjectivity feature, as it were, negatively in relation to the other. In other words, that the political field can never become closed in on itself, because something in subjectivity resists its closure and reopens it to radical contingency even in the most totalitarian of regimes (for instance, in the senseless violence that humans are capable of, which Freud saw fit to discuss as a metaphysical death drive); and that psychology and subjectivity, in turn, are not closed systems but interact, ultimately unpredictably, with politics (so, for example, gender is just as much the core of one's psychological identity as a sociopolitical, and therefore collective, construct).
2 'There are more things in heaven and earth, Horatio, than are dreamt of in your philosophy'.
3 I thank Prof. Rob Walker for this suggestion.
4 Lacan distinguishes, following the French and other romance languages, between knowledge as *connaissance* and knowledge as *savoir*. Very roughly stated, *connaissance* is the individual's consciously held understanding of an object – therefore implicitly deceptive – whereas *savoir* is the 'objective' knowledge embodied in a system and determining a given mode of subjective, political, economic, etc., functioning.

References

Althusser, Louis. 2001. 'Ideology and Ideological State Apparatuses'. In *Lenin and Philosophy and Other Essays*, translated by Ben Brewster, 1st ed., 85–126. New York: Monthly Review Press.

Berlant, Lauren. 2011. *Cruel Optimism*. 1st ed. Durham, NC: Duke University Press.

Bruno, Pierre. 2010. *Lacan passeur de Marx*. 1st ed. Toulouse: Érès.

Chitty, Christopher. 2020. *Sexual Hegemony: Statecraft, Sodomy, and Capital in the Rise of the World System*. Durham, NC and London: Duke University Press.

Coletti, Lucio. 1992. 'Introduction'. In *Early Writings*, by Karl Marx. London: Penguin.

Crenshaw, Kimberlé. 1989. 'Demarginalizing the Intersection of Race and Sex'. *University of Chicago Legal Form* 1: 139–167.

Declercq, Frédéric. 2006. 'Lacan on the Capitalist Discourse: Its Consequences for Libidinal Enjoyment and Social Bonds'. *Psychoanalysis, Culture, and Society* 11: 74–83.

D'Emilio, John. 1996. 'Capitalism and Gay Identity'. In *The Material Queer: A LesBiGay Cultural Studies Reader*, edited by David Morton, 1st ed., 263–272. Oxford: Westview Press.

Donahue, Charles. 2016. 'The Legal Background: European Marriage Law from the Sixteenth to the Nineteenth Century'. In *Marriage in Europe, 1400–1800*, edited by Silvana Menchi, 33–60. Toronto, ON: University of Toronto Press.

Duggan, Lisa. 2003. *The Twilight of Equality? Neoliberalism and the Attack on Democracy*. Boston, MA: Beacon Press.

Duggan, Lisa. 2012. 'After Neoliberalism? From Crisis to Organizing for Queer Economic Justice'. *Scholar & Feminist Online* 10 (1). https://sfonline.barnard.edu/after-neoliberalism-from-crisis-to-organizing-for-queer-economic-justice/.

Dustan, Guillaume. 2013. 'Dans ma chambre'. In *Oeuvres I*. Paris: P.O.L.

Ferguson, Roderick. 2003. *Aberrations in Black: Towards a Queer of Color Critique*. 1st ed. Minneapolis, MN: University of Minnesota Press.

Foucault, Michel. 1977. *Discipline and Punish: The Birth of the Prison*. Translated by Alan Sheridan. 1st ed. New York: Vintage Books.

Foucault, Michel. 1978. *The History of Sexuality I: The Will to Know*. Translated by Robert Hurley. 1st ed. New York: Pantheon Books.

Freud, Sigmund. 1955. 'Two Encyclopedia Articles'. In *The Standard Edition of the Complete Psychological Works of Sigmund Freud*, vol. XVIII, translated by James Strachey, 1st ed., 235–259. London: The Hogarth Press.

Freud, Sigmund. 1964. 'New Introductory Lectures on Psycho-Analysis'. In *The Standard Edition of the Complete Psychological Works of Sigmund Freud*, vol. XXII, translated by James Strachey, 1st ed., 3–183. London: The Hogarth Press.

Frith, Hannah. 2015. *Orgasmic Bodies*. Cham: Palgrave Macmillan.

Goux, Jean-Joseph. 1990. *Symbolic Economies: After Marx and Freud*. Translated by Jennifer Curtis. Ithaca, NY: Cornell University Press.

Hennessy, Rosemary. 1996. 'Queer Theory, Left Politics'. In *Marxism Beyond Marxism*, edited by Saree Makdisi, Cesare Casarino, and Rebecca Karl, 1st ed., 214–242. New York: Routledge.

Hocquenghem, Guy. 1993. *Homosexual Desire*. Translated by Daniella Dangoor. 1st ed. Durham, NC and London: Duke University Press.

Hocquenghem, Guy. 2022. 'A Shameless Transversalism'. In *Gay Liberation after May '68*, translated by Scott Branson, 107–118. Durham, NC and London: Duke University Press.

Jagose, Annamarie. 2012. *Orgasmology*. Durham, NC and London: Duke University Press.

Lacan, Jacques. 1962. *Le Séminaire de Jacques Lacan, Livre IX: L'Identification*. Unpublished.

Lacan, Jacques. 1992. *The Seminar of Jacques Lacan, Book VII: The Ethics of Psychoanalysis*. Translated by Dennis Porter. 1st ed. London: W.W. Norton.

Lacan, Jacques. 1998. *The Seminar of Jacques Lacan, Book XX: Encore*. Translated by Bruce Fink. New York: W.W. Norton.

Lacan, Jacques. 2001a. 'Préface à une thèse'. In *Autres écrits*, 1st ed., 393–402. Paris: Seuil.

Lacan, Jacques. 2001b. 'Radiophonie'. In *Autres écrits*, 1st ed., 403–446. Paris: Seuil.

Lacan, Jacques. 2001c. 'Réponses à des étudiants en philosophie'. In *Autres écrits*, 1st ed., 203–211. Paris: Seuil.

Lacan, Jacques. 2001d. 'Télévision'. In *Autres écrits*, 1st ed., 509–546. Paris: Seuil.

Lacan, Jacques. 2006. *Le Séminaire de Jacques Lacan, Livre XVI: D'un autre à l'autre*. Paris: Seuil.

Lacan, Jacques. 2007a. *The Seminar of Jacques Lacan, Book XVII: The Other Side of Psychoanalysis*. Translated by Russell Grigg. 1st ed. New York: W.W. Norton.

Lacan, Jacques. 2007b. *Le Séminaire de Jacques Lacan, Livre XVIII: D'un discours qui ne serait pas du semblant*. Paris: Seuil.

Lacan, Jacques. 2011. 'La Troisième'. *La Cause freudienne* 79 (3): 11–33.

Lacan, Jacques. 2014. *The Seminar of Jacques Lacan, Book X: Anxiety*. Translated by A.R. Price. Cambridge: Polity.

Lacan, Jacques. 2017. *Talking to Brick Walls*. Translated by A.R. Price. Cambridge: Polity.

Lacan, Jacques. 2019. *The Seminar of Jacques Lacan, Book VI: Desire and Its Interpretation*. Translated by Bruce Fink. 1st ed. Cambridge: Polity.

Lacan, Jacques. 2023. *Le Séminaire de Jacques Lacan, Livre XIV: La logique du fantasme*. 1st ed. Paris: Seuil.

Lacan, Jacques. 2024. *Le Séminaire de Jacques Lacan, Live XV: L'acte analytique*. Paris: Seuil.

Lacan, Jacques, and Madeleine Chapsal. 1957. 'Les clefs de la psychanalyse: Entretien avec Madeleine Chapsal'. *L'Express*, 31 May. https://www.lexpress.fr/actualite/societe/1957-lacan-livre-les-clefs-de-la-psychanalyse_2095718.html.

Lewis, Holly. 2016. *The Politics of Everybody: Feminism, Queer Theory, and Marxism at the Intersection*. 1st ed. London: Zed Books.

Lyotard, Jean-François. 1993. *Libidinal Economy*. Translated by Ian Hamilton Grant. Bloomington, IN: Indiana University Press.

Marshall, Bill. 1996. *Guy Hocquenghem: Theorising the Gay Nation*. London: Pluto.

Marx, Karl. 1969. *Value, Price, Profit*. New York: International Co.

Marx, Karl. 1976. *Capital*, vol. 1. Translated by Ben Fowkes. London: Penguin.

McGowan, Todd. 2016. *Capitalism and Desire*. 1st ed. New York: Columbia University Press.

Millar, Isabel. 2021. *The Psychoanalysis of Artificial Intelligence*. Cham: Palgrave Macmillan.

Miller, Jacques-Alain. 2024. 'Tout le monde est fou'. *La Cause du désir* 112 (3): 48–57.

Morton, David. 1996. 'Changing the Terms: (Virtual) Desire and (Actual) Reality'. In *The Material Queer: A LesBiGay Cultural Studies Reader*, edited by David Morton, 1st ed., 1–34. Boulder, CO: Westview Press.

Mouffe, Chantal, and Ernesto Laclau. 2001. *Hegemony and Socialist Strategy*. 2nd ed. London: Verso.

Penney, James. 2014. *After Queer Theory: The Limits of Sexual Politics*. London: Pluto Press.

Preciado, Paul B. 2018. *The Countersexual Manifesto*. Translated by Kevin Gerry. New York: Columbia University Press.

Rabaté, Jean-Michel. 2009. '68+1: Lacan's année érotique'. *Parrhesia* 6: 28–45.

Reich, Wilhelm. 2012. *Sex-Pol*. London: Verso.

Schehr, Lawrence. 2009. *French Postmodern Masculinities: From Neuromatrices to Seropositivity*. Liverpool: Liverpool University Press.

Sibalis, Michael. 2010. 'L'arrivée de la libération gay en France'. Translated by Nathalie Paulme. *Genre, Sexualité et Société* 3. https://journals.openedition.org/gss/1428.

Soler, Colette. 2016. *O que faz Laço?* Translated by Elisabeth Saporiti. São Paulo: Escuta.

Sous, Jean-Louis. 2017. *Lacan et la politique: De la valeur*. 1st ed. Toulouse: Érès.

Tomšič, Samo. 2015. *The Capitalist Unconscious*. 1st ed. London: Verso.

Tomšič, Samo. 2019. *The Labour of Enjoyment*. 1st ed. Berlin: August Verlag.

Vighi, Fabio, and Heiko Feldner. 2015. *Critical Theory and the Crisis of Contemporary Capitalism*. 1st ed. London: Bloomsbury Academic.

Žižek, Slavoj. 1989. *The Sublime Object of Ideology*. 1st ed. London: Verso.

Zupančič, Alenka. 2018. *What IS Sex?* 1st ed. Cambridge, MA: MIT Press.

Conclusion

For a Queerer Lacanism

I Whose Lacan?

One thing that emerges, I hope, clearly and unambiguously in this discussion of Lacan, queer theory, and sexual politics is that 'Lacan', much like 'man' and 'a woman' and, for that matter, 'queer', is nothing but a signifier (Lacan 1998, 39); and the order of the signifier has too many gaps in it to presume that there is any fixed and correct apportionment between signifier and signified, let alone one that allows us to deal with whatever escapes language. 'Lacan', it follows, means very different things to different people, and it is plainly the case that Lacan himself proposed various, often both concurrent and contradictory, theoretical systems – all of them equally riddled with holes. This is why Lacanian terms have such a dazzling polysemic quality to them, and why his statements can be puzzling even to those who have been reading him for years, and often decades: the (big O) Other is language, but also the earliest caretaker (as its 'depository') and the body (as its surface of inscription), just as it can be the Other sex (as what escapes the signifier); the (small o) other can be myself in the mirror or my fellow man, just as it can be the impossible object that falls away as a result of symbolisation (*objet a*), and so on. Similarly, 'Lacan' and 'Lacanian' can stand for the epitome of heteronormativity – there is but one law, and it states that a woman is a phallus to be exchanged among men – or for the proposition that this heteronormative fiction is a laughable sham – there is no Other of the Other; 'Lacan' can be a funny anecdote about psychoanalytic sessions lasting less than a minute, or a serious thinker of the deadlocks of analytic theory and technique; and so on.

Even so, there are some demonstrable interpretive problems in the major queer uses of Lacan. Chapters 1 and 2 took to task two leading queer scholars, Judith Butler and Lee Edelman, in respect of their interpretations of Lacan, who is undoubtedly one of their most important interlocutors and sources. I argued that if, as Butler holds, the Lacanian concept of the phallus is indeed the signifier of a heteronormative cultural norm (the carrier of the propositions 'I am owed a woman', 'I am owed to a man'), that is not all it is.

DOI: 10.4324/9781003424604-6

On the one hand, if the phallus is the signifier to a cultural norm, it is not that which imbues that norm with its power. Lacan ascribes that role to the father, a concept he will subject to relentless critique for two decades thereafter, and already in the seminar year following the classical statement of the Lacanian Oedipus in *Seminar V*, a fact Butler all but ignores. On the other hand, the phallus is not merely a signifier to a cultural norm. It is also a solution to a problem that is independent of it, namely the lack of grounding of the symbolic order to which humanity owes its purportedly exceptional rank among other animals, a lack the subject cannot but try to fill up with the avatars of their renounced enjoyment. A few implications follow; for instance, even if non- or less heteronormative societies are possible – which should of course be strived for – the underlying problem of enjoyment that motivates heteronormative social arrangements will remain forever intractable. More interestingly, the maintenance of a heteronormative social order is not merely a cultural matter to be resolved by cultural work, but is a much more intractable libidinal one. As Lacanian clinicians have been demonstrating, the progressive weakening of heteronormative social institutions is not unambiguous: despite the enormous violence and injustice they have historically sanctioned, Lacan allows us to see in them a standard collective solution to a problem they themselves did not create – and there does not seem to be another such collective solution to hand.

Lee Edelman, on the other hand, is much more attentive to the problematic of enjoyment in respect of a social order built around efforts to keep it at bay. However, I argued that Edelman remains too close to the European libertine tradition epitomised in the Marquis de Sade and repurposed by some of queer theory's antisocial heroes. Edelman's argument that the ethical duty befalling the queer person is to represent a sexual enjoyment that serves no productive or reproductive purpose is posed at the level of what psychoanalysts call the superego, which is precisely not the desire that psychoanalysis purports to speak of. For Lacan, the ethical stakes of the psychoanalytic experience cannot be resolved by recourse to the form of commandment, be that Kantian or Sadean (which, Lacan argues, amount to the same). Rather, the use Lacan makes of Kant, and of Sade's parody of him, is to delineate the floorplan, as it were, of the field of desire as it presents itself to us moderns. Psychoanalysis replaces the field of Kantian morality – guaranteed by the postulates of freedom, the immortality of the soul, and the God who will pronounce the Last Judgement, and striving towards the marriage of virtue and happiness in the *summum bonum* – with the place where desire is articulated, the order of the signifier framed by the fantasy of enjoyment. If '[t]he dimension of the signifier is … the very thing an animal finds itself caught up in while pursuing its object, in such a way that the pursuit of this object leads it into another field of traces', psychoanalysis' ethical goal is to confront the subject with the traces making up 'that indefinite chain of significations called destiny' (Lacan 2014, 66). It is the uncovering of whatever roots us in our peculiar fate – family myths and desires, cultural ideals, social contexts, and all the accidents of a human life – that is given priority in the ethics of psychoanalysis, and its imbrication with a question to be posed in a hypothetical beyond-death: 'have you acted in conformity with the desire that is in you?' (Lacan 1992, 314). That an analysand might be given the opportunity to sketch out an answer to this question before they die is undoubtedly one of the major ethical innovations of analysis.

Whatever their exegetical merit, queer theorists' creative misreadings of Lacan have been productive to the discipline and its critique of all things heteronormative. One of their major strengths is to make it clear that psychoanalytic knowledge has a necessary, rather than incidental, relation to society and to the image that psychoanalysis gives itself of society. Chapters 3 and 4 considered aspects of the account of society that Lacanian psychoanalysis works with and how it influences, or does not influence as it should, core psychoanalytic concepts, such as that of the father or that of enjoyment. The interrogation these chapters undertake is important in light of the macrosociological theses and political positions arising from contemporary Lacanian scholars and institutions. For example, many contemporary Lacanians espouse some variant of the thesis of the decline of the father (for discussion, see Zafiropoulos 2001; Tort 2007), whereby modern and contemporary changes to the hegemonic Western family form have led to the weakening or disappearance of paternity as a privileged relay for social authority. Other Lacanians prefer the notion of the decline of symbolic efficiency, whereby science and capitalism destroy traditional modes of human togetherness and cause symptoms of social isolation and unbridled enjoyment. The question as to whether these are defensible social theories in respect of contemporary sexuality and relational regimes therefore imposes itself.

Chapter 3 considered three forms of the Lacanian account of the father and of the phallus – the pivots of the child's resolution of the Oedipus complex – as implicating an underlying theory of society. I argued that contemporary Lacanians' disavowal of aspects of Lacan's conservatism, for instance in respect of a great many pronouncements he made that today we cannot regard as anything but homophobic, is damaging to our ability not only to honestly assess the clinical implications and societal assumptions of Lacanian theory but also to decide which parts of it are essential in the face of the major societal changes of the 20th and 21st centuries. So, for example, the thesis of the decline of the father only makes sense if it is read in relation to the earliest Lacan who, from 1938 until 1950, held on to the proposition that the Oedipus complex was a function of a set of social conditions, chief among which was the dominant form of Western families. This was itself a function of Lacan's adherence to Durkheim's theory that the Western family was contracting, having gone from larger, intergenerational and patriarchal households to more intimate, conjugal ones, and that its contemporary tendency was towards increased individualism, for instance in the recognition that mothers and children had individual rights that limited the father's authority. For the 1938–1950 Lacan, the conjugal family Durkheim described, made up of father, mother, and minor children, all the while holding an exceptional capacity to maximise the tension between repression and sublimation, was on course to disintegrate under the weight of the forces of 'progress' – by which he meant liberal individualism in its various guises – which would have increasingly pathological effects, not only in respect of character but also in respect of criminality and other alleged signs of social disintegration.

If Lacan's thesis at this time was that there was a set of phenomena that could be called the 'social conditions of Oedipalism', chief among which was the dominant family form, it follows that he was a relativist in respect of the Oedipus complex, and accordingly not a Freudian. He only partly retreats from this thesis during his classic period, in which he universalises the function of the father but makes it so abstract that it could notionally be fulfilled by any signifier elevated to the rank of a socially viable *point de capiton*. Functionally, the father at this stage is simply the operator of the subject's consent to the grounding fictions of their social group, a function modelled after Lévi-Strauss's structural interpretation of Mauss. However, this did not change the fact that Western societies, the grounding fictions of which can be broadly described as patriarchal, phallocentric, and heteronormative, could only countenance a father function that assured successful sexual normalisation – or, in other words, that produced virile heterosexual men and virginal heterosexual women. The dying breath of this interpretation will be *Seminar XIV*, which presents a somewhat caricatural theory of kinship as the means whereby men attempt to retrieve a masturbatory and homosexual enjoyment they renounced by means of the exchange of women.

However much one might agree that Lacan is a sharp critic of heterosexuality and that he followed Freud's problematisation of any notion of sexual normality, the fact remains that Lacan's social reflection throughout the first 30 years of his psychoanalytic career relies on the proposition that the core social institution in the West – the one without which there would simply be no society and accordingly the one towards which Oedipal normalisation contributes – is heteronormative kinship. Lacan's reliance on the hypothesis that heteronormativity is society-founding would be only briefly suspended by the events of May 1968. Faced with the radical demands of student protesters and the willing accommodation of workers and the French Communist Party, Lacan proposed several, sometimes prescient, sometimes rather strange political theses. Most important among these for contemporary Lacanians is the macro-historical argument Lacan proposes to the effect that modern science and capitalist social relations destroy traditional – that is, patro-phallocentric and heteronormative – forms of the social bond.

Lacanian commentators have generally accepted Lacan's take on this issue, but their theorisation of the social fails to acknowledge that the effects of science and capitalism over human sociality, desire, and enjoyment are not exclusively negative, in the sense of an undoing of heteronormative institutions without any replacement or remainder. Quite to the contrary, Lacan viewed the imbrication of scientific know-how and capitalist social relations as a novel regime whereby social control was assured directly through the creation and administration of desire and enjoyment. What we are faced with today, in other words, is not simply the result of the erosion of traditional heteronormative institutions buttressing the socius, and the generalisation of the scientific real to the detriment of a previously enchanted world, but primarily the proliferation of modes of generating and regulating desire and enjoyment that amount to new forms of the social bond. These, finally, should be analysed in their own right, and I provided a brief and impressionistic example of what such an analysis might look like in my consideration of how the gay male lifeworld mimics some procedures that Lacan describes as characteristic of the capitalist system.

I want to highlight a couple of substantive conclusions to this itinerary. First, and despite the implicit division of labour between practising analysts and cultural, social, or political queer and Lacanian scholars, the rapport between the Lacanian theory of subjectivity and its account of society is one of mutual, direct, and strict co-implication. In other words, the Lacanian theory of subjectivity is always already a social theory, whereas the Lacanian theory of society is always already a theory of subjectivity. It follows that, whenever one might find these two issues being discussed separately, one can be sure that some form of obfuscation is taking place. So, it is the case, for example, that Butler's too strictly social and cultural reading of Lacan is partial in that it cannot even begin to consider the subjective problems that the phallus and the father purport to solve in Lacan's account of the Oedipus complex. Butler's Lacan, in other words, is only half a Lacan, the half whose work is coterminous with Lévi-Strauss and his account of kinship. Lacanian clinicians, on the other hand, tend to make the opposite mistake: starting from a set of new symptoms betraying their analysands' difficulty in symbolising enjoyment, they content themselves with near-caricatural accounts of society that often boil down to elegies to some hallucinated ideal of the good old days of patriarchal authority under which such disorganisation would have been axiomatically impossible. Lacanians' Lacan, finally, is too often also a half Lacan: faced with contemporary forms of domination premised on the productive channelling of enjoyment rather than its prohibition, and therefore with the desuetude of a patro-phallocentric social theory, Lacanians proceed as if society had all but disappeared for the contemporary subject. What is at issue, however, is not that society has disappeared or that its symbols have become ineffective, but simply that it has changed – it is the average Lacanian's theory of it that has failed to keep up.

Second, there is a sexual politics to be found not only in Lacan's work but also in contemporary Lacanian practice. This conclusion, of course, follows directly from the last one: if Lacanian theory is subjective and social at once, and if speaking of the one means also speaking of the other, it follows that, for Lacanians, any change to society should entail a change to subjectivity, and therewith to their understanding of their practice and of its goal; and, conversely, that any change to their practice should have some grounding in an account of society. Furthermore, changes to society are always of necessity political, having to do with the way in which power is distributed and exercised among social actors, including in respect of sexuality – which, finally, makes the entire edifice political in some sense or another. This is not an abstract problem, but a crucial and concrete one, speaking not only to the major changes to sexuality and the dominant relational regimes of the developed West of the last century, but also to the clinic's rapport with the social. To exemplify this problem in somewhat stark terms: should a contemporary Lacanian analyst assume, as Lacan did, that one subsidiary or central goal in the analysis of a homosexual is to change his or her sexual practice, object-choice, or identification[1] (Lacan 2017, 190)? It is obviously the case that any answer to this question will be at least partly political and social, since it will have to do with the subsidiary question as to whether the concrete coordinates of how this or that analysand lives out their object-choice lead to a more or less liveable and enjoyable life within a given social setting. So, as I elaborate further down, contemporary Lacanians do not even wonder about the extent to which a homosexual analysand might be or become more open to heterosexual practices – and psychoanalysis properly understood can only be emphatically opposed to conversion 'therapies' – but they do make substantive judgements about whether their analysands' (homo)sexual practice is, for example, too dangerous or asocial. In sum, this means that their preconceptions as to what counts as too dangerous or asocial, and therefore what is less dangerous or asocial, come into play in each and every analysis they facilitate, just as Lacan's preconceptions came into play in his anti-Freudian *Seminar V* opinion that homosexuals are curable.

In light of these conclusions, it seems clear that queer theory can offer psychoanalysis what feminist and LGBT+ organising and thought have, in fact, always offered psychoanalysis: on the one hand, a critique of inessential psychoanalytic assumptions, those that psychoanalysis makes in relation to sexuality and society that are, in fact, a function of the reigning prejudices of a given state of a given society that has been de facto superseded; and, on the other hand, a catalogue and analysis of contemporary changes to the regulation of sex and kinship, to the differential ascription of social and economic vulnerabilities, etc., all of which engage, not incidentally but centrally, the very presuppositions of Lacanian psychoanalysis. Conversely, psychoanalysis can offer queer theory and other such militant disciplines not only many indispensable conceptual tools, but also a constant reminder that the socius simply cannot do away with the contradictions and impasses that define human life, most especially, though certainly not only, in respect of the erotic. Desire and enjoyment, as core Lacanian concepts, are important indexes of those contradictions and impasses, and also signal the hard limit of queer theory's radical social constructionism and antinormative sexual utopianism. As a final addendum to this book, I want to risk some further observations on the topic of how Lacanian psychoanalysts have been engaging with changing sexual and gendered landscapes, and in what respects, if any, they have been politicising their practice. A reflection that starts with a few remarks about politics and psychoanalysis.

2 Psychoanalysis and Politics

Psychoanalysis' rapport with politics and society has always been a vexing topic for psychoanalysts and psychoanalytic scholars alike, although political matters feature prominently, if sometimes implicitly, in Freud's work. Despite his well-known aversion to organised politics, for example, Freud himself did not hesitate to employ political and military metaphors in his description of the psychic apparatus (especially after the 1920s introduction of the second topography), while his early work often suggests that psychopathology could be a direct result of the strength and quality of the renunciations modern societies impose on their subjects. Sometimes Freud's statements in this latter respect verge on the militant. His '"Civilized" Sexual Morality and Nervous Illness', for example, comes incredibly close to a paraphrase of Marx's 'Critique of the Gotha Programme' in its denunciation of the unfair apportionment of the societal demand for renunciation:

> It is one of the obvious social injustices that the standard of civilization should demand from everyone the same conduct of sexual life – conduct which can be followed without any difficulty by some people, thanks to their organization, but which imposes the heaviest psychical sacrifices on others.
> (Freud 1959, 192)

> From each according to his ability, to each according to his needs!
> (Marx 1970, 27)

Despite the occasional militant statement, Freud took a kind of 'can't live with it, can't live without it' attitude towards society and politics: social life demands renunciation necessarily rather than incidentally, including and prototypically the renunciation of incest, and not all of us can bear it without important social or psychological sequelae. Solutions other than private, neurotic ones to excessive social demands do exist, and sometimes take their toll on social peace: some might turn to crime, immorality, or even to the philosophically elevated perversions of a Marquis de Sade, as ways of refusing to let go of enjoyment. Even so, Freud exempts some perversions – homosexuality foremost – from the negative connotations of the category, which suggests a certain ambivalence in his stance towards the asocial potential of sexuality. '[H]omosexuality', Freud famously writes to a concerned mother, 'is assuredly no advantage, but it is nothing to be ashamed of, no vice, no degradation, it cannot be classified as an illness' (Freud 1951, 786).

LGBT+ and queer thinkers and activists have long been attuned to the Freudian oeuvre's potential for the redemption of sexual minorities' seeming refusal to renounce their sexual attachments to people of their own gender or to their differently gendered ego-ideals. The men who were active in the gay liberation movement of the late 1960s and 1970s often describe their encounters with Freud, Wilhelm Reich, and Herbert Marcuse in liberating terms. As Jeffrey Escoffier, who more or less is representative of many intellectuals formed by gay liberation, writes: '[t]hese ideas reassured me that, as a queer, I was not destined for a socially meaningless life' (Escoffier 2018, 11). In this respect, gays and lesbians have always read Freud politically. There is no question, for them, that there is a politics to analysts' account of the Oedipus complex, for example, and they have always been attuned to psychoanalysts' and psychiatrists' shifting stances on the question as to whether or not their perversion was to be morally (or medically, which, in this and many other instances, amounts to the same thing) condemned.

This is not so for psychoanalysts themselves, who are notoriously circumspect when it comes to political matters. Freud himself became increasingly disillusioned with the political dimension of psychoanalysis as his work progressed. If one can read a certain militantism into works such as the *Three Essays* or '"Civilized" Sexual Morality', that is certainly no longer the case for his post-World War I work. The Freud of *The Future of an Illusion* has few hopes that psychoanalysis might critique, mitigate, let alone resolve, the problem of repression. In fact, repression is not even conceived as a problem anymore, but as part of a solution, and sometimes even as a justification for an enlightened elite's repression of the masses:

> It is only through the influence of individuals who can set an example and whom masses recognize as their leaders that they can be induced to perform the work and undergo the renunciations on which the existence of civilization depends … there are two widespread human characteristics which are responsible for the fact that the regulations of civilization can only be maintained by a certain degree of coercion – namely, that men are not spontaneously fond of work and that arguments are of no avail against their passions.
>
> (Freud 1961, 8)

It might well be surprising to hear this from the Freud who, not a decade earlier, had written in *Group Psychology* that the effect of identifying with a leader was, quite to the contrary, 'the weakness of intellectual ability, the lack of emotional restraint, the incapacity for moderation and delay, the inclination to exceed every limit in the expression of emotion and to work it off completely in the form of action' (Freud 1955, 117). Whatever the case, the only constant in Freud's work is an unwavering pessimism: even at his most militant, the political ideal of collective happiness remains stubbornly, structurally out of reach. The intractability of the human drive – in respect of aggressiveness, for example, or the ambivalence of any and all affective ties – seemed to Freud to suggest that the only political belief appropriate to the psychoanalyst would be a benign political indifference.

In the contemporary Lacanian field, however, Freud's political circumspection may no longer be the rule. French Lacanians, despite the de rigueur psychoanalytic political reticence, have been remarkably vocal about society and politics over the past few decades. Two themes approached by the publications of the École de la Cause freudienne (ECF), founded by Lacan's son-in-law, Jacques-Alain Miller, stand out in the political work produced by its analysts. On the one hand, French psychoanalytic discussion has closely followed, and participated in, debates relating to the legal regulation of kinship and sexuality, including the recognition of homosexual relationships and, more recently, the so-called trans* question. Psychoanalytic interventions into these debates prominently feature work on the contemporary family form, the LGBT+ movement, the clinic of sexual diversity, and the sociological, anthropological, and philosophical underpinnings of the psychoanalytic account of sexuality. On the other hand, French Lacanians have recently started taking an open political stance on more traditional, mainstream issues, particularly in response to the threat in the shape of Marine Le Pen, the far-right Front National candidate, during the 2017 presidential election (which independent centrist Emmanuel Macron ended up winning).

Although it is important to remember that the Lacanian psychoanalytic world is split into various institutions with no necessary presumption that there exists some unifying doxa among them, the Millerian camp is probably the strongest and most militant player among them, which makes its opinion on these matters arguably hegemonic. In respect of changes to the family and sexuality, ECF psychoanalysts have argued that psychoanalytic practice generally welcomes family and sexual diversity, even as they note the persistence of traditional family forms, ideologies, and inspirations, as well as the different subjective difficulties that 'new' family forms might pose (Vinciguerra 2007; Miller 2013). They do not, on the other hand, tend to approve of either the alternative social environments in which LGBT+ people transit, or the political positions of the LGBT+ movement, often reiterating the argument that all these spaces and movements do is provide an identificatory crutch that might give LGBT+ people some relief from anxiety, but that can only impede analytic work (Deffieux 2003; Miller 2003). This position sometimes translates into a quiet presumption that some traits associated with less heteronormative sexual identities, and especially with gay male sexuality – anonymity, the large number of partners, the occasional preference for unprotected penetrative sex, the avoidance of penetration altogether, etc. – are *ipso facto* harmful, and that any retreat from these practices signals a positive clinical development. Furthermore, analysts' acceptance of contemporary changes to gender and sexuality extends only insofar as they do not threaten what these analysts consider to be *passages à l'acte* aimed at abolishing or threatening sexual difference, which in practice has meant that they oppose surgical and hormonal gender-affirmative care for trans* people on often plainly transphobic grounds (Miller 2021; Miller and Millot 2022). So, for instance, an analyst might accept homosexuality as a normal sexual variant and even 'polite' transvestism as a normal sexual practice (meaning that they do not constitute symptoms in and of themselves, but only if the analysand speaks of them as symptoms), but will typically have trouble countenancing a trans person's demand for surgery or for puberty blockers, especially if they have not reached majority.

In respect of their positions on more 'traditional' political topics, a thesis has emerged, principally in the Millerian camp, that liberal democratic regimes are the only political forms compatible with psychoanalytic practice, and therefore that liberal democracy is the only real political system under which psychoanalysis might flourish (Miller 2017; for discussion Nobus 2020). This credo became a sort of core belief of the Millerian field during the course of the 2017 French presidential dispute, when it seemed as though Marine Le Pen stood a good chance of winning, and when the left-wing *France Insoumise* candidate Jean-Luc Mélenchon resisted endorsing Emmanuel Macron's candidacy. From a pragmatic electoral standpoint, Miller's political argument is of course banal and has faced many of us on the left (who vote) in the last decade: there are times when one must choose between the neoliberal (or the not-left-enough) candidate or party and the (far-)right one, and one may well accept the need to endorse the neoliberal-or-not-left-enough candidate or party because at least they do not openly oppose the basic formal structures of liberal democracy. By way of example, this conundrum has been posed in some form (depending on political system) in the elections pitting Trump and Clinton (United States, 2016), Macron and Le Pen (France, 2017 and again in 2024), Sunak and Starmer (United Kingdom, 2024), Trump and Harris (United States, 2024) with varying degrees of success (or of lesser failure). However, Miller made a wider theoretical point when he disqualified left-wing candidate Jean-Luc Mélenchon's arguments against endorsing Macron, which Gabriel Tupinambá summarises in the syllogism:

(I) psychoanalysis depends on freedom of speech, (II) only the State of Law guarantees this freedom, (III) both the radical Right as the radical

Left are willing to suspend the State of Law, hence (IV) to defend the practice of psychoanalysis is to fight against both of these political fields.
(Tupinambá 2019, 345)

What is interesting is not so much the Millerian argument per se (which is probably just a personal preference rephrased in Lacanese: Slavoj Žižek has claimed that it was well known in French Lacanian circles that Miller's electoral darling was centre-right candidate Sarkozy; Žižek 2021, xv), but rather that Miller did not take this political stance as a citizen. In fact, he mobilised the entire institutional apparatus of the ECF and of the World Association of Psychoanalysis around his argument, which even led to what Gabriel Tupinambá has called a 'smear campaign' against left-wing Lacanian thinkers (Tupinambá 2021, 7–8).

There is obviously ample room to question the positions taken by the Millerian camp on these issues. For one, some of these positions are demonstrably untrue. To take the 'psychoanalysis is only compatible with democracy' argument as an example, the first thing to note is that psychoanalysis can very well coexist with, and indeed thrive under, authoritarian regimes. It persisted under Nazi Germany – in a sense, it even Nazified itself with the acquiescence of Ernest Jones' International Psychoanalytic Association – just as it flourished under Latin American dictatorships (Brazil, Argentina). Psychoanalysts may even have collaborated with the agents of repression, and they certainly did in the Brazilian case (for a review of the literature, see Nobus 2020; for the Brazilian case, see Alves Lima 2021), such that it is difficult to see in what respect psychoanalysis would be incompatible with authoritarianism, which it plainly is not, or indeed why it would have some elective affinity with liberal democracies – which may be true in some cases, but certainly not all. The idea that psychoanalysis is incompatible with authoritarian regimes rests, more accurately, on a prior judgement as to what constitutes psychoanalysis, a judgement that includes the proposition that 'if it is practised under an authoritarian regime, it is not psychoanalysis, because psychoanalysis is subversive by definition and authoritarian regimes do not like subversion'. In this respect, analysts' argument is not empirical at all, but a matter of definition. Which means that it is an entirely meaningless argument in the absence of an agreement as to what constitutes psychoanalysis, democracy, or subversion – an agreement that has never existed, and probably one that cannot exist even and especially within the analytic field.

The problem cannot be chalked up to some psychoanalytic aversion to historical and empirical study, although that aversion exists, and is certainly part of an explanation. Lacanian positions in respect of contemporary sexual diversity sometimes also make little sense in light of these psychoanalysts' own theory and practice. Although Jacques-Alain Miller retreated from this argument in 2013, he had argued in 1997 that homosexual relationships should receive some form of legal recognition, in which he was reasonable enough, but for which he gives an interesting explanation. 'I am in favour', Miller writes, 'because I have clinically ascertained the authenticity of these relationships [*liaisons*] between [male] homosexuals' (Laurent 1997, 9, my translation). Setting aside the question as to what exactly might count as 'authenticity' for a psychoanalytic discourse in which every emotional tie can be presumed ambivalent, Miller goes on to claim that the recognition of homosexual relationships should not be called 'marriage', for the reason that 'we do not find', in these otherwise 'authentic' relationships between men, 'the demand for erotic fidelity' (Laurent 1997, 9, my translation). In short, gay men supposedly do not want to be monogamous, which means they should be barred from marriage. Anyone who has read any psychoanalytic literature will see the obvious arbitrariness of this argument, which bizarrely implies that straight couples who cheat are *ipso facto* 'psychoanalytically unmarried'. Not only does the psychoanalytic literature by no means sanction the equation marriage = erotic fidelity (as a matter of fact it is the impossibility of that fidelity that makes up the greater part of Lacanian theory, in a way, one might add, suspiciously consonant with the lax personal stance that Lacan, some of whose mistresses survived him, held towards that ideal), Miller does not even deign to raise the far more important question as to why his opinion as a psychoanalyst should even matter in respect of this obviously political issue (Eribon 2019). In which case, one must presume that he is not voicing his opinion as a psychoanalyst, but as a clinician with pretentions closer to those of a psychiatrist (the latter of which, finally, he is not).

In sum, not every reason given by these psychoanalysts to take up the political stances they claim are consistent (and, in respect of the democratic argument, the only consistent stance) with psychoanalysis is convincing. Faced with these arguable lapses in judgement by scholars and practitioners who one should not assume are simply ignorant, it may well be worth pondering what other reasons might inform their positions, if not the ones they offer explicitly. I think it would be dishonest to answer anything to this question other than that the Millerian camp have made these arguments not for any psychoanalytically defensible reason, but because they have come to subscribe to a more fundamentally conservative account of society, and that they are supported in their adherence to this conservative account of society by (to my mind, inessential) aspects of Lacan's work. It is therefore all the more concerning that parts of the Lacanian institutional apparatus may have been instrumentalised by these thinkers' increasingly non-psychoanalytic agenda.

This is not merely a political problem, such that one might simply say that psychoanalysts' political beliefs are only ever held as citizens and never as psychoanalysts, and such that what they think about politics does not matter to how well they can do what they do as analysts. Quite to the contrary,

Lacan himself militated against this argument. Speaking of ego psychology in *Seminar VIII*, Lacan characterises his *Seminar* in these terms:

> Regarding what I am endeavoring to do here, one might say – with all the caveats implied by it – that I am attempting to provide an analysis, in the strict sense of the term, of the analytic community insofar as it is a mass organized by the analytic ego-ideal, such as it has in fact developed in the form of a certain number of mirages [especially that of the 'strong ego'] …
>
> For the analyst himself is inscribed in and determined by the effects that result from the analytic mass – by which I mean the mass of analysts – given the current state of their constitution and their discourse.
>
> (Lacan 2015, 335)

There is, therefore, a rapport between the state of the 'analytic mass' and the practice of psychoanalysis. One can therefore assume that it is the task of the psychoanalyst to continuously critique not only their practice and its theoretical bases, but also the form of the social bond they participate in alongside other analysts, out of which they themselves arose in their capacity as analysts. If this bond acquires a political meaning, for instance in the proposition that 'the psychoanalyst is a centrist democrat because psychoanalysis only functions under centrist democracies', that meaning will thereby be in direct relation to, and have a bearing upon, every other aspect of analysis. It is at least arguable, then, that the appropriate Lacanian stance before the form of the social bond formed among Millerian analysts' new political militancy can only be that of a self-critique as ruthless as Lacan's critique of the psychoanalytic movement of his time.

In light of these issues, it becomes relevant to ask whether the contemporary Lacanian movement, if one heuristically considers Jacques-Alain Miller and the institutions that generally defer to him as privileged representatives of it, are sufficiently Lacanian. I believe that the only answer consistent with the discussion I have presented in this book is negative. Whole swathes of the contemporary Lacanian movement are not sufficiently Lacanian, in other words, and it is at least arguable that their becoming more Lacanian might require them to think more queerly about their own discipline and practice. In concluding this book, I want to exemplify this argument by paying closer attention to how contemporary French Lacanians have been treating the issue of sexual and gendered diversity in their late 20th and 21st century work. Specifically, I will try to demonstrate in the next section that, despite the correct theoretical arguments that the Millerian camp has advanced to the effect, for instance, that conjugal heterosexuality cannot be taken as the standard sexual solution in psychoanalysis, whenever Millerians are faced with a concrete challenge to traditional gendered and sexual norms, they tend to ratify these norms implicitly against that challenge. This tendency has more benign versions, in the case of homosexuality, and more malign versions, in the case of trans* identities, but it unambiguously points towards a need for greater self-critique on Lacanians' part. To indulge in a little Lacanian cliché, it may be reasonable to speak of a need to return to Lacan, as he himself once returned to Freud.

3 What Is Lacanian …

The Millerian psychoanalytic camp has paid significant attention to the issue of sexual and gendered diversity, including most notably the theory and clinic of homosexuality, the politics of the (homosexual) family, and the so-called trans* issue. Much worthwhile work has emerged from their discussions, as a brief look at the editions of the ECF's institutional journal editions dedicated to 'The Homosexual Unconscious' (1997), 'Gays in Analysis?' (2003), 'the Residual Family' (2007), and others show. The developing stance on homosexuality found an important negative summation in a cautionary letter against the use of psychoanalytic knowledge in the French *mariage pour tous* debates of the early 2010s, signed by many French psychoanalysts. This letter, penned by Miller, states quite simply that psychoanalytic theory and practice provide no support to the proposition that marriage ought to be restricted to a couple formed by a man and a woman, which is a thesis taken from the book of Genesis rather than from Freud. Lacanian psychoanalysis, the letter goes on, does not see in the Name-of-the-Father an anthropological invariant, nor does it sanction the imaginary belief in a complementarity between men and women, a presumption that Lacan's work clearly and consistently militates against. This means, as Miller puts it elsewhere, that the normal Oedipal solution is not qualitatively different to perverse solutions to the lack of the sexual rapport – it is one solution among others (Miller 2003). It is up to each subject, the letter concludes, to find their own way in respect of desire, and a religious, heteronormative, conjugal solution to the problem of finding one's way cannot be presumed to be universal or indeed universally applicable (Miller 2013). In this sense, one might surmise, psychoanalysis should keep apace with societal developments having to do with gender, sexuality, and kinship, since these developments do change the nature of the subjective solutions arrived at by their analysands, and indeed the goals of analysis.

Miller's letter might seem to constitute a sort of last word on the matter of gay marriage for Lacanian psychoanalysis, but it makes no positive claim in respect of any other aspect of the sexual politics of homosexuality as viewed by psychoanalysis. While the letter's silence on this issue is probably more consistent with psychoanalytic theory and with its general political stance than the prior writings, the fact remains that Miller's school does make positive claims about the sexual politics of homosexuality in its prior work, and that these claims are not without specifically political problems. These are partly exemplified by the obvious arbitrary of such propositions as Miller's 1997 'yes, let them get together, but not marry, since apparently most of them are in open relationships', from which he correctly retreats in the 2013 letter, but they include a routine condemnation of the gay and lesbian community and movement (Laurent 1997). The gist of this condemnation is interesting in that it can be seen as a version of the homonormativity argument in queer theory: the signifier 'gay', Miller and other analysts suggest, is a master signifier cementing a group effect mediated by capitalist social relations and the globalisation of U.S. lifestyles. Like all group effects, it is destined to foster resistance to, and ultimately fall away through, psychoanalytic work. A short 2003 piece by Jean-Pierre Deffieux, with the incredibly gauche title '*The Gay Way of Life* and psychoanalysis' (italicised English in the original), makes this point clearly and directly:

> The question ... is of knowing what collective form has instituted itself around this signifier [gay]. It is a complex question because, on the one hand, we find in it the Freudian dimension of the collectivising ego ideal of the *Massenpsychologie* [group psychology] – the instituted manifestation of *gay pride* in many countries of the world, the creation of the pride flag, speak of this sort of identification.
>
> But, more fundamentally, what this signifier has constituted over the course of decades is a collective of consumers of identical products, it's far from concerning only the sexual [*le sexuel*] ... clothing brands, diets, interior design and furnishing, the mode of travel, etc. ...
>
> To begin an analysis is, for a gay [*pour un gay*] a choice that almost always changes, sooner or later, his relation to the community, if only because the entrance into analysis ... leads the subject to expect a response from that Other, which does not really correspond with the gay position.
>
> (Deffieux 2003, 22, my translation, emphasis in the original)

A few motifs in this piece can be taken, I think, as representative of the Millerian stance on (or against) the gay movement. The title of the piece already makes the point that contemporary gay identity is not a French or European construct, but rather a U.S. import. *The Gay Way of Life* is obviously a play on the better-known 'American way of life', an ideological construct that one might more or less identify with some vague notion of the U.S. ethos of capitalist free enterprise and the pursuit of an individual happiness basically reducible to relentless consumerism. Much like its national counterpart, the 'gay way of life' is understood to be a somewhat paradoxical communal identity (the reference here is to Freud's *Massenpsychologie*) centred around consumerist individualism and a set of shared, quasi-national symbols: what gives consistency to the gay community is not only the flag, the pride slogan, etc., but also and more importantly the community's patterns of consumption embodied in allegedly standardised modes of dress, preferred gym memberships, etc.

If one's allegiance to the gay community is, in this sense, a group effect and, moreover, a group effect that is 'libidinally consumerist', so to speak, it is guilty of the two cardinal Lacanian sins, namely giving up on one's desire in favour of an identification to a collective master signifier, and buying into the 'fake surplus-enjoyment [*plus-de-jouir*]' that is offered to us in the form of commodity and gadget (and therefore denying castration). The signifier 'gay', Miller writes in the same dossier, follows 'the same procedure as Alcoholics Anonymous – it takes care of castration anxiety with a master signifier' (Miller 2003, 50, my translation) and, one might add, it also helps the subject to escape a form of enjoyment taken to be a priori harmful (as the parallel with alcoholism makes clear – it is unclear whether what is harmful is gay people's sexuality per se or the consumerism it is modelled after). Accordingly, 'a gay's' entrance into analysis cannot but problematise the subject's adherence to their gay identification, since entry into analysis questions both the presumption that identification can deliver the truth to desire and the presumption that enjoyment can be procured through consumption or through 'frenetic' sexual activity, sidestepping castration and the entire problematic of loss and sexual difference. In place of these two presumptions, analysis offers the operative illusion of transference (the idea that there is a truth to one's desire, and that this truth is known by a subject more or less embodied by the analyst) and the suspension of established modes of enjoyment during the session (the fundamental rule stating that one must speak, and only speak, what comes to mind) as supports of a newfound desire to know one's unconscious.

Deffieux leaves open the possibility that the gay analysand might retain a connection to 'the community', but notes that the nature of this connection will certainly change as the subject questions their adherence to the image of the good life that their gay identification promises. This questioning will not, in most cases, be accompanied by a change in object choice – psychoanalysis does not purport to 'cure' homosexuals of their homosexuality, to the contrary of Lacan's own explicit opinion to the effect that they are perfectly curable (Lacan 2017, 190) – but at the very least it is likely to accompany an increase in the joy [*gaieté*] possible to the analysand. The principle guiding analytic work in this respect is not the analysand's conformity to a pre-established normative and communitarian sexual position, whether gay or straight, nor their orderly progression through a series of predetermined (oral, anal, etc.) phases, but rather arriving at the 'best possible' position for that analysand's subjective structuring. As Miller explains, analysts search for

> the point where the patient accords with himself, with his being, and we
> consider that each subjective position can find its point of equilibrium ...

its best impasse ... We say he develops his possibilities, that he manages to work, to love, to enjoy [or to come, *jouir*], etc.

(Miller 2003, 48, my translation)

Miller's is a beautiful statement of principle, even if it is buttressed by a somewhat suspect social theory (largely reducible to the proposition that capitalism and science undo traditional forms of the social bond; see Chapter 3) and a general lack of interest in the debates that take place within the LGBT+ movement. It does not, however, translate into the proposition that psychoanalysis is queer, in an antinormative sense, or indeed neutral in respect of the individual, social, and medical concepts of the good (of the person, of society, of the organism). The case reports accompanying the 2003 dossier implicitly concur that a successful analytic itinerary should thicken, so to speak, the analysand's social bond in a rather traditional (psycho-analytically) sense, particularly by allowing them to have penetrative sex with a stable partner, to love another person continuously rather than merely have sex with multiple and fleeting partners, and to sustain gainful and socially valued work. So, Hervé Castanet's (2003) analysand Justin's progress comes in the form of a new male partner's demand to be penetrated, which disturbs the cycle of anonymous cruising consisting of mutual masturbation Justin had been stuck in after the break-up of a prior heterosexual marriage. Jac-queline Dhéret's (2003) Julien is a leather fetishist whose sexual activity consists in passively being masturbated by anonymous men who donned the (Tom of Finland-like) insignias of hypermasculinity, and his progress in analysis is described vaguely as that 'his sexual activity changed' upon taking up a professional role he had abandoned to become a priest. Meanwhile, Massimo Recalcati's (2003) Riccardo is negatively judged for his exclusively masturbatory sexual activity, supported by fantasies of fellatio. He manages to become more assertive at work, but Recalcati appears disappointed about the lack of change in Riccardo's sexual activity. In sum, changes away from solitary or otherwise unsettling and unconventional enjoyment are seen as positive by the analysts, and failure to effect change is viewed as negative. These are not unreasonable opinions; indeed, most people may well agree with these analysts' assessments of their analysands' journeys; however, they are judgements that betray a set of substantive goals to the analytic itinerary that are not immediately reducible to Miller's statement of principle that each subjective structure has a 'best impasse', a best 'know-how' with the symptom, and so on, since nothing could possibly buttress an analyst's jud-gement that it is not the best possible impasse for someone that they go to leather bars to be masturbated by hypermasculine men besides some set of criteria external to analysis. What could 'best' even mean, if not that?

Despite the fancy rhetoric, then, Lacanian psychoanalysts' judgement on the success or otherwise of their analytic work with these gay men is clearly measured by their analysands' increasing capacity to form responsible, stable, and pleasurable bonds with other people. In other words, however much Lacanians might retreat from this suggestion, what seems to guide their clinical judgement in these cases where homosexuality comes front and centre is a rather traditional, dare I say simply reasonable, set of concerns – whether the analysand can sustain gainful employment, maintain a satisfying social life, etc., and indeed a very traditional psychoanalytic motif that has gone by such names as 'genitality' and 'oblativity', or the capacity to love another person (minus the requirement that such a person be of the other gender) selflessly, responsibly, cooperatively, and with appropriate recognition of their subjectivity. Even if this conclusion does not sound all that Lacanian, it seems clear that the Millerians are at least willing to extend homosexuals some goodwill.

4 ... And What Is Not

At the other end of the spectrum, Miller's goodwill flies out the window entirely when it comes to the demands of trans* people. If Miller was willing to countenance the proposition that psychoanalysis does not enforce normative standards in respect of object choice and sexual identity, that sexuation is a problem even to the most normatively inclined subject, that there is no preordained rapport between men and women, that masculinity and femininity are both symbolic fictions reliant on the phallic signifier, and other Lacanian truisms, whenever the supposedly natural body and its strict sexual dimorphism is in question, psychoanalysis itself, in its very essence, is threatened. It is worth quoting one of Miller's interviews on this topic at length:

> Today, after the political victory of homosexuals, the question moves on to the trans. We know them from our consulting rooms, from institutions, we see them one by one, we find them suffering, fragile beings, sometimes suicidal, and it is a question whether doctors and surgeons should intervene. We know that [trans* people] may be led to taking hormones of the opposite sex for their whole lives, leading sometimes to surgical complications. These are beings who will be under medical surveillance their whole lives ... this picture contrasts clearly with the style of trans activists' demand. They say: 'it's not a pathology, it's only a pathology because of you, because you make it a pathology' ...
>
> In the trans movement, in fact, it is necessary to listen to the *parlêtres* [the speaking-beings], it is necessary to listen to people, it is necessary to listen to children ... but at the same time it is forbidden to interpret. If the four-year-old says 'I want to be a girl' and you say: 'well he is saying this now, will he say it later? What is it that he understands by "girl"?' Etc you are out, because you have had the gall of putting in question what he has said. It's like an infraction of his human rights and therefore you are already a reactionary, already in the far right, you want to

subjugate [*dominer*] him ... This break between the listening to which we give all our assent and the interpretation we forbid ... I would say it's mortal for psychoanalysis ... It's what we have seen with the documentary [*Little Girl*, dir. Sébastien Lifshitz, 2020] ... [which] truly is proof of a very extensive trans offensive, that has powerful relays in our media ...

I hold the property of myself, and everything is a social construct ... this started with a treatise, a little American book on social construction, published in 1966 [presumably Berger and Luckmann's *The Social Construction of Reality*] ... a social construction that makes the natural given be considered as an illusion. We have a subject that has no more natural given, that has annulled, annihilated, the natural given.

(Miller and Millot 2022, 158–60, my translation)

These fragments make for difficult reading, especially when compared with the goodwill extended to homosexuals since as early as 1997. Some things might be noted from the outset without the aid of the trans* thinkers and activists Miller is seemingly ignorant of, and against whom one might reasonably presume he would be biased anyway. In no particular order, some common sense and/or psychoanalytic objections to Miller's opinion here might include the following:

- Miller assumes that the subset of trans* people French psychoanalysts tend to see is representative of the whole population of trans* people. This is an obvious selection bias, one that has coloured much psychoanalytic thinking on sexual diversity, for instance in its presumption that there was a natural affinity between psychosis and male homosexuality (for this bias in respect of male homosexuality, see Lewes 1999).
- Miller assumes that the poor situation he finds his trans* patients in is wholly attributable to something about the trans* condition itself, and not at all related to the social reaction to transness: for example, the fact that trans* people are very often bullied in educational and family settings, kicked out of their homes, forced to become economically independent at a young age, discriminated against in formal employment, forcibly engaged in informal and often criminalised work, vilified in the media and in specialist literature, subject to transphobic violence, etc., all of which are factors denying trans* people the thickness of the social bond that psychoanalysts tacitly aim at in their work with non-heterosexuals.
- Miller assumes that it is consistent with a psychoanalyst's task to pronounce on the appropriateness or otherwise of one's request for transition (I would say, quite to the contrary, that a psychoanalyst who consents to make that determination is already not acting as an analyst (see, on this point, Gherovici 2010, 14–15).

- Relatedly, Miller fails to distinguish between the task of the doctor and the task of the psychoanalyst. Knowing what is good for a patient is a doctor's job, but most certainly not an analyst's. The analyst's task is to lead the analysand to a sufficiently satisfactory enunciation of their unconscious desire and, at least in respect of Lacan's major theoretical statements (*Seminars VII* and *XV* being the controlling instances here), there is relatively little wiggle room to the definition. It follows that the two positions – doctor/therapist and analyst – may sometimes be at odds, and therefore that Miller is arguably speaking from the position of a medical doctor or therapist and not as an analyst.
- Miller misconstrues the psychoanalytic concept of interpretation, which is not about determining for the analysand the truth of what is being said in their words despite their conscious intention, but rather about generating subjective effects by opening up a space for the analysand to interpret their own message, spoken back at them.
- Miller presumes that a subgroup that is consistently discriminated against on the grounds of their gender identity has some sort of media conglomerate in its pocket and seems to be quite lax in respect of what kind of evidence is sufficient to prove this point (more on this point below).
- Miller assumes that the specific situation of trans* people is in some sense an existential threat to psychoanalysis, which, at a minimum, is a claim that requires some more explanation than one reliant on a psychoanalytically erroneous concept of interpretation.
- Miller has recourse to a notion of 'nature' or 'the natural given' [*le donné naturel*] that is plainly anti-psychoanalytic. One wonders what he would say to Lacan's 'man and a woman ... are nothing but signifiers' (Lacan 1998, 39).
- Miller misinterprets the notion of social constructionism as a form of idealism when he claims that social constructionists believe nature to be an illusion. The claim, more accurately, is that nature – not simply as it is, but as an object knowable to a human being – is obviously not independent from how people speak about nature at any given stage of scientific knowledge.

In brief, it is difficult to consider Miller's opinion as psychoanalytically sound. At the very least, one would be perfectly justified in asking him to explain – as a psychoanalyst and to other psychoanalysts – how he might respond to these very simple objections, which can be raised against him by any psychoanalytically informed reader or practitioner. Now, with some input from queer and trans* perspectives, Miller should also be challenged on a few other grounds:

- Miller cites, in this interview, French psychiatrist Colette Chiland, who has characterised gender-affirming care in these terms: 'The fact that the medical profession offers the possibility of sex conversion … imprisons [trans* people] in their crazy dream and closes the path of wisdom to them' (Chiland 2003, 165). Chiland has, more recently, argued that the goal of some fantasised cabal of 'neo-feminists' is to abolish sexual difference and therefore to deny 'biological reality', and furthermore that these (largely hallucinated) crazed feminists have declared war on heterosexuality and heterosexuals (Chiland 2015). These are both well-established right-wing rhetorical devices mobilised to disqualify queer, feminist, and trans* thinkers who find the concept of gender useful to analyse and challenge social structures that systematically disadvantage women and sexual minorities (Butler 2024).

- The interview is given alongside Catherine Millot, who is infamous among queer and trans* scholars for having drawn a too-strict association between trans* identities and psychosis. Millot's core theoretical source is Lacan's discussion of Schreber, who should certainly not be taken as typical of the trans* experience (Millot 1990; see, for a review of the literature, Coffman 2022).
- Miller assumes that transness is a pathology to be corrected, rather than, for instance, a possible, and possibly liveable, variation in one's ego-ideal.
- Miller resorts to a tactic of fearmongering whereby some shadowy trans* cabal would be attempting to manipulate the medical and psychiatric establishment into opposing good common-sense, which is also a well-established far-right tactic. He cites as evidence a single documentary (*Little Girl*, dir. Sébastien Lifshitz, 2020) and a known anti-trans 'charity' (La Petite Sirène) whose founders and main spokespersons should be regarded with far more circumspection, if not suspicion, than he does (Fassin 2023).
- Miller's argument that the trans* movement tends towards an abolition of interpretation is not only a misapprehension of the psychoanalytic concept of interpretation. It is probably also Miller's way of repurposing the very arguments he had rejected in the case of homosexuals, those having to do with the universality of the Name-of-the-Father and of the Oedipus complex as heterosexualising. In this sense, the alleged trans* demand to abolish sexual difference (which is, at any rate, wrongly attributed) would be intrinsically inimical to a psychoanalysis that can only think itself in terms of the traditional Oedipus complex.

In brief, there are enough elements in the interview I have been commenting on to cement the impression that Miller does not discuss the trans* phenomenon from a psychoanalytic perspective, let alone from a defensible Lacanian one. Rather, Miller uses Lacanian theory retrospectively to justify a position he has already chosen on other grounds, which, from the tone and style of this interview and other interventions, seem to be personal and political, as well as generally conservative and transphobic. The longer-form piece 'Docile to Trans', written against Paul B. Preciado's *Can the Monster Speak?*, is a case in point: even if one concedes that Preciado's intervention, pronounced before an audience of ECF psychoanalysts, was calculated to be polemical and provocative, Miller's response is written in such relentlessly mocking tone and with such apparent pride in his own ignorance of the issues he addresses that one would be forgiven for doubting his good faith (Miller 2021; Preciado 2021). As a side note, it should be added that Preciado relates that a psychoanalyst in the audience even called on her colleagues to stop listening, accusing Preciado of being 'a Hitler' to the auditorium's applause. It takes some goodwill to presume that there is a deeper meaning to be recovered in what is likely no more than garden variety transphobia but, in fact, the analyst in question was reciting another well-known French Lacanian's overtly homophobic rant against the recognition of homosexual relationships: 'to give homosexuality the status of a family is to put the democratic principle in service of a fantasy. It is fatal insofar as the law [not Oedipal law but positive law, *le droit*], founded on the genealogical principle, would then give place to a hedonistic logic inherited from Nazism [*héritière du nazisme*]' (Legendre, cited in Perreau 2003, my translation).

Despite many Lacanians' best efforts, and as many other thinkers have quite reasonably argued, I do not think that psychoanalysis in general, and Lacanian psychoanalysis in particular, are intrinsically inimical to sexual and gendered diversity, or that their theoretical apparatus and clinical practice are ultimately reducible or restricted to heteronormative accounts of the Oedipus complex. However, as I hope to have shown in the two preceding sections, there is a perfectly feasible case to the effect that, despite Millerian Lacanians' grand statement of principle, some of them do conceive of their practice as so inimical and so reducible, if not unambiguously in respect of homosexuality, certainly when it comes to trans* lives. One would be forgiven the impression that some among them even seem to think of themselves as the guardians of a set of traditional values, and of a natural order, which any defensible interpretation of Lacan's work should take to be dead and buried. In light of this discussion, it strikes me as imperative that Lacanians firmly denounce the use of their discipline and practice towards reactionary ends, just as it is imperative that they acknowledge that their political positions are undertaken as citizens and not on behalf of psychoanalysis, and finally that their position as citizens is not indifferent to their work with their analysands – such that it can and must be subject to a critique as rigorous as the one they undertake in respect of their theory and practice. As the examples of Patricia Gherovici (2010) and other self-consciously non-transphobic work by Lacanian clinicians (Gozlan 2015) demonstrate abundantly, this is not only possible but also clinically desirable and consistent with Lacan's own work.

5 A Couch for Queers

I wish to conclude this book with a brief statement of principle. It is true that, as Tim Dean put it more than two decades ago, 'hostility toward psychoanalysis remains a sign of allegiance, a necessary credential for one's political identity as lesbian or gay' (Dean 2000, 5). It is also true that anyone who sees themselves as part of the LGBT+ acronym and is hostile towards psychoanalysis has good historical and theoretical reason for that hostility. However, the opposite contention is also arguable, and indeed persuasive, namely that the contemporary tolerance and even acceptance of those of us who identify as LGBT+ is at least partly due to the psychoanalytic problematisation of the notion of sexual normality. Not only that – psychoanalysis is also undoubtedly the only practice currently available in the catalogue of 'mental health' offerings (although 'mental health' is not what psychoanalysis itself offers) that might systematically allow a gay subject to interrogate their desire otherwise than merely or primarily as a member of the gay community. This is an important aspect of the psychoanalytic clinic, and it is an important methodological caution that psychoanalysis brings to scholarship concerned with sexuality. 'Gay', whatever else it might be to each of us, is primarily a collective construct that sexual minorities have used, and continue to use, to make political demands; the moment it morphs into an overarching identification, into what queer theorists call an 'identity', there is sure to be a betrayal of desire.

It is perhaps exemplary (although very much anecdotal) of this betrayal that what strikes me as the 'standard' coming out narrative today is pitched as though the acquisition of the signifier 'gay' were a revelation of a deep truth, one that will, from that moment on, come to (have) define(d) every aspect of one's life. There is always, it seems, an aha moment in which the signifier 'gay' is adopted as an overarching grid making sense of the subject's sexuality from the beginning, a transition between 'I have always known I was attracted to boys or girls' and 'I am gay'. As any homosexual who has found themselves on the couch long enough can testify to, however, that collective signifier does not provide any sort of truth about oneself, but merely one more or less convenient solution to a problem that is much more complicated than simply naming what one has always already been, what desires one was supposedly born with, or what essence one may have been bequeathed by a capricious nature. As Leo Bersani put it decades ago, the fact that one might be appropriately described as gay does say something about oneself, but nothing all that interesting. 'Even if we are straight or gay at birth', Bersani writes, 'we still have to learn to desire particular men and women, and not to desire others; the *economy* of our sexual drives is a cultural achievement' (Bersani 1995, 64, emphasis in the original); and the history of gay thought seems to prove that it has been all too easy to forget that, if there is such a thing as a method to uncovering the history of the renunciations and fixations that make up the economy of the sexual drives, it is psychoanalysis.

In this sense, despite the justifiable distaste that LGBT+ people and sometimes even queer theorists entertain towards psychoanalytic thinking and practice, psychoanalysis is a *sine qua non* to any inquiry about sexual diversity that is not content to reiterate our ambient common sense that 'gay is OK' and other platitudes of the 'born this way' and 'gay rights are human rights' era. These are important political and cultural slogans, but they should not purport to monopolise the field of what counts as a legitimate sexual politics, let alone a legitimate sexual identity, for those who fail to conform to a heteronormative caricature of sexuality. Psychoanalysts are right in their suggestion that identificatory handles such as 'gay', through the enormous cultural and political labour that has been placed in them, have become means through which one might stop thinking, and ultimately arrest the ability of truth to generate subjective effects. Rephrased in psychoanalese, 'gay' may have become something like a master signifier: it has come to provide those who would see themselves in that designation with an ego-ideal capable of making them feel loveable before a notional gaze. This may well have pacifying effects, allowing them to deal with the anxiety that comes with the lack or inadequacy of other such labels besides those of heteronormative heterosexuality. Yet, as Lacan made it clear, pacification is not and should not be the goal of a psychoanalytic itinerary: there are no guarantees that the pursuit of knowledge of one's desire will be pleasant or peaceful, nor does its ultimate statement usually result in some zen-like, post-analytic bliss, despite Lacan's famous but cryptic and misleading musings on the experience of the drive after the traversing of the fantasy (Lacan 1978, 273–4).

Even so, it is important to reiterate that this argument does not disqualify the political work that the signifier 'gay', or, for that matter, other collective signifiers such as 'worker', does. This is the greatest mistake that psychoanalysts commenting on the new landscape of sexual and gendered practice and identity, and on politics more generally, make. They correctly diagnose a too-strict individual identification to a signifier such as 'gay' as problematic in respect of the analytic itinerary, but they extend that argument illegitimately into the political and social arena, as if the fact that a signifier may pose resistance to the analytic itinerary were sufficient reason to disparage that signifier politically. In doing so, they forget two crucial things: first, the limits of their practice and expertise, since psychoanalysis is emphatically not politics; and, second, a point that their own theoretical framework forces them inexorably to accept, namely that it may well be that the signifier 'gay' might be a way to assuage anxiety by avoiding some stubborn real, but that 'straight' (as well as 'man', 'woman', etc.) does exactly the same work. To subject one to critique and fail to mention the other is therefore already to take a heteronormative position stating that 'straight' is, for whatever reason, a less reprehensible mode of avoidance of the real than 'gay'. Perhaps this is because psychoanalysts believe that 'straight' is less political, since heterosexuality has never been forced to argue for its legitimacy – but the entirety of the sociology of sexuality, including, of course, queer theory, is there to disprove that presumption.

In this sense, and although I recognise the great difficulty in this procedure, it strikes me as absolutely crucial that queer theory, psychoanalysis, and the contemporary politics of sexuality should increasingly be thought of together, rather than in isolation. It is clear that each field still has something to learn from the others, and it is clear too that a greater interface among them could only turn out to be productive. At the very least, it seems to me that such an interface might force each field to more honestly reckon with its own presuppositions, and to discard what presuppositions no longer serve it. I have tried to work through some general issues posed by this triangulation of sorts, focusing on some core points of mutual misunderstanding and (sometimes wilful) ignorance of one field of the others. Yet this book is only a very preliminary effort in what should strike psychoanalysts and queer scholars alike as a more important task posed to their disciplines by the disorientating effects – some salutary, some not so much – of capitalist, scientific modernity. The founding act of Lacan's school speaks of 'a duty that befalls' psychoanalysis 'in our world' (Lacan 2001, 229, my translation). Lest psychoanalysis become the contemporary echo of an archaic phallocentrism, and lest queer theory become the theoretical arm of the superego's 'enjoy!', that duty should be thought of as a collective one.

Note

1 Before one sounds the homophobic alarm bell, it ought to be remembered that gay and lesbian activists in the 1970s often raised this possibility themselves in their argument that heterosexuality and homosexuality were both ways of limiting human erotic fulfilment.

References

Alves Lima, Rafael. 2021. *A Psicanálise na Ditadura Civil-Militar Brasileira*. Doctoral Thesis, São Paulo: University of São Paulo. https://www.teses.usp.br/teses/disponiveis/47/47133/tde-12082021-220350/publico/lima_do.pdf.

Bersani, Leo. 1995. *Homos*. 1st ed. Cambridge, MA: Harvard University Press.

Butler, Judith. 2024. *Who's Afraid of Gender?* London: Penguin.

Castanet, Hervé. 2003. 'Un célibataire'. *La Cause freudienne* 55 (3): 37–39.

Chiland, Colette. 2003. *Transsexualism: Illusion and Reality*. Translated by Philip Slotkin. London: SAGE.

Chiland, Colette. 2015. 'Le genre: Du statut social au déni de la réalité biologique'. *Bulletin de l'Académie Nationale de Médecine* 199 (6): 1017–1028.

Coffman, Chris. 2022. *Queer Traversals: Psychoanalytic Queer and Trans Theories*. 1st ed. London: Bloomsbury.

Dean, Tim. 2000. *Beyond Sexuality.* 1st ed. Chicago, IL: University of Chicago Press.

Deffieux, Jean-Pierre. 2003. '"The Gay Way of Life" et la psychanalyse'. *La Cause freudienne* 55 (3): 22.

Dhéret, Jacqueline. 2003. 'Julien'. *La Cause freudienne* 55 (3): 68–69.

Eribon, Didier. 2019. *Écrits sur la psychanalyse.* 1st ed. Paris: Fayard.

Escoffier, Jeffrey. 2018. *American Homo.* London: Verso.

Fassin, Éric. 2023. 'An Epidemic of Transphobia on French Turf'. *DiGeSt: Journal of Diversity and Gender Studies* 10 (2).

Freud, Sigmund. 1951. 'Letter to a Mother of a Homosexual'. *The American Journal of Psychiatry*, 786.

Freud, Sigmund. 1955. 'Group Psychology and Analysis of the Ego'. In *The Standard Edition of the Complete Psychological Works of Sigmund Freud*, vol. XVIII, translated by James Strachey, 65–133. London: The Hogarth Press.

Freud, Sigmund. 1959. '"Civilized" Sexual Morality and Nervous Illness'. In *The Standard Edition of the Complete Psychological Works of Sigmund Freud*, vol. IX, translated by James Strachey, 177–204. London: The Hogarth Press.

Freud, Sigmund. 1961. 'The Future of an Illusion'. In *The Standard Edition of the Complete Psychological Works of Sigmund Freud*, vol. XXI, translated by James Strachey, 3–58. London: The Hogarth Press.

Gherovici, Patricia. 2010. *Please Select Your Gender.* 1st ed. New York: Routledge.

Gozlan, Oren. 2015. *Transsexuality and the Art of Transitioning.* London: Routledge.

Lacan, Jacques. 1978. *The Seminar of Jacques Lacan, Book XI: The Four Fundamental Concepts of Psychoanalysis.* Translated by Alan Sheridan. 1st ed. New York: W.W. Norton.

Lacan, Jacques. 1992. *The Seminar of Jacques Lacan, Book VII: The Ethics of Psychoanalysis.* Translated by Dennis Porter. 1st ed. London: W.W. Norton.

Lacan, Jacques. 1998. *The Seminar of Jacques Lacan, Book XX: Encore.* Translated by Bruce Fink. New York: W.W. Norton.

Lacan, Jacques. 2001. 'Acte de Fondation'. In *Autres écrits*, 1st ed., 229–242. Paris: Seuil.

Lacan, Jacques. 2014. *The Seminar of Jacques Lacan, Book X: Anxiety.* Translated by A.R. Price. Cambridge: Polity.

Lacan, Jacques. 2015. *The Seminar of Jacques Lacan, Book VIII: Transference.* Translated by Bruce Fink. Cambridge: Polity.

Lacan, Jacques. 2017. *The Seminar of Jacques Lacan, Book V: Formations of the Unconscious.* Translated by Russell Grigg. 1st ed. Cambridge: Polity.

Laurent, Éric. 1997. 'Normes nouvelles de l'homosexualité'. *La Cause freudienne* 37 (3): 5–10.

Lewes, Kenneth. 1995. *Psychoanalysis and Male Homosexuality.* 1st ed. London: Jason Aronson.

Marx, Karl. 1970. *Critique of the Gotha Programme.* Moscow: Progress Publishers.

Miller, Jacques-Alain. 2003. 'Des gays en analyse?' *La Cause freudienne* 55 (3): 45–50.

Miller, Jacques-Alain. 2013. 'Non, la psychanalyse n'est pas contre le mariage gay'. *Le Point* (blog). 14 January. https://www.lepoint.fr/invites-du-point/jacques-alain-miller/non-la-psychanalyse-n-est-pas-contre-le-mariage-gay-14-01-2013-1614461_1450.php#11.

Miller, Jacques-Alain. 2017. 'Le bal des lepénotrotskistes (farce)'. *La règle du jeu* (blog). 27 April. https://laregledujeu.org/2017/04/27/31308/le-bal-des-lepenotrotskistes-farce/.

Miller, Jacques-Alain. 2021. 'Docile to Trans'. *Lacanian Review Online*. https://www.thelacanianreviews.com/docile-to-trans/.

Miller, Jacques-Alain, and Catherine Millot. 2022. 'La question trans dans la psychanalyse et pour le psychanalyste'. *Figures de la psychanalyse* 43 (1): 151–162.

Millot, Catherine. 1990. *Horsexe.* Translated by Kenneth Hylton. New York: Autonomedia.

Nobus, Dany. 2020. 'Psychoanalytic Geopolitics'. In *Routledge Handbook of Psychoanalytic Political Theory,* edited by Yannis Stavrakakis, 355–368. London: Routledge.

Perreau, Bruno. 2003. 'Faut-il brûler legendre?' *Vacarme* 25 (4): 62–68.

Preciado, Paul B. 2021. *Can the Monster Speak?* Translated by Frank Wynne. Cambridge, MA: MIT Press.

Recalcati, Massimo. 2003. 'La maison des femmes'. *La Cause freudienne* 55 (3): 71–73.

Tort, Michel. 2007. *La fin du dogme paternel.* 1st ed. Paris: Flammarion.

Tupinambá, Gabriel. 2019. '"Pandora's Box Has Been Opened": Lacanian Psychoanalysis and Politics after 2017'. *Crisis & Critique* 6 (1): 341–363.

Tupinambá, Gabriel. 2021. *The Desire of Psychoanalysis.* 1st ed. Evanston, IL: Northwestern University Press.

Vinciguerra, Rose-Paule. 2007. 'La psychanalyse à l'endroit des familles'. *La Cause freudienne* 65 (1): 81–85.

Zafiropoulos, Markos. 2001. *Lacan et les sciences sociales: Le déclin du père.* 1st ed. Paris: Presses Universitaires de France.

Žižek, Slavoj. 2021. 'Foreword: For Lacan, against Lacanian Ideology'. In *The Desire of Psychoanalysis,* by Gabriel Tupinambá, 1st ed., xi–xvii. Evanston, IL: Northwestern University Press.

Index

For Product Safety Concerns and Information please contact our EU
representative GPSR@taylorandfrancis.com
Taylor & Francis Verlag GmbH, Kaufingerstraße 24, 80331 München, Germany

www.ingramcontent.com/pod-product-compliance
Lightning Source LLC
Chambersburg PA
CBHW070336270326
41926CB00017B/3890

9 781032 543802